ALEXANDER KORDA

PAUL TABORI

ALEXANDER KORDA

OLDBOURNE
LONDON

OLDBOURNE BOOK CO. LTD.,
121 Fleet Street, London, E.C.4.

© *Oldbourne Book Co. Ltd.,* *1959*

First published in 1959

Set in 12-point Bembo, 2-point leaded, and
printed in Great Britain by
Wyman & Sons Ltd., London, Reading and Fakenham

CONTENTS

LIST OF ILLUSTRATIONS

Facing page

CHAPTER I

THE MEN WITH THE BIG CIGARS

LONG BEFORE I met him, Alexander Korda was both a legend and a symbol for me. The boy from the *puszta*, the young journalist who had made films in Vienna, Berlin, Rome, Paris, Hollywood and London embodied the dreams of thousands of Hungarians who longed to break out of the narrow confines of their small country.

He was the local boy who had made good—had achieved a fabulous career. And he hadn't forgotten his origins, his friends. He was always willing to help any of his fellow-countrymen; when I visited London, I heard that the five Union Jacks flying over Denham Studios represented five British employees—all the rest were Continentals. This was pardonable exaggeration; but many of my friends and colleagues had tales to tell about Korda's bounty.

Yet I did not meet Korda until half-way through the Second World War when my friend, John Brophy, the novelist, took me to see him. Korda was then in charge of Metro-Goldwyn-Mayer-London Films, installed in a large and aristocratic mansion in Belgrave Square. He received me with flattering kindness and within half an hour we had agreed that I was to work for him.

It was only later that I discovered Alex had twenty-seven writers on his pay-roll, from Enid Bagnold to Evelyn Waugh, from James Bridie to Nevil Shute. He had announced sixteen films 'ready for production'. There was only one snag. He didn't have studio-space in which to make them. Twenty-seven writers and twice as many actors, innumerable technicians, secretaries and other staff were eating their heads off—with no work at all to do. The single picture which he produced for M-G-M. London Films, the brilliant 'Perfect Strangers', had seventeen of us working on the screenplay. In the end, of course, only one of us got the screen-credit; indeed, it would have been impossible to sort out our individual contributions.

I felt a little guilty cashing my handsome weekly pay-cheque but after a while these pangs of conscience disappeared. During the buzz-bomb plague, perched over a table in our basement kitchen, I wrote a novel about the first year of a completely ruined city in Eastern Europe after the war. I sent the typescript to Korda and a week later I received a summons to Belgrave Square. This time Mr. Ben Goetz, the M-G-M. executive, was also present.

"I want to buy your book," Korda said. "You kept me awake all night. It will make a great film."

He went on talking; I was a little dazed by this sudden good fortune. Mr. Goetz jabbed a blunt forefinger into my midriff.

"*You* listen to Sir Alexander!" he warned me.

I did. I even dared to voice my opinion that when the picture was made I'd be happy if it followed the style of a great M-G-M. film that had impressed me deeply some years before—King Vidor's magnificent 'Our Daily Bread'.

Mr. Goetz frowned. "Ai," he said, "if you knew what a lot of money we lost on that picture!"

But Korda's manner had changed suddenly, mysteriously. Until then he had been the great executive, the professor giving a lecture, maybe even a very wise, very gentle father talking to a small boy. Now he looked at me and winked. Unexpectedly, we were fellow-conspirators.

It wasn't until I started to gather material for this biography that I discovered the reason behind that change. In 1935 Alex had given an interview to the *New York Telegraph* in which he said: "That magnificent epic of the American depression 'Our Daily Bread' is a film I shall never forget. I consider that King

Vidor has here produced a picture that will create screen history. He has taken his courage in both hands, and his inspiration from the headlines in the newspapers of the world, and presented a vivid account of what can happen, and very probably is happening, to thousands rendered destitute by the world depression. Seldom, if indeed ever, have I seen a motion picture which asks the question, 'what do you think?' oftener than 'Our Daily Bread'. And to me that is one of the chief interests of films."

So he liked it, too—and if I had deliberately chosen some way of winning his sympathy, his friendship, I couldn't have done better. There is always something gratifying, even heart-warming if two people unexpectedly discover the same tastes.

A few days later his secretary called me. Could I go and see Sir Alexander at Claridge's? He expected me Saturday afternoon. The girl chuckled: "I'd take my pyjamas if I were you . . ."

A little puzzled by this invitation, I turned up in Brook Street in the middle of the afternoon. I was shown up to Korda's penthouse suite and found him deep in Voltaire's *The Age of Louis XIV*. For an hour or so we talked about the Sun King and his glittering reign. Tea was served; a little later Korda stepped to the sideboard on which two fair-sized china barrels rested—one labelled 'whisky', the other 'brandy'. This, in the middle of the war, was lavish luxury indeed. We both had a brandy and talked on.

He began to speak about my book and became completely absorbed. Brilliantly, persuasively, he told me *why* I had written it, what exactly I had in mind, what the different characters stood for. I listened spellbound. I do not mean to be sarcastic when I say that the novel had become entirely *his*; I felt it was a mere accident that I had written it. He knew far more about it than I did. He told me that he had already made arrangements for Spencer Tracy to play the lead and for Ian Dalrymple to produce it; we discussed directors and the approach to the screenplay.

Dinner was served and we talked on. About three a.m. Korda said:

"Why don't you spend the night? Then we can talk some more."

I remembered the warning about the pyjamas and mumbled something about being unprepared; but he waved my objections aside. I was shown into a bedroom which was completely equipped for unexpected guests, down to a brand-new tooth-brush in cellophane. It was Monday noon before I got home, dazed, a little sleepy but wonderfully stimulated and inspired.

A few weeks later the producer, the production manager and myself went up to Wales to look for locations. Work started on the screenplay—R. C. Sherriff was doing the first draft—and my original contract was renewed for two more years. But production was postponed because of lack of studio-space.

Soon after the end of the war, Korda gave me leave-of-absence to make a tour of the Middle East and the Balkans. I managed to get into Hungary and when I returned in February 1946, I brought him a little gift. In my father's library which had miraculously escaped destruction in the seven weeks' siege of Budapest, I found a copy of the first issue of *Pesti Mozi*, the film-paper he started as a very young journalist. Alex was as pleased as a child and for two hours we talked about his youth, his friends in Hungary and the state of the post-war world. He asked me about dozens of writers, actors, journalists and made careful notes of their addresses and what help they needed. In the next few months he sent several thousand pounds' worth of food and clothing parcels to Budapest.

At the very end of our talk he mentioned my novel and the film we had planned. While I was away he had severed his con-nection with M-G-M. London Films was on its own again. The rights of my book had been bought by the American company; now Korda wanted to get them back. "You go and see them," he said. "Tell them someone wants to turn it into a stage play and insists on having the film rights as well. They'll sell it to you much cheaper than they would to me."

I dutifully went along to Mr. Ben Goetz—but Korda's plan did not work. M-G-M. wanted exactly seven times as much for the

property as they had paid originally and this was a bit too steep
even for Alex. The film was never made; but my contract was
renewed, now with London Films, until 1948.

A few months later, one Saturday morning, my phone rang;
Korda's secretary asked me to come down at once to 146 Piccadilly. I found Alex with Karl Hartl, the Austrian producer and
director who had been his first assistant when he started in
Vienna in 1920.

"We want to make a picture in Austria," he told me. "It'll be
a comedy, it will star Cary Grant and the basic idea is 'invisible
frontiers'. I want you to do a treatment as quickly as possible."

I asked how quickly and Alex said: "Monday afternoon will
do…"

I begged for a little more time and finally was granted until
Wednesday. Korda's instructions hadn't been very detailed; but
I went home and with the help of several pints of black coffee and
my memories of occupied Vienna (I had been there early in 1946)
I managed to put together a reasonably funny story. On Wednesday morning, bleary-eyed and exhausted, I rang London Films
and asked when I could come and see Sir Alexander.

"Oh, didn't you know?" his secretary told me. "He's flown to
New York yesterday. He won't be back until next week."

When he came back, we discussed the story at length and he
liked it. But mysterious things happen in the film world. In
the end Korda did make a film in Austria. It wasn't a comedy;
it didn't star Cary Grant; and as far as I know, it had nothing to
do with invisible frontiers—and practically nothing with my
story. 'The Third Man' was quite a success.

Later I spent six months with Lajos Biro working on a script
of 'Carmen'. Korda gave us only two instructions: he wanted to
include the famous and beautiful Easter Procession at Seville and
he wanted Prosper Mérimée, the author of the original story, to
be one of the characters in the film. Carmen was to be Paulette
Goddard. He had also decided to discard the Bizet music completely and use lovely *flamencos*, the folk-songs of Spain instead.

I learned more about scriptwriting from Biro than from anybody else; but again, the script was put aside and Miss Goddard did 'An Ideal Husband' instead, which was a far cry from Carmen.

When my contract ended, I departed for Hollywood. Korda gave me a final bonus and said: "Here are three letters. These are my only real friends in California—two of them are crooks, the third is the soul of honour. Go to the first two—don't call on the third unless you are in real trouble."

I followed his advice. I discovered that the first two men were highly successful; the third wasn't. But they all helped me and they all talked to me about Alex as their teacher, their model— almost, I would say, their spiritual father.

After that I met Korda only a few times—mostly in connection with needy Hungarians who used me as go-between when they wanted help. A few weeks before his death I went to him on behalf of an old journalist who was trapped in Spain and needed rescue badly. I discovered that he had worked on Korda's early film-magazine for a few months; the two men hadn't met for forty years. Yet for almost a decade Korda had paid the storage fee of this man's furniture in Paris and now he arranged at once for a monthly stipend to be paid to him by his Madrid office. In the last few years of his life I took at least twenty similar cases to him—and always help was forthcoming, promptly and generously.

On that last visit, after dealing with the matter in hand, we talked about television.

"It's stupid to be afraid of it," he told me. "Some of my fellow-producers just keep moaning about the menace. I think it'll offer us great new chances—especially if pay-television is introduced— and I, for one, will be quite prepared to devote ten or fifteen years to both films and TV."

Alas, he only had a few weeks—not all those years he wanted. He loved life more than anything else; but life for him was the creative art of producing films.

*   *   *   *

It would be best, I thought, to start this book with my personal experiences—because, in a way, they contain in a miniature Korda's whole character and philosophy. To me and to my former fellow Hungarians he was, as I said, both a legend and a symbol. He was certainly a legend to the whole of show business. Master impresario, financial wizard, discoverer of a hundred stars, spendthrift—a newspaper complained once that he was spending money with 'the abandon of a drunken sailor on a spree'—he was a visionary and a man of deep erudition, he attracted publicity as a bathing beauty attracts cameras. In England he was something exotic, fascinatingly strange and original. Especially because few knew his background, his origins, his past history. I must confess that I was equally puzzled by him until I began to explore his youth and his career before he founded London Films.

He was a film producer—but also a great many other things. A Hollywood psychiatrist once told me, quite seriously, that the protagonist, the archetype of our century *was* the Producer—as in some other centuries it had been the Saint, the Warrior or the Revolutionary. Korda, true to type, was one of the Harun al Rashids of our age; one of the men who could pick up the phone, and the loveliest women were wafted into his presence on the magic carpet of a Super-Constellation; who pressed a button and the greatest story tellers of the world went to work to turn out plots and scenarios; a man who lifted one finger and a herd of elephants or a pride of lions were caged for his pleasure. To his countless associates he was a charmer with a foreign accent and a wonderful command of invective; to his actors, directors, technicians he was something of a father-figure—as, indeed, he often called them 'my children'.

And Korda played this part both in public and in private; unlike another producer whose brother told me: "Joe gets to the studio at half-past nine in the morning, takes off his jacket and promptly becomes a genius. At six he puts on his jacket, walks through the gate—and immediately turns back into what he's always been—an idiot." Whether in his palatial offices, in his

Claridge suite or Millionaire Row penthouse apartment, on the studio floor or on board his yacht—characteristically called *Elsewhere*—Alex ran true to type.

But what was his type?

The earliest type of the film producer was the *pioneer*. Men like Sam Goldwyn, William Fox, Adolph Zukor or the Warner Brothers; immigrants or sons of immigrants who started in the fur or the garment trade, bought a few of the early nickelodeons and, like giants, created huge companies and blazed the trail to Hollywood. Their life-stories have been told in scores of books; most of them have disappeared though a few still survive, for theirs was an extremely tough race. For many years their rôle was to produce money; their power and prestige were measured by the amount they could raise—and in the early heroic days this often meant pawning the wife's jewellery or mortgaging the home.

This is the type about which most of the jokes, true and legendary, are told. The producer of the 'super-colossal' who demands a hundred-and-twenty apostles instead of the paltry twelve at the Last Supper; the other who sees a sundial for the first time, has its principle explained to him and exclaims: "My, whatever will they think of next?" One of my favourite stories concerns Mr. Sam Goldwyn. (When I met him some years ago in London I found him a quiet, self-assured man with little flamboyance or truculence; he told me that he rather encouraged the stories invented about him; they were good publicity.)

One day, Mr. Goldwyn was sitting in his private projection theatre, with his eleven-year-old son, Sam jr. who has since become a successful producer himself. He was looking at the 'rough-cut', the unedited version of one of his films, with the director watching anxiously for his reactions. At one point, Sam Goldwyn stopped the film and said, somewhat testily:

"I don't understand this. What's it supposed to mean?"

The director who was rather proud of the particular sequence, explained it at some length.

"I still don't get it," Sam said.

The director, eager to save his favourite scene, hit upon a simple expedient:

"Why don't we ask young Sam? I'm sure he understands it."

They did. Sam jr. explained clearly, intelligently what the scene was all about. The director beamed with delight and relief. But Goldwyn poked him in the ribs.

"Since when," he demanded angrily, "since when, I wanna know, *are we making pictures for children?*"

And of course, he was perfectly right—from his own point of view. Pictures, by and large, are not made for precocious children; they are made for filmgoers whose mental age and I.Q. are sometimes very low indeed.

I had a personal encounter with one of the great pioneers of the motion picture industry. With a colleague I went along to discuss the story he had commissioned to star Miss Rita Hayworth. The mere fact that he was willing to receive us was a tremendous concession. We found him in his air-conditioned office, large enough to have served as an hotel lobby. He had our story in front of him in a leather folder and he said:

"Sit down. I tell you what I'll do—I'll read it right now."

We waited tensely while he flipped over the pages, now and then stabbing at a line or paragraph with a red pencil. When he finished—in ten minutes flat—he turned to us with a frown:

"I like it—except for one thing. You make her a cho . . . a choreographer. Won't do!"

"Why not?" asked my co-author who had more courage than I.

"All choreo . . . all dance designers are without glamour. And we gotta have glamour."

Hesitantly, I mentioned one lady-choreographer who was certainly famous for glamour.

"She's a nigger," he dismissed her with a jab of the pencil.

My collaborator brought out another name, this time of a most celebrated dance-designer, of pure Caucasian race.

"She's old an' ugly," snapped the big man.

As our story was based on the fact that Miss Hayworth *would* play a choreographer, we gave up. The film was never made.

Korda was the contemporary of some of these early titans (though perhaps a little younger) yet he had nothing in common with them. Someone called him once the 'Sam Goldwyn of Britain', a misleading and inappropriate comparison. For in Korda the businessman was usually dominated by the artist even if, like all men in show business, he had to make compromises. Art, culture and inspiration were only interesting to the trail-makers of Hollywood if they paid off in dollars or pounds. Korda, too, was conscious of money—but he went on record as saying: "Money promises you everything and gives you nothing. But you have to have it in order to despise it."

After the early pioneer period, the era of the Keystone Cops, of Mary Pickford, the 'Perils of Pauline' and all the heroic, almost pre-historic experiments, the film industry became big business. There was now little scope for the lone wolf; the wife's jewels or the mortgaged house were no longer sufficient for a million-dollar budget. The nickelodeons and penny arcades were replaced by movie palaces, cinema circuits, organized world-distribution and huge advertising campaigns.

Many of the pioneers found themselves nudged out or taken over by big capital. The new masters were the bankers or financiers who sat in their New York and London offices. The men in the studios became straw-bosses who had to get on the phone whenever a major decision was to be taken and who were more likely than not put on the carpet if anything went wrong. The Grey Eminences of the City or Wall Street were impersonal; they were powers behind the throne which was either vacant or filled with rapidly changing 'kings'. There were a few years when the American film industry was perilously close to becoming a soul-less 'dream factory'.

Korda rebelled against this from the beginning. The men who provided him with money were never his bosses—or never for long. He made even the toughest believe that he, Korda, was doing him a favour by accepting his money; and those who did not agree with his attitude he soon abandoned. He wanted to be his own master and for the greater part of his career, he succeeded.

The talkies brought another change. When Al Jolson opened his mouth and sang 'Sonny Boy', a whole era ended. For one thing, the *Word* came into its birthright again. By now the pioneers were old or middle-aged, and a new generation, a new type of producer arose. Unless he was an independent, he no longer had to find the money. He was a salaried employee—often with a fabulous income—who was given certain orders and rarely created the subject or determined the budget on which it would be made. This is somewhat over-simplifying an enormously complex and varying arrangement which changed from studio to studio, from country to country; but by and large it applied everywhere.

Though Korda filled such a rôle for a short time when he became production chief of British M-G-M.-London Films, again he could not fit into a minor, subordinate part. For this reason he parted from M-G-M. and resuscitated his own company shortly after the war.

The last ten years have again brought a complete revolution in the producer's rôle and his personality—a revolution due to two things: taxes and television.

In the last ten years the star has become all-important. Television forced upon the film industry, almost throughout the world, the need to make fewer but bigger pictures; these had to be spectacular and star-studded. Salaries went up and up—and so did taxes. So stars, in order to keep a reasonable proportion of their earnings, became owners of skating rinks and hotels, of baseball teams and oil wells. It was a natural development that they should become their own producers, forming their own companies, with themselves as principal assets; though some went so far as to produce films in which they did not appear.

Korda believed in making stars—but he was more interested

in actors than in names. The only star with whom he worked on the basis of co-producer was Sir Laurence Olivier; their co-operation was a most happy one.

Television both contributed to the downfall of the movie tycoons—the men with the big cigars—and accelerated it. Sidney Gilliat, the well-known British producer said a few months ago: "We may very well be witnessing the break-up of Hollywood as the world centre of movie-making, accompanied by a tremendous scaling-down of the power of the big distributors." Korda was not afraid of television but wanted to put it into the service of films—through pay TV which, in theory, would enable a film producer to recoup his entire production cost in a single night. I think if he had lived he would have been in the vanguard of the producers who could move with the times and turn the latest form of mass entertainment to their advantage.

The pioneer, the financier, the salaried executive, the star and, more recently, the chartered accountant—the pattern of the film producer has changed considerably in the last fifty years. But Korda did not fit into any of these categories—because, to a certain extent, he belonged to all of them though he was far more creative artist than financier. Indeed, Lord Rank once said a little testily: "I wish Korda would stick to making pictures and not meddle with high finance!" Perhaps he was right; but I doubt if Alex would have taken the advice.

*   *   *   *

Few modern producers have impressed themselves on the public as has Korda. Most films are being presented today as being this or that star's or director's; there are few Hitchcocks, Disneys or DeMilles who have created an unmistakable trademark. And the popular image of the producer is still the man with the big cigar or the slightly shady fly-by-night *entrepreneur*.

For this, I think, we writers are partly to blame. Perhaps because we have suffered most at the hands of producers—or perhaps because we were the most sensitive and articulate victims. In a thousand novels and plays, in countless stories and satires, in every tongue, the writer has tried to revenge himself by following the principle of 'give a dog a bad name . . .'

But we had some provocation.

There was the charming English lady novelist who sat through the screening of a picture supposedly based on one of her successful books. At the end she turned to the producer and said:

"D'you remember that lion, roaring in the third reel?"

"Yes, of course. What about it?"

"I believe you took that *straight* from my book."

And there is the tale told about Korda himself. It was a long and difficult story conference; an eminent author had to be persuaded to accept numerous changes in his masterpiece. Korda could be very persuasive, so with very little trouble, the writer accepted the changes. But then they came to an episode of little or no importance—and the writer dug his heels in. Nothing Alex or the director said would budge him. This went on for several hours—until Korda sighed and signalled to the director. They left the recalcitrant writer alone with Lajos Biro. Perhaps he would have better luck, talking author-to-author.

When they were alone, Biro asked:

"Tell me, old chap, you've agreed to all these changes—why are you so stubborn about this minor point?"

"Minor?" cried the writer, with tears in his eyes, "damn you, it's the last little bit left of my whole original!"

There are far worse, true stories of betrayal and exploitation. No wonder that from Cedric Belfrage's 'Promised Land' to Jeffrey Dell's 'Nobody Ordered Wolves' from Budd Schulberg's 'What Makes Sammy Run' and 'The Disenchanted' to Clifford Odets' ferocious 'The Big Knife' it is always the same —the producer is presented as a tyrant, an illiterate, a white slave trader in men's and women's souls and minds.

Even more curious is the fact that Hollywood and other film-centres have accepted this convention. Film producers on the screen are rarely more sympathetic or human than in books and plays. Perhaps this self-deprecatory attitude is a sort of propitiation of the gods or the public; perhaps it is due to a contempt for humanity. The fact remains that, except in a few film-biographies, the fictional presentation of the producer is always unflattering; utterly unlike the image one would gather from the numerous hand-outs the studio publicity departments put out with such fabulous industry. Of course, neither the films, books, plays nor the publicity releases bear much relation to real life. But this 'split image' makes it a hundred times more difficult to present the facts when writing the biography of any film producer.

* * * *

Hollywood and Denham, Joinville and Neubabelsberg have coined many a *bon mot*, invented many a joke about Hungarians in the film industry. The typical Hollywood success story, they said, began: "My parents were poor but Hungarian . . ." Not to mention the savage warning: "If you have a Hungarian friend, you don't need an enemy."

Sometimes I tease my English friends by reminding them that the paragon of all Englishmen, the perfect fool who is all the time immensely clever is the creation of *three* Hungarians. *The Scarlet Pimpernel* was written by Baroness Orczy, daughter of a Hungarian aristocrat who left his native country in the middle of the last century. The film version was produced by Korda; and the title was played by Leslie Howard who, born Leslie Stainer, came to England in his early teens.

If you accept the idea that the Film Producer is, in a way, the symbol of our age, the personification of twentieth-century civilization, I believe Korda can be called the archetype of the Film Producer. He, too, smoked big cigars—but as one of his stars told me "it was a different cigar". Films were his life and his obsession; ever since his schooldays he wished to make them. He became one of the greatest technicians of the cinema and had every detail of its very complicated techniques at his finger-tips; in set design or camera angles, problems of sound recording or make-up he could speak with equal authority. That he was something of a financial wizard, his career has amply proved; he created vast enterprises out of practically nothing; and if his detractors sometimes accused him of thinking too lavishly, spending too much, the results usually justified his actions. He was a voracious reader, a discriminating art collector, a gourmet and a connoisseur of wine and cigars. He was a Universal Man as far as this could be achieved in our age of specialization; and what he created on celluloid will endure.

This biography, in a way, has been written by many people. His school-mates whom I have tracked down in half a dozen countries; his cousins and kinsmen still alive in Hungary; his secretaries and associates in Vienna and Berlin, Paris and Hollywood; the stars and writers, directors and producers who worked with him—they have all come forward to help me. I owe special thanks to my friend and colleague Peter Noble who put a vast amount of material at my disposal. The film archives and institutes of Vienna, Wiesbaden, New York, London and Rome have also supplied me with certain data.

When Korda, a few years before his death, was asked who could be his successor, he said, with a smile: "I don't know. You see—I don't grow on trees." He was conscious of his achievements though he never became pompous; he could afford to be modest yet self-assured. Films have an ephemeral life; but I believe that Korda will live in his work, in the scores of men and women he inspired and taught, directly or indirectly. This book as well as being written about him is written for him.

CHAPTER II

THE BOY FROM THE *PUSZTA*

SÁNDOR LÁSZLÓ KORDA was born on September 16, 1893, in Pusztaturpásztó, County Jásznagykunszolnok, Hungary.

The name of his birthplace is far more impressive than the spot itself. Only the largest-scale maps show it; not even a hamlet, just the name of a settlement, the centre of a large estate owned by the Salgo family. A few houses, barns, stables, silos. No electricity, no running water or post-office. The nearest little town, Turkeve, was about six miles away.

This was the heartland of Hungary, the Kunság. It had been settled centuries before by the *kun* tribe, a thrifty, hard-working, taciturn and stubborn clan; though they lived on the plains, they had many things in common with the Highland Scots.

The eighteen-nineties were peaceful and prosperous in Hungary. A quarter of a century before, the Habsburgs had made their peace with the rebellious Magyars and the Dual Monarchy came into being. There were violent fights in parliament over civil marriage and other minor reforms; but the country seemed to be well-fed and contented, looking forward to 1896 when the first millenium of the nation would be celebrated with festivities lasting a whole year.

Yet under the serene surface there was considerable tension and strife. Most of the land was owned by a few thousand aristocrats, the Church magnates and capitalists. Smallholders had to fight hard for survival. The landless agricultural workers formed a large proletariat. Few people had to starve but money was scarce. Peasants bought matches four or five at a time; they couldn't afford a whole box. In the cities agrarian and industrial socialism was making more and more converts.

Korda's father was called Henrik (Henry) Kellner. He was the bailiff of the rich and powerful Salgos, a member of the lower middle class. Most of his salary was in kind—so much grain, so many pigs, so many sacks of flour or salt per year, with a modest house thrown in—but, at least in the early years, very little cash. His salary never rose over 3,000 forints (about £300) a year. Still, while the job lasted, he had authority and a certain prestige. He was a sturdy, handsome man who had served in a Hussar regiment, rising to the rank of sergeant, and he preserved a soldierly bearing. He took his family responsibilities very seriously and was generous to a fault; he provided his sisters with dowries and was always sending cartloads of firewood or sacks of flour to needy relatives and friends.

Mrs. Esther Kellner was a beauty, considerably better-read and more cultured than her husband. A bailiff's wife had also to be his deputy; she looked after hen-house and buttery and directed all the minor operations of a large estate. She was a proud woman with an indomitable spirit.

When her first child was born, one of the farmhands was sent off to Turkeve on horseback to register the birth at the village notary's office. The father had chosen the name 'Sándor', the Hungarian equivalent of Alexander. But when she heard of it, Mrs. Kellner protested violently. She didn't like the name at all. She wanted her son to be named László (Leslie). Back the messenger rode, making another twelve miles' round trip. By then it was too late—all the registrar could do was to add Leslie as a second name. Though Korda never used 'László', his family and his early friends all called him 'Laci', the Hungarian diminutive of Leslie.

Puszta in Hungarian literally means prairie. But it has also the meaning of farm or ranch. The small settlements in the *puszta* are *tanyas*, thousands of isolated farmhouses, at varying distances from the nearest village or town, cut off in the winter by snow-drifts, in the autumn and spring by muddy roads which are often little better than cart-tracks. This was the place where Korda spent his childhood.

The Kellners had two other boys—Zoltan, born in 1895, and Vincent in 1897. The three boys were very close, with Alex as their natural leader, and they remained close for the rest of their careers.

Until they went to school, they led the lives of the peasant children, running around bare-foot, playing endless, mysterious games in the fields, the paddocks, the barns and the yard in which agricultural machinery was kept. The mansion of the Salgos, their employers, was a few hundred yards from their modest cottage. It was surrounded by a tall wire fence. Sometimes the boys caught a glimpse of the lady of the manor, reclining on a couch on the long veranda, a huge Newfoundland on guard beside her. They rarely entered the mansion themselves—and then only through the back door. In the kitchen there was a wonderful, exciting smell—not of food, but of fresh paint, which they sniffed like puppies.

There was always plenty of food, and boys and girls of the family came for visits and spent their holidays with their country cousins. Later Alex used to invite his schoolmates and whole classes of boys descended upon the bailiff's home, being fed to repletion by Mrs. Kellner.

At five Alex insisted on being sent to school. There were no schools on the *puszta*—he had to be taken on a farm-cart to Turkeve. A couple of years later Zoltan joined him. It was impossible to make the journey every day so the boys were boarded out. At weekends and holidays they were fetched on a buggy; riding high on the box, Alex was immensely proud. Sunday evenings they were taken back to town.

Alex was a brilliant scholar with a fabulous memory; once he read a page, it stuck in his mind and he could repeat it verbatim. He entered secondary or high-school (in Hungary it is called *gymnasium*) on a scholarship when he was nine. First in Kisuj-szállás, an overgrown village which called itself a town and later in Mezötur, which had an old college and a flourishing home-industry of pottery. He was a lively boy who loved all sports. Whenever his form went on a hike, he would refuse to stay in line or stick to any group; he hated the shackles of discipline and always tried to walk alone. His temper was gay and carefree; he loved to sing and whistle. Some of his classmates thought him stubborn, self-centred, not easy to get on with; perhaps because they thought that he felt superior to them. He was a voracious reader, seldom without a book in his hand. His favourites were the science fantasies of Jules Verne; but he also devoured thrillers and adventure stories. But above all, he watched over his brothers. Zoltan, being younger but more pugnacious, got into many a fight; but Alex was always there to rescue him if he took on more than he could manage. At one time they nicknamed him 'The Boy with the Bone' because he had got hold of a sawn-off antler which he used with devastating effect whenever his foes threatened to overwhelm him.

Then, in October 1906, when Alex was barely thirteen, his father fell ill. The small-town doctor diagnosed appendicitis but applied the wrong treatment. Henrik Kellner was taken to Budapest. By then it was too late and within a few days, the vigorous man of forty-three was dead.

Alex and Zoltan had been living with their grandmother in Kecskemét, the fat, prosperous city which later became famous for its wonderful fruit and the delicious apricot brandy which it brewed. One autumn day she called them into the house, brushed their clothes and handed them black ties to put on. Alex protested—he did not like the colour. Zoltan followed his lead. But their grandmother insisted and in the end they humoured her. They travelled, third-class, to Budapest for their father's funeral.

★   ★   ★   ★

A bailiff in Hungary couldn't gather riches even if he was dishonest; and Henrik Kellner had been well known for his scrupulous integrity. For the last two years he had been working for the Jakabffys, another rich family of landowners. Though they were sympathetic, another bailiff was appointed and their home had to be vacated. Mrs. Kellner herself moved to Kecskemét, where her father-in-law, Károly (Charles) Kellner was living. She took a small house in Cow Street and eked out her small income by taking in a couple of girl-lodgers. The move meant that the family's life had changed from comparative affluence to grinding poverty. They stayed in Kecskemét almost two years; but long before that Alex had gone to Budapest. He was lodged with some cousins and entered the *gymnasium* in Barcsay Street, a tough day-school which had the reputation of a male St. Trinian's.

Then, in 1909, the Kellners decided to take the great step and follow Alex to the capital. It would be easier for the boys to find part-time jobs and a lodging-house or some similar enterprise could be run at a greater profit.

Life, especially in the first years, was extremely hard. They moved three times within a few months in order to find a more suitable apartment. Mrs. Kellner kept lodgers for whom she cooked; she was an excellent cook and the huge helpings she heaped on her student-lodgers' plates didn't leave her much profit. The boys, of course, lived at home. She loved them all, but Alex was the apple of her eye. He was given the maid's tiny room for his own while the peasant slavey slept in the kitchen. Zoltan, Vincent and an occasional relative or friend whom Mrs. Kellner took in, slept on the floor in the hallway or one of the rooms.

By this time Alex had transferred from the *gymnasium* to a commercial high school in Mester Street and Zoltan joined him. It is a strange fact that quite a few of his fellow-students later became connected with films as directors or screenwriters; while others ended up as writers and journalists. How much of this was due to the influence of Alex, would be difficult to say; although his friends were quick to acknowledge him as a natural leader. He had little interest in school or his regular studies (though he did well enough to keep his scholarship) but he could charm his teachers with the same self-assurance as he later used on the City bankers or the Hollywood executives.

He was still a schoolboy when he began to contribute to the liberal daily *Független Magyarország* (Independent Hungary) for which he wrote topical articles, dramatic criticism, book reviews and short stories.

Some time in 1908 one of his schoolmates took him to the Café Venice. Schoolboys weren't expected to frequent coffee-houses in Hungary; but there was a special attraction in this case. Three or four times a day the windows were darkened and a short show was put on for the customers. A movie show! It lasted only about half an hour and no film was longer than five or six minutes. Korda watched with absorbed interest. When they left the smoky café, he was unusually excited. "This is the future!" he cried, grabbing his friend's arm. "This is what I want to do!"

It was more than boyish enthusiasm; at sixteen he had chosen his profession and all his efforts were directed towards getting into the infant motion picture industry.

For the time being this seemed as remote a possibility as becoming a millionaire. However hard Mrs. Kellner worked, she could not make ends meet. Zoltan, after school-hours, did some tutoring and the household chores, carrying coal from the cellar, running errands, cleaning the lodgers' boots; Vincent was too small to be of much help yet. Alex had to provide whatever was needed to balance the pitiful family budget. He tutored his less bright class-mates, sometimes five at a time, getting maybe ten shillings a month from each. Luckily, with his photographic memory, he had no need to do much homework. It was about this time that he began to play his favourite party game, another proof of his fabulously retentive mind. This consisted of taking a novel and conducting a quiz about its characters. Not the heroes and heroines but the 'bit-parts', the minor figures—a maid, a coachman, the most obscure member of the Pickwick Club or the crew of the *Nautilus*. In time his friends refused to play it— because they knew that Alex would always win. Thirty years later he was still playing it, his favourite partner being Baroness Moura Budberg, for two decades his story-editor who could give him a fair run for his money though he was still winning two out of every three games.

Every Hungarian secondary school had a literary club which was called, rather quaintly, 'Self Improvement Circle'. Korda became quickly prominent in his own school, serving as president in his final year. He made his debut with a short story. Characteristically, its villain was a hard-hearted landlord who ejected a poor family for not paying the rent. As the Kellner family was constantly faced with the same difficulty, it wasn't surprising that the landlord was presented as a blackguard. The realistic story had no happy ending; the dispossessed family was left homeless, sitting on the pavement, with its poor furniture piled up in the rain.

His first film-show had fixed Korda's ambitions; one of his masters had just the same deep and enduring influence over him. In Hungary there were few boarding-schools and boys spent far less time with their teachers than boys did in England. For a schoolmaster to make a real, decisive impression on any of his pupils, he had to be an extraordinarily strong character. Young Alex Kellner came under the spell of Oscar Faber, who taught him history and Hungarian literature.

Faber was a Catholic priest who had left the Church. He was a Christian and a Socialist. His students admired him and followed him in his progressive and liberal views which often caused him to clash with those in authority. It was Faber who had placed his favourite pupil's articles and stories in the liberal daily *Independent Hungary* and even got him a job in the editorial offices where he could earn more than by tutoring. It was against all rules for a secondary school student to work at night in a newspaper office but Alex did not care. It was Faber who introduced him to the latest, most provocative political and philosophical books. Their relationship wasn't that of master and student, not even that of a substitute father and son; they were friends, in spite of the great difference in their ages. Alex's quicksilver mind was shaped and broadened under Faber's influence.

He was still at school when he took part in the first (and last) political demonstration of his life. It was the early autumn of 1909. The reactionary Spanish government had arrested Guardia Ferrer, the humanist champion of free education, author of the famous *Modern School* whom Oscar Faber admired greatly, having published several books of the same spirit. Ferrer's arrest caused world-wide protest in which Hungarian students also took part—especially those in the Galilei Circle, a left-wing club of high-school and university youth. Alex had read everything he could find about Ferrer and he knew more about him than Oscar Faber himself. He read a long essay in the Literary Circle about the Spanish educator whom he compared to Pestalozzi; an essay which was honoured by the greatest distinction the Circle could grant—to be inscribed in the '*Golden Book*' by the author himself. With his best friend, Andor Zsoldos, Alex retired to a small coffee-shop where impecunious students could get a roll and a cup of coffee for a penny and set to work. But he was interrupted by the newsboys crying the headlines of the evening papers. Ferrer had been sentenced to death. "They won't dare to execute him!" his friend said, trying to calm him down. "Of course they will," replied Alex, who was far more of a realist. "You don't know them—you're a poet and this is politics, dirty politics! Oscar Faber thinks the same as I do!"

A few days later Alex and some of his friends stood outside a small cinema on the main boulevard of Budapest. The newsboys again rushed down the street, carrying the fresh copies of the papers, still wet with printer's ink. The headlines proclaimed that Ferrer was to be executed the following day. The papers were grabbed eagerly by the passers-by and especially by the students whose favourite promenade this stretch was. Groups formed, angrily discussing the fate of Ferrer. A group of fifteen or twenty young men gathered on a corner and Alex started to make an impassioned speech. He called upon them to follow him to the Spanish Embassy and register an immediate protest. They set out along the boulevard and soon gathered a sizeable crowd as they marched in the roadway, shouting loudly: "Down with Ferrer's murderers!"

Alex Kellner, in his thin, short, light-brown overcoat, his long fair hair tousled, marched along with a set face in the evening drizzle. By the time they reached the Octogon, one of the main squares of the city, the crowd had grown to several hundred; students, workers and curious passers-by. People swarmed from the cafés until the whole square was filled. A few policemen appeared. Alex, usually so quiet and self-possessed, seemed completely changed—he was the loudest, most excited among the demonstrators. Outside one of the cafés the chairs and tables were still standing on the terrace. Trams and cars had to stop because of the multitude blocking the road. People were hanging from the windows. One of the pedestrians, caught in the crowd, turned to Alex and asked: "What's going on, young man? Who's this chap Ferrer you're shouting about?"

This was the last straw for Alex. He jumped on a café table in the drizzling rain, his long hair flowing, his face flushed, his large Adam's apple moving up and down, and began to make an impassioned speech about Ferrer. "Down with the hangmen of Spain!" he cried. The students cheered him wildly. He spoke for about four or five minutes when policemen appeared along the broad Andrassy Avenue. Alex took no notice of them; but one of the policemen rushed up to the café terrace and dragged him from the table. He resisted with all his strength but his companions couldn't give him much help. The policemen were armed with revolvers and heavy sabres; but there was no need for force, they simply dispersed the demonstrators, letting them move on in various small groups. Within half an hour it was all over.

Late that night Alex sat with one of his friends on his usual bench in a small square. He was deeply dejected; he knew that nothing could save Ferrer. But he wondered how such judicial murders could be prevented in the future; what he and his friends could do to shape a better and happier world.

A few weeks later Alex Kellner left school, only two or three months before he would have graduated. There were several reasons for this drastic step. Zoltan had been in trouble before with his teachers; now, once again, he was involved in a fight and the headmaster had advised him to leave the commercial high school. Alex tried to argue against this decision; but it was no use. At the same time he felt that school had very little to offer him. True, in Hungary high school graduates received a special treatment when they did their compulsory military service; but there was also a special 'intelligence certificate' which one could obtain and which exempted one from serving in the ranks. But the most important consideration was money. His tutoring, his part-time journalistic job did not earn enough to provide regular and substantial help for his family. Besides, attending school and working all night were too much of a strain. And so, at seventeen, he ended his formal education. The fiasco of the Ferrer demonstration also cooled his fervour for social reform. All his life he kept a deep sympathy for the underdog; but he had become a realist.

⋆　　⋆　　⋆　　⋆

When young Kellner published his first short story in the liberal daily, he had to choose a pseudonym—lest his headmaster discover that he was breaking the school rules. He had already contributed to the school magazine, using the Latin tag of 'Sursum Corda'. The admonition of 'lift up your hearts' must have sustained him in the dark days of dire poverty and the harsh years of an apparently hopeless struggle. Now he adopted the second word for his regular *nom-de-plume* and it was as Alexander Korda that he began his professional journalistic career.

B

Independent Hungary, like most opposition papers in Hungary, didn't have much money. Korda had to start as a general handyman, covering fires or the meetings of the municipal council, writing an occasional theatrical review or feature article. To eke out his income, he would sell short stories to the news editor of the paper who was running a syndicated fiction service for the Hungarian provincial journals. He was paid about five shillings for each of them, which wasn't exactly princely; but the family needed every penny.

Though he was beginning to earn money, he was still restless. Journalism could only be an intermediary stage; he remembered what he had told his school-friend about films—the 'only future'. Hungarian film production was still in its earliest, most primitive stage. There had been an abortive effort by a theatrical producer to make pictures, using the actors of the famous Gaiety Theatre in Budapest. A photographer, Edmund Uher, made the first professional and profitable Hungarian films but his financial means were very modest. Above all, there was nothing to *learn* about film-making in Hungary, where most technicians were still amateurs.

Korda wanted to see the world. He asked to be sent to Paris as a foreign correspondent. His editor told him that they couldn't afford it; all he could give him was a journalist's card and the promise to publish his articles without any regular commitment. Korda sat down and wrote a letter to one of his relatives:

"I would like to go to Paris and study at the Journalists' Academy. But as you know, I am poor. Would you lend me two hundred crowns? I'm sure that I'll pay you back and I guarantee to become a great man.

"Most respectfully, Alex."

In spite of this 'guarantee', his relative refused to lend him the money. In the end it was Mrs. Kellner who managed to scrape together a hundred crowns—by borrowing, pawning the less essential furniture and sacrificing her pitifully meagre savings. It was a small enough sum but Alex was supremely confident that he would soon become 'somebody in films'. His two young brothers watched with big, solemn eyes as Mrs. Kellner, crying bitterly, packed her oldest son's few belongings in a green wooden box. Alex was feverishly impatient to set off—and in June 1911, not quite eighteen, he started for Paris and the greater world.

In the two decades before the first world war Paris was the Mecca of Hungarian writers and artists. Hungary's greatest modern poet, Endre Ady, wrote a whole cycle of poems which were fervent declarations of love for the French capital. Twentieth-century Hungarian literature had been immensely enriched by the months or years scores of writers spent in the City of Light.

Most of them were young and poor; they lived in small hotels on the Left Bank, spent the days roaming the streets, visiting museums; at night they sat and argued in the cafés. They formed a loosely-connected, amorphous community, helping each other when they had a little cash (which happened rarely) and making the most of their opportunities. One of Korda's friends, a painter, had developed an ingenious system for obtaining credit. He always kept a pile of empty sardine tins on the top of his dresser. That created the impression that the grocer was still trusting him —so the milkman would do the same.

Alex's money didn't last long. The fourteen months he spent in Paris were hard and cruel. For the first time in his life he was entirely on his own. He wrote almost every other day to a friend in Budapest, long letters in which he poured out his heart, describing his hopes, his dreams, his disappointments. Some of the time, his letters revealed, he had no roof over his head; he slept in cafés, on the floor of the hotel-rooms of friends. There were days when he lived on a couple of croissants. Some of his articles were published in Hungary but payment was often delayed, and in any case it wasn't much. But all the time he followed his lodestar, being drawn as if by a magnet to the Pathé Film Studios. When he arrived in Paris, he knew no French, though by the time he returned to Budapest he spoke it fluently. At first all he could do was to hang around the studios; but gradually he managed to gain entry and occasional employment. There were no unions in those days and he took anything he could get; shifting scenery or working as an extra. When there was nothing for him, he would sneak on the floor and stand, watching the director, the cameraman, for whole days. He was determined to learn everything he could about films—even if he starved in the process. He soaked up knowledge; often he itched to take over from a bungling director, set a scene, change the position of the actors—for he felt already that he could do better. But he was never given the chance.

At the end of fourteen months he returned to Budapest. He didn't have the money for the fare and had to be sent back at the expense of the Hungarian Consulate. His mother had been puzzled for some months by the fact that Alex's letters arrived without stamps—he never told her that he couldn't even afford the few centimes. He sat up for three days and nights in the third class railway carriage. When he walked into the family home, his fair hair was almost shoulder-length—a haircut was another luxury he couldn't afford—and he was hungry enough to eat everybody's breakfast at home. He was thinner, taller and more determined than ever to become 'somebody in films'.

★   ★   ★   ★

When Korda came back from Paris, he had acquired a certain prestige; he had seen the world, spoke French and seemed to know a good deal about films. But he was still far from making them.

He continued working for *Independent Hungary* and a publication called *Entrepreneurs' Journal*, contributing regular articles to a trade paper, the *Illustrated Movie World*. All this, however, wasn't getting him closer to his goal.

The café in which Alex had watched his first 'flicks' was owned by the rich Ungerleider family. From showing those early one-reelers, it was a logical step for them to become film distributors. They formed the Projectograph firm which handled French, German, Scandinavian, Austrian, Italian pictures. A few weeks after his return, Korda became the company's secretary. His job was to edit the weekly throwaway programme which contained details of the films and their players; to look after publicity and do any odd chores that cropped up. It wasn't a very well-paid job and he always needed money. Among other things, he had acquired a taste for cigars—good ones, which were expensive even in pre-1914 Hungary. Luckily for him, the Hungarian Minister of Interior issued a new decree about this time, making it compulsory for all foreign films to have Hungarian sub-titles. As many of these were being imported by Projectograph, it wasn't difficult for the company secretary to get a large share of the work. This provided, in addition, an invaluable training, as he had to look at each film several times, study the release scripts when these were available and learn to sum up the action succinctly, simply and clearly in the titles. It was during this time that Korda taught himself the rudiments of English, German and Italian—the languages which he later learned to speak fluently if not always grammatically.

Even though all this meant ten or twelve hours' work a day, it still didn't provide enough for a secure, comfortable life. In 1912 Korda became film editor of the Hungarian weekly *Szinházi Élet* (Theatre Life).

For twenty-five years this lively magazine played an important part in Hungarian culture. It was denounced by its rivals; but its editor-in-chief, Alexander Incze, had developed it from a small publication into a large and vastly prosperous enterprise. Although its title only mentioned the theatre, it dealt with the entire show business. Every issue contained a complete play; short stories, poems, reviews, gossip, fashion, puzzles, sports, radio, travel, society column, advice to the lovelorn—everything but politics. Alexander Incze (who now lives in New York, still happily active in the theatre) had a great affection for Korda, who was a few years his junior. They remained friends for the rest of Alex's life. Korda was already holding three jobs but all this did not exhaust his quicksilver energies. In October 1912 the first issue of *Pesti Mozi* (Budapest Cinema) appeared, edited by Alexander Korda and Istvan Varnai, a well-known journalist. The very word *mozi*, the Hungarian for 'movie', had been coined only a few years earlier by Eugene Heltai, one of the brightest young Hungarian writers and Korda's life-long friend. The paper was published every Saturday, had thirty-two pages with a well-designed, coloured cover and cost less than the price of a roll and a cup of coffee at the students' coffee-house Alex used to frequent.

Turning the yellowing pages of those early issues of *Pesti Mozi*, one can easily trace the development of Alexander Korda as journalist, writer and man-of-the-cinema. He created a lively, colourful and almost aggressively independent paper. He himself, sometimes using the pseudonym '*Sursum*', wrote comparatively little, as he had managed to attract a great many talented and enthusiastic young collaborators. In April 1913 his co-editor retired from the editorship but remained a contributor. The same month the magazine acquired a larger format and was printed by a more professional firm, which showed that it was prospering. But though it was gratifying, it still did not mean the real thing —the making of films instead of writing about them.

Pesti Mozi lived for two and a half years and was replaced by another weekly, *Mozihét* (Ciné-Weekly). Korda began as its sole editor and retained his connection with it until he left Hungary. But long before then he had built his first studio, directed his first score of films and had achieved at least part of his youthful ambitions.

CHAPTER III

THE MEETING AT THE CAFÉ NEW YORK

WHILE Alex was struggling to get into the film industry, his brothers were starting their own careers. Zoltan managed to finish commercial high school and became a checker for a large firm of coal merchants, getting up at dawn to weigh and mark the loads of coal at the freight-yard. For a time he also helped his brother by distributing Alex's little movie magazine among the wholesalers and news-kiosks. Shortly after Korda's return from Paris, a family council was held; the respectable uncles and aunts were alarmed by the unorthodox behaviour of the three boys. It was decided that Vincent should become a dispensing chemist—that was a safe and sensible career. But both Alex and Zoltan protested, threatening to leave home if their young brother was to be forced into a pro-fession he loathed. And so Vincent was entered at the College of Industrial Art, working at the same time in an architect's office. His talent for drawing and painting wasn't discovered until he was fourteen; but he soon made great strides and later was taken on as a pupil by Béla Iványi Grünwald, one of Hungary's fore-most painters, who headed an artists' colony at Kecskemét.

When the first world war broke out, Zoltan Korda was called up and went almost immediately into the army; two years later Vincent followed him. Alex, too, had his medical but the army doctors rejected him as unfit because of his poor eyesight. As a child he had a stubborn eye-ailment which was wrongly diag-nosed as trachoma. For long months the country doctor treated him with blue-stone—a terribly painful treatment—and, as eye-specialists told him much later in London, almost destroyed the sight of one eye. So he found himself at liberty—but financially still insecure.

Through his *Ciné-Weekly* he met Nicholas M. Pasztory, who was a prosperous florist but at the same time a passionate film-addict. Pasztory wanted to make films and he was willing to let Korda help him. Korda promised that he would get him a star —and a story.

The star he found in Gabor Rajnay, one of Hungary's most popular actors, member of the National Theatre. Alex's approach was simple and direct. He walked up to Rajnay's table in the Café New York and said:

"My name's Alexander Korda. There's a friend of mine who wants to make moving pictures and has some money. We thought a war-picture might be a good idea if you were willing to star in it."

"Really, young man," protested Rajnay, "you shouldn't waste my time. There are no studios, no cameras—how d'you expect to make pictures?"

"We've got everything," replied Korda confidently. "There's Zsitkovszky, the lame photographer, he has a camera. There's a small studio in Elizabeth Square—we'll do the interiors there. In any case, it's the exteriors that matter—genuine war-stuff."

"What's the story about?" the actor demanded to know.

"A captain of the Hussars is cashiered because of his gambling debts. War breaks out, he enlists as a sergeant, is promoted in the field for heroism; later he is wounded, falls in love with his nurse —a happy ending!"

"That sounds fine," said Rajnay, almost capitulating, "what about the money?"

"A thousand crowns," Alex promised without any hesitation.

"A thousand crowns? It's a deal, my friend. When do we start?"

"Tomorrow we'll drive out to Kelenfold railway station. You'll be dressed as a Hussar sergeant. We'll wait until we find a

marching company entraining for the front, you'll join them—
that's how you'll go off to war."

Rajnay turned up in his uniform. After a few minutes a company marched into the station and he simply slipped into the
ranks. The cameraman cranked madly under Korda's direction.
Suddenly an officer accosted the actor:

"Are you coming with us, Mr. Rajnay?"

"Not very far," the star grinned. "This is for a movie!"

"Wonderful!" cried the officer. "Are we going to be in it,
too?"

"Of course."

"Then let's make it look real! We'll give you all you want—
tears and kisses and embraces . . ."

The whole company proved to be most co-operative. A giant
Hussar, with flowers around his neck and in his cap, a two-year-
old girl in his arms, with another child clinging to his tunic,
stopped in front of the camera, saying a fond farewell to his
family; tears flowed by the bucket, everybody was acting his
head off.

"Thank God," said Korda, "we've got your departure—now
we need a bit of a battle. Let's go to Rakos, maybe we find
something."

Rakos was the huge drill-ground of the Hungarian Army.
Rajnay, Alex and the cameraman drove out to the vast plain
and waited for a couple of hours. Then a company of Hussars
arrived—a company of cadet-officers. They were led by an
officer on a big black horse. Rajnay was delighted to recognize
an old friend of his named Lulu Topics. He turned out to be the
C.O. The actor explained to him what he wanted; again, the
idea was received with great enthusiasm. They wanted a battle?
Happy to oblige! A real Hussar attack? Glad to help. Zsitkovszky,
almost out of his mind with excitement and delight, went to
work. The scene was so realistic that two Hussars were thrown
by their mounts. Luckily no one was hurt—the only casualty was
a slightly bent cavalry sabre.

Korda beamed with happiness—but he wanted some fighting in the trenches, too. Fortunately, Rakos could provide everything.

A few hundred yards away infantrymen were engaged in target-practice, lying in shallow trenches. Korda told Rajnay to jump into the trench while the cameraman shot the scene. The actor took a flying jump, landing on a young cadet-officer whom he almost scared out of his wits. Rajnay explained that they needed a bayonet attack and some hand-to-hand fighting. Once again, the army proved co-operative. The infantrymen staged an attack—nothing could have been more heroic or bloodthirsty! Several men fell and died most convincingly, others rushed with gnashing teeth, at the invisible enemy; there was a lot of shouting and shooting. No real battle could be more impressive and Korda was truly happy.

Next day the interiors were shot. Around the gambling table, the star, dressed as a captain, lost a fortune to various unpleasant characters. Then there were a few sequences in a hospital with a final love scene in a rose-arbour—and the picture was finished, in three days flat.

It was called 'The Story of a Career', though later it was re-titled 'An Officer's Sword-Knot'. It did wonderful business and turned Gabriel Rajnay into a full-fledged film-star.

*   *   *   *

The Café New York, in which he first approached Gabor Rajnay, played a very important part in Alexander Korda's life.

It was a big, luxurious place, the favourite haunt of journalists, writers, artists. It never closed. It had a high gallery, a vast ground floor and a sort of open basement which was called 'deep water'. Above all, it had a most understanding head-waiter who acted as pawnbroker, moneylender, father confessor and agent to his large, varied clientèle. You could always get a cup of coffee and a roll on tick or sit for hours over a glass of water, solving the problems of the world or developing a new masterpiece; you could read all the foreign and Hungarian newspapers and, if you happened to be temporarily homeless, even catch a little sleep on the red plush seats.

After the hastily improvised first picture, Korda waited in vain for another chance. He went on with his four jobs—but all this meant unsatisfactory drudgery. A whole year went by and then one fortuitous day a tall, well-dressed gentleman walked into the Café New York. He was Eugene Janovics, a man of many parts. Scion of an old Transylvanian family, he began life with an academic career; first a university lecturer and newspaper editor, he became later the Managing Director of the Hungarian National Theatre at Kolozsvár, the capital of Transylvania. He was a man of boundless energy, considerable business acumen and a flair for making a success of his bold experiments. He, too, had been to Paris, but as a well-heeled visitor. He had been shown over the Pathé studios and decided to produce pictures in Kolozsvár. He had the actors, his large and excellent repertory company—and he had space. He made arrangements with Pathé to hire a cameraman and had already shot a few films. His directors included Michael Curtiz and Marton Garas; but production was being expanded, Curtiz had left for Denmark—and he needed a new director.

Alexander Incze, the editor-in-chief of *Theatre Life*, had been called up at the beginning of the war. In 1915 he was wounded and was sent to Kolozsvár for convalescence. He had known Janovics for some years and now, while recovering from his wounds, he began to direct and produce films for his friend. The 'studio' was a tent in the backyard of the theatre; the regular company provided the casts. The average film took a week— six days, to be precise. Often the actors only had a few minutes between finishing their film work and starting a stage performance. It was a cheerfully amateurish business with much improvisation; most people connected with it were blissfully young and ignorant. Janovics had signed a distribution contract with Projectograph—the same firm for which Korda worked. He was a kind man but he hated indolence. One week when the current picture happened to finish Friday afternoon, he insisted that Incze should find a story and write a script overnight so that they could utilize Saturday for starting the new one. "Those hams!" Janovics said, "they'll be paid for doing nothing! My heart breaks over such waste!"

Incze had talked to Janovics about Korda, who was editing *Theatre Life* in his absence and whose longing to direct films he knew. Janovics probably forgot all about it; but the following summer he went to Budapest—and, of course, his first call was at the Café New York where he was certain to meet his friends. As he entered, he looked around; the place was teeming with writers, journalists, musicians and actors. He stopped at one of the tables to greet his old friend Ivan Siklosi, the manager of the Royal Apollo, one of the Hungarian capital's biggest cinemas. Siklosi, who was also a film-journalist, scenarist and title-writer, invited the director of the Kolozsvár National Theatre to join him.

"Tell me, Ivan," Janovics came straight to the point, "could you recommend somebody to direct a few pictures for me in Kolozsvár?"

"Of course I can," replied Siklosi promptly. "Look . . . up there, in the gallery . . . at the back, in the right-hand corner . . . can you see that young, fair-haired fellow?"

"What about him?"

"He's a most versatile, talented chap. He's been working at Projectograph but left his job recently; he's also editing the *Ciné-Weekly*, which you know—but I'm sure he'd love to work for you . . ."

"But Ivan . . ." Janovics was puzzled, "has he ever directed a film?"

"I think he's done one with Rajnay . . . a small war picture . . ."

"That doesn't sound as if he'd had much experience . . ."

"Well, he's been in Paris and worked at the Pathé studios—and he's always wanted to be a director. Last year the *Trikolor* Company was formed here, planning several films. One of its directors would have been Korda. It wasn't his fault that they never started production. I really think he's the man for you . . ."

Janovics pondered this for a while, watching Korda, who sat fifteen feet above them, blissfully unconscious that his fate was being decided down below.

"All right," the producer said at last, "can't do any harm to talk to him . . . Ask him to come downstairs . . ."

Siklosi introduced the two men and then left for his office. He returned five hours later for an after-lunch cup of coffee. Janovics and Korda were still sitting at the same table, which was littered with cigar-butts, sheets of paper covered with figures and names, half-empty glasses of water and cold cups of coffee.

A week later *Ciné-Weekly* published the following item:

> "Our editor, Mr. Alexander Korda, has left this week for Kolozsvár to direct some pictures during the summer in Dr. Eugene Janovics's Transylvania Studios. In his absence Istvan Varnai will act as editor."

Five weeks later this was followed by another announcement:

> "Alexander Korda, our editor, who is working as director in Dr. Eugene Janovics's Kolozsvár film studios, has signed a three year contract with the Transylvania Film Company."

Korda's first salary was 18,000 crowns a year. A little more than the salary a Hungarian Cabinet Minister received at that time.

*   *   *   *

This was the great chance, the fabulous coincidence, the long-awaited opening for which Korda had hoped and worked ever since he had stood on the floor of the Pathé Studios, eagerly watching the director's work and envying him with all his heart.

Yet at the last minute he had a little stage-fright. He knew that however much he had learned about films, it had been from the outside; that apart from that crazily haphazard venture a year before, he had never carried such responsibilities.

"I just don't know enough," he confided to Incze, whom he still found in Kolozsvár.

"Never mind—you'll learn," his friend reassured him. "I knew even less—and I managed somehow."

Korda's misgivings turned out to be justified. Not because he failed to master his craft; he had seen so many pictures and thought so much about films that he was more than ready to start. But when the veteran actors of Janovics's theatre saw the 'young boy', they revolted and sent a deputation to their boss.

"We won't work under such a 'snotnose'," declared the veteran Istvan Szentgyörgyi, Hungary's Henry Irving. "Why, he's hardly out of the cradle; his mouth's still wet with his mother's milk!"

"He's crazy, anyhow," said another actor. "We've been making pictures for over a year—and we've done them exactly in the same style of acting as we used on the stage. Now this Korda starts to spout that films are different, that we've got to learn our profession all over again!"

Korda, of course, found out about the 'conspiracy'. He told Janovics that he would return to Budapest on the first morning train. Janovics asked him to wait and called a general meeting of the company.

"All I'm asking you is to wait until the first picture is finished," he told them. "Until then do whatever Mr. Korda asks you— even if it's against your convictions. When the film's ready, we can decide whether he's right or wrong. I promise you he won't direct a second picture unless the first is successful."

This first picture was an adaptation of Sardou's famous melodrama 'Fedora', retitled 'White Nights'. Shocking Janovics to the core, Korda took two weeks instead of the usual six days over it. He had a beautiful, talented leading lady, Lily Berky, supported by half-a-dozen of Janovics's best actors. They grumbled and groaned but followed Korda's direction.

The picture was trade-shown in August, 1916, in Budapest. The reviews spoke of 'artistic perfection', 'a new revelation', 'a milestone in Hungarian films'. The picture made a great deal of money and was the first Hungarian production to be shown outside the country.

A little sheepishly, the actors admitted that they had been wrong. The matter was clinched with Korda's second picture, 'Grandmama'. This was based on a Hungarian stage classic and the title role was played by Lujza Blaha, probably Hungary's best-loved actress, a combination of Marie Lloyd and Irene Vanbrugh. She took to Korda from the first moment and never questioned his authority. The others had to follow her lead whether they liked it or not. Korda wrote the script himself and among his players was Michael Varkonyi, who later became very successful in the silent Hollywood films as Victor Varconi.

This second picture was an even greater success. Now the actors changed their attitude completely—they insisted on being told every small detail, besieged Korda for advice. Janovics renewed his contract for three years.

During the summer and early autumn Korda made five more films in the Transylvanian capital. Three of the seven were released in 1916, the others were spread over the next two years. Among them were 'Tales of the Typewriter', the film-version of a best-selling novel, the first to present in Hungary the modern career girl which also starred Lily Berky; Mark Twain's 'The One Million Pound Banknote' which Korda and Janovics scripted together, transferring it to a Hungarian setting. Korda was constantly searching for better, more literary material. It was he who did the first of a whole series of dramatic pictures based on the novels of Maurus Jókai, Hungary's greatest novelist who combined the rich narrative talent of a Walter Scott with the realism and humour of a Charles Dickens.

*   *   *   *

Korda's next clash was not with his actors but with his employer. Throughout his life he would always chafe under authority and never feel happy unless he was his own master. Janovics himself began to realize that his brilliant young director was a problem-child. Korda's reputation grew apace—and so did his budgets. Janovics warned him repeatedly to stick to the agreed figures. Korda replied that he couldn't work with his hands tied; he would either make good pictures or none at all. Within a few months his self-assurance had grown tremendously. He wouldn't stand for any interference in the choice of the screenplay, the cast or his technical staff, though he listened patiently to the opinions of the smallest bit-player or the property man. In the end, however, he always made his decisions himself.

Early in 1917 Janovics came to the conclusion that the backyard of his theatre was too small for the large-scale productions Korda wanted. The Rumanians had invaded Transylvania and though they had been beaten back by the Hungarian-German armies, there was still the danger of war spreading to the province. He transferred his production firm renamed Corvin Films after Matthias Corvinus, Hungary's great Renaissance king —to Budapest, where at first they found a modest home near the Town Park, in Colony Street.

Soon after the transfer Janovics realized that while Korda was the king-pin of his organization, he himself couldn't remain its chief. Korda wouldn't work under him; and he couldn't very well subordinate himself to the man he had hired only a few months before in the Café New York.

When he returned to the capital, Korda called on his old friend and ex-editor, Alexander Incze. Incze had recently produced the first Hungarian 'all-star' picture based on one of the plays of Ferenc Molnar. This film, called 'Mr. Doctor', had been financed by Richard Strasser, son of a wealthy dynasty of grain-merchants. Strasser was far more interested in pretty actresses than in the hemp-yarn factory his family had bought him; it was logical that he should become an angel of the film industry. Incze introduced him to Korda.

In April 1917 the Hungarian trade papers announced that Alexander Korda and Nicholas M. Pasztory had bought Corvin Films from Dr. Janovics. The new owners announced an ambitious production programme. A few days later Korda appointed Frederick Karinthy, one of the most brilliant Hungarian writers, head of his scenario department. Karinthy, whose mordant 'Journey Around My Skull' made him known both in America and England, was to write original stories, adapt classics and recruit a staff of the best authors as his collaborators.

In the autumn of 1917 Corvin Films was transformed into a company with a nominal capital of one million crowns. Large offices were leased on Rakoczi Road, one of the main boulevards. The studios had cutting rooms and ample space for expansion. Here Alex, the eternal cigar clamped between his lips, used to cut his films with Gustav Kovacs, his faithful cameraman. Outsiders often watched him with fascinated horror—for if a few embers or particles of glowing cigar-ash were to have dropped into the baskets holding the waste film, the whole house would have gone up in flames.

About a dozen well-known actors were placed under contract: Oscar Beregi who, in his eighties, is still making an occasional film in Hollywood; Victor Varconi who was signed for six pictures; Lily Berky, Korda's first star and Gabor Rajnay, who had so good-naturedly helped Alex to start his career as a director.

But Korda wanted to have his own studios. With Strasser's financial resources this became possible and, in the summer of 1917, in spite of wartime shortages and restrictions, construction began in Zuglo, a north-eastern suburb of Budapest. The Corvin studios were built in record time and were soon busily turning out pictures.

Between April 1917 and October 1919 Korda directed and produced about a dozen films. The first picture made at the new studios was Edward Knoblock's 'Faun' which had been a great stage success in Hungary. Gabor Rajnay starred in it with an enchanting blonde named Ica Lenkeffy. It was followed by 'St. Peter's Umbrella', the film version of Koloman Mikszath's fine novel, a half-mystical, half-humorous tale which poked good-natured fun at miracles. Victor Varconi and Ica Lenkeffy were the stars, supported by Martin Ratkai, the best-known Hungarian comedian. Korda's next venture was a most ambitious film, based on 'The Stork Caliph', a psychological novel by the great Hungarian poet Michael Babits, adapted by Frederick Karinthy —the psychological study of a young man who in a series of nightmares slips deeper and deeper into the criminal underworld until he reaches the point of no return. It was followed by 'Magia' (Magic), an original story by Kalman Sztrokay and Frederick Karinthy, which also dealt with the occult. 'Harrison & Barrison' was a light-hearted farce with a complex plot, set in a lightly caricatured America and starring Hungary's best-known comedians with Martin Ratkai at their head.

In eighteen months Korda had acquired considerable experience, great authority and a large income. He dominated his staff, and his partner, the ex-florist Nicholas Pasztory. He had left the family home and established himself at the Hotel Royal, a few blocks from his offices on the main boulevard of Budapest. His cigars had become bigger and more expensive.

Alex had very decided views about film-scripts which he considered the most essential part of any picture. In an article which he contributed to *Theatre Life* in 1917—it carried a very youthful photograph of the author—he pointed out that screenwriters were finding entirely new opportunities and that the old-fashioned, over-literary approach was being discarded. A screenplay must be visual and the story told in a series of images. It wasn't easy to acquire the technique but it was essential to learn it. The mere idea wasn't enough; it had to be developed in a form which had nothing to do with any other form of writing. "Only action that can be expressed in images is suitable for the screen . . ." he said.

This advice, more than forty years old, is still pertinent today even though Korda was writing about silent films.

In November 1917 he published a two-part article in *Ciné-Weekly* about the position of Hungarian films. This was reprinted by a Berlin trade paper with a hostile comment. The Germans considered Hungary an 'exclusive colony' as far as films were concerned and resented the growth and success of the native product. Korda replied to the German attack in the Christmas issue of *Ciné-Weekly*. It is a striking fact that if one substituted 'British' for 'Hungarian' and 'American' for 'German', these statements would be completely valid today. Interesting, too, is that in his interview he envisaged a post-war world in which Germany would be a defeated or at least a considerably chastened country.

"I'm almost ashamed to say it again as I have done it so often before, but I have a deep faith in Hungarian films. You must understand—this is not just whistling in the dark, nor a *credo quia absurdum* belief. I do not expect Hungarian film production to vegetate among the many other national film industries; I believe unflinchingly and have been shouting it at the top of my voice for four or five years: we Hungarians will soon get to the top. The doubters I cannot convince. It would be better for them to wait. In a year's time I'll present them with the proofs.

But what will happen once peace comes? I am an optimist. Good films have always done well, whatever the economic conditions; and if the Hungarians follow their present bent, they'll survive in the new, salutary and longed-for cataclysm which peace must bring. We mustn't be afraid of film prices being lowered rapidly. Do not misunderstand me: I am not speaking as a producer now. I don't mind if films are cheap—but only if their production costs are low. It would be a disaster if at the rate of the present costs the revenue of films would be suddenly cut by 75 per cent. But this cannot happen. The times when films were sold at so much per yard can never return.

It is certain that for us—but also for the German studios— times will be difficult for a while. In this transitory period we must find our home-market again—which is bound to change—and sell our pictures to the world, as the frontiers are opened again. The Germans feel the crisis the hardest of all. They try to protect themselves against us. Now they have formed a new concern with a capital of twenty-five million marks.

Just like all new enterprises this, too, is starting with glittering phrases; but behind the big lies and untold millions something is missing: the basic motive of the whole organization is not superior vision and force but defensive timidity, based on purely local resources. What is the truth? The Nordisk company which the Allied Powers have boycotted in the war, is the paramount film power in Germany today. It owns most of the big cinemas and is almost dictating to the German film-world. On the other hand Germany will represent a small territory after the war and the Nordisk company must regain the world market. How can it do this? By acquiring certain assets which it can later use as bargaining counters with the Western film studios. It must create, if possible, a monopoly in Germany, Austria and Hungary— if the latter two countries are given a share in the world markets.

It will be a great battle. No doubt about it, the German market has already been taken over by this concern. We don't believe that it will take over Hungary. It would be greatly to our disadvantage.

In the future battles for the world markets of films the decision won't be brought about by the millions of marks but by good films. And in this respect I consider the German mammoth enterprise far weaker than the studios of the

Western Powers. That is why I do not believe that the coming film-war will bring a victory for Germany or turn Hungarian film-production into a servile appendage of the Germans."

*   *   *   *

In 1917 Korda met a strikingly beautiful young woman. She had started her career very early in show business and then married a rich young man who was an amateur composer. She was a dazzling blonde, tall, with a perfect figure and a character that someone described as that of a 'royal tigress'. Her name was Antonia Farkas; her friends called her 'Toncsi'. The world came to know her as Maria Corda.

Alex fell deeply in love with her; after her divorce, they were married. By that time he had starred her in five films, surrounding her with the best and most experienced actors for support.

This last series of Korda's Hungarian films was a varied lot. As the Central Powers were beginning to face defeat, film production was running into difficulties. The blockade led to shortages everywhere and practically everything was rationed. Raw materials to build sets were almost impossible to obtain; wood, plaster of paris, even nails were getting scarce. Yet Korda went on, with unflagging enthusiasm, although sometimes he couldn't help complaining:

"We must consider the tremendous financial superiority, the highly developed technical equipment of the German, French, and especially American studios," he said in an interview. "We have only the minimum of technical resources; sets, costumes, transport and many other requirements present tremendous problems and one must give up many an idea which our foreign colleagues could easily realize. I was unable to get ten pounds of plaster of paris in the whole of Budapest. The public, of course, cares little if one scene of the film, passing through the hands of sixty smugglers, is spoiled and it is hard to obtain a substitute; the main thing is that it should be a good picture and stand comparison with the foreign produce . . ."

His most ambitious and successful film of these final Hungarian years was 'Man of Gold', based on Maurice Jokai's classic novel. This was actually a 'super-colossal', shown in three parts. The scenario had been written by Ernest Vajda, who became an internationally-known playwright and screenwriter under the pen-name of Sydney Garrick and who died in Hollywood quite recently. The cameraman was Steven Eiben—a boy of sixteen whom Korda discovered and who remained active in Hungarian films until his death in 1958. Korda took his company, which included Oscar Beregi, Gabor Rajnay and his close personal friend Gyula Szöreghy, on location to the Lower Danube, the romantic Iron Gate and the picturesque little island of Ada Kaleh, to shoot 'Man of Gold'. This, perhaps his most ambitious film to date, was a triumphant success.

The second picture of this period was 'Number 111', based on Eugene Heltai's charming, slightly nostalgic novel. Korda's discovery, Antonia Farkas, was co-starred in it with Gabor Rajnay. An old, rather supercilious actress was playing the part of Princess Olympia in the picture. Korda had a great deal of trouble with her. She wouldn't follow directions, sit at the right angle or react properly. After five or six takes, Korda went up to the box in which she was sitting (the scene was in a theatre), removed his cigar and said, very gently:

"Your Royal Highness, if you spoil one more take, I'll kick you so hard that you'll land in exile!"

The old actress bridled, undecided whether to scream or faint. She did neither; but she was so indignant that she looked just right and the scene was perfect.

'Yamata' starred Emil Fenyvesi, one of Hungary's matinée idols, Gabor Rajnay—in the unlikely rôle of an Ethiopian servant

—and Ila Loth, a lovely young actress. Miss Loth was rather frightened by the already famous young director. When she was doing a love scene with Fenyvesi, Korda suddenly called to the actor: 'Don't be so sincere!" The brief instruction summed up the whole character, the essence of the scene—and the young actress suddenly gained confidence.

Korda was by now accepted as the leading producer in Hungary. He was elected to the board of the National Cinema Association. In May 1918 he finally said good-bye to his *Ciné-Weekly* which he had started three years earlier.

"It is not easy for me to forsake my place," he said in a farewell interview, "for I have loved this magazine dearly; but my present work leaves me no time for editorial chores. My friends with whom we had struggled together for three whole years, have been carrying on this work for months on their own, anyhow."

Later that year he gave another interview to *Ciné-Weekly*, repeating his contention that Hungarian film production would stand up to post-war competition:

"In the last three years of the war Hungarian studios have achieved more than in the previous fifteen. We began to approach the standards of the great European film-makers and our results are without parallel in the history of the cinema. I believe that in the future we'll keep above the level of Austrian and German production though unavoidably lag behind America and Britain . . ."

A week later he attacked the Hungarian film distributors who preferred the foreign product, pointing out that in 1917 and 1918 fifty per cent of screen-time was occupied by successful Hungarian films.

Nineteen-eighteen was a momentous year for Hungary. Ten

days before Armistice Day, the so-called 'Revolution of the Autumn Roses' took place in Budapest. War-weary Hungarian soldiers streamed back from the front. Count Michael Karolyi, a popular though somewhat weak liberal leader, became head of the government. Everything was in ferment; centuries-old institutions were destroyed, the ties of Austria and Hungary were cut, the Habsburg Monarchy collapsed.

Months before these events Korda was already thinking of greener pastures, wider fields. In the summer of 1918, as he sat at his desk in the Rakoczi Road offices of Corvin Studios, he talked to his friend and former schoolmate, Andor Zsoldos. Korda was twenty-five but he barely looked twenty. His dark-blond hair was hanging over his forehead; he wore his usual stiff, high collar. He told his friend that in Hungary no one occupied himself seriously with the problems of films; there was so little capital for worth-while pictures. The managing director of Svenska Films had written to him, asking him to send prints of two of his films; he was seriously considering going to Stockholm, where he felt he would have far more scope.

The new Hungarian democracy was a shaky régime. The surrounding so-called successor states were preparing to carve up the country, claiming large chunks of territory; inside Hungary the Communists were plotting against Karolyi. In the midst of all this danger and strife, Korda went on making pictures as long as he could. In March 1919 the Communist dictatorship of Bela Kun took over. Film production was first interrupted and then subordinated to Red propaganda. Korda, who had two films on the floor, couldn't finish them for many months. Nineteen days before the Communist *coup d'état* he was still talking about ambitious plans in an interview. He intended to film several of Jokai's novels; Hungary had to prove that she could compete with the top pictures of other countries. The success of his own 'Man of Gold' had proved that it was stupid to waste time on silly detective stories, petty love tales, over-sentimental rubbish —all that was called 'average film'. He planned three Jokai-

films with a total budget of 2½ million crowns. After that he
would tackle Victor Hugo's 'Notre Dame', Goethe's 'Faust',
Washington Irving's 'Rip Van Winkle', 'The Bells of Corneville'
and one of Walter Scott's novels.

Of all these impressive plans only the first two Jokai films
ever came to fruition.

★　　★　　★　　★

The Bela Kun régime lasted a hundred and thirty-three days—
from March 21 to the middle of August, 1919. The very first day
the 'Governing Council', the new body running the country,
issued a decree nationalizing the entire film industry. The same
evening producers, distributors, exhibitors and technicians of the
industry met to be harangued by Bela Paulik, the 'film commissar', who told them they had all become 'workers of the
state'.

Apart from the so-called nationalization, nothing much happened. Everybody kept his job; only the titles changed. The
producer or managing director became the 'studio-responsible'.
But soon enough the heat was turned on.

In 1957 the fortieth anniversary of Korda's Corvin Studios was
celebrated in Budapest and a Communist paper published a long
article about him. Istvan Lengyel, a veteran journalist, wrote:

> "Two years after the opening of the studios Korda left
> not only his job but also changed his country. As the director
> of the propaganda and newsreel films of the Hungarian
> Soviet Republic, the Counter-Revolution singled him out
> for persecution and he had to flee from the terror of the
> White Reactionaries."

Then Lengyel added a curiously apologetic paragraph:

> "The historians of our country's culture, engaged in
> building Socialism, must strive for objectivity and put all

achievements of Hungarian culture in the proper perspec-
tive. That is why on the fortieth anniversary of the Corvin
Studios we placed the founder's, Alexander Korda's, rôle
and activity in the foreground of this study, sketching the
heroic age of our film production."

This double-talk meant, of course, that in Communist Hungary
at that time a eulogy of a 'capitalistic' film-magnate had to be
seasoned with considerable distortion of facts. It would be
ridiculous to defend Korda against the charge of having been a
Communist. If Korda had really filled such post, this would have
been prominently and repeatedly mentioned in the columns of
Red Film—the weekly review published during the brief Bela
Kun régime. The Communists—as they always do in the early
stages of their dictatorship—were anxious to make use of all
'bourgeois talent', the well-known and important figures in the
arts and sciences. But Korda's name appeared only twice in 'Red
Film'. In the second issue there was a brief notice about a committee appointed to screen and grade the Hungarian actors. Its
members were Michael Curtiz, Alfred Deesy (a well-known
director, now in his eighties, still living in Budapest), the popular
author Paul Forro, another director named Bela Balogh, two
stage and film-stars and Dr. Pakots, a writer and editor. Not one
of these was known as particularly left-wing. Korda was the
eighth member.

The only other reference to Korda was in No. 12 of *Red Film*,
announcing him as director of the film-version of Israel Zangwill's
'Mary-Ann', followed by another picture called 'Ave Caesar'.

Korda had always been a humanist but never a party politician.
And during the short-lived Communist régime in Hungary
there was precious little humanism. In these months Korda
frequented the Café Balaton, not far from his mother's home,
talking the nights away with his closest friends, Andor Zsoldos,
Ivan Siklosi, Istvan Varnai. One evening he told them how the
Communist film bosses wanted to force him into making a

propaganda picture but that he had refused. They chose Alexander
Petőfi's great poem 'The Apostle'; all Alex could do was to play
for time though he was under considerable pressure. Financially
he was very well off; he received a monthly salary of five thousand
crowns in so-called 'blue money' (the worthless Communist
currency was, strangely enough, called 'white money' because
one side of the banknotes was blank) and he drew as much for
expenses as he wanted. Naturally, his less prosperous friends
shared his affluence. He deposited a large amount with the head
waiter of his favourite café against which his friends could draw
in settling their bills.

The Communist régime collapsed in August 1919 and there
was a brief interregnum before Rumanian troops occupied the
Hungarian capital. (They stayed for several months until Admiral
Horthy's White Army marched in.) By then Korda was determined to leave Hungary. One night, after visiting his usual café,
he went for a long walk with Zsoldos. They sat down on a
bench outside the ancient Rudas Baths and Korda explained that
he had made all his arrangements for his departure. "I haven't
been able to fix the Swedish contract," he said, "so I'm going
to Vienna. There's a count who's started a studio, he has
unlimited funds—I'll try to do something with him. He's sent
me an invitation . . ."

But somehow he couldn't tear himself away from Budapest.
He finished 'Mary-Ann', which had been interrupted during the
Communist régime, and put the finishing touches to 'White
Rose', based on another Jokai novel, starring Antonia Farkas in
the title-rôle of 'Gul Beyazet', a Turkish beauty of the sixteenth
century. Both films played to packed houses when they were
released a few months later.

★   ★   ★   ★

As Admiral Horthy established his régime, a purge began in
Hungarian life. In the first year there was a full-scale White

Terror, balancing the Red Terror that had ruled between March and August 1919. Hundreds of people were arrested, scores murdered or executed under martial law. The Horthy régime was anti-Semitic and anti-Liberal.

In Hungary all cinemas had state licences. The new government revised them; most Jewish owners were deprived of them. Corvin Studios lost the two large cinemas they owned. In January 1920 an entirely new company was formed with British, Italian, Austrian and German capital. The new board consisted of Colonel Stead (a member of the British Military Mission), Dr. Simonyi-Semadam, for a brief time Prime Minister of Hungary, Julius Hegedüs, a well-known actor, Richard Strasser and two Austrian financiers. Korda was named as production chief.

This was a piece of window-dressing. Within a few weeks the Corvin shares were sold to a Hungarian businessman, Alexander Barna. Korda had already left Hungary.

Late in October 1919 he was arrested. There was nothing dramatic about it—a sergeant of Horthy's army collected him at his home, politely and almost apologetically. But his family and friends discovered that he had been taken to the Hotel Gellert, the headquarters of the White Terrorists.

Toncsi Farkas and Zoltan Korda hurried to the hotel to enquire about his fate. They thought that a beautiful actress and an ex-officer might intervene effectively if they combined forces. As they were taken up in a lift, they overheard two Horthyist officers talking about a "tall, fair-haired film man" whom they intended "to teach manners" by a thorough beating that night.

As it turned out, they missed their little bit of sadistic fun.

Zoltan and Toncsi managed to see Horthy's chief aide-de-camp. At the same time Korda's friends, among them Eugene Heltai, whose Number 111 Alex had filmed, also came to the rescue. Actually, a mistake had been made. Alex had a namesake, an obscure actor who had been a prominent Communist; the mis-understanding was cleared up and he was released in less than twenty-four hours.

One thing is certain: no proceedings were ever started against him, no accusation made of Communist affiliations in any Hungarian paper. His films continued to play in the Budapest cinemas; in October and December 1920 while the White Terror was still at its height, the *Ciné-Weekly* published articles about him and he contributed a letter to the Christmas number. Unlike so many Hungarian writers, artists, journalists, actors who left the country rather than live under the new régime, Korda was never denounced or attacked in the Hungarian Press.

CHAPTER IV

YOUNG MAN GOING WEST

K ORDA arrived in Vienna in November 1919. He drove
straight to the luxurious Grand Hotel and took the
largest suite. Then he gave orders for a large limousine
to be at his disposal day and night. A year or so before he had
grown a beard—Van Dyck style—about which his friends teased
him mercilessly. He also took to wearing a monocle. But he knew
what he was doing. He wanted to look older—and therefore
have more authority. The suite, the hired limousine—they were
all part of his plan to conquer the West. It didn't bother him that
he had very little cash in his pockets.

He had told his friends about the 'count' who wanted him to
make pictures in Austria. At that time he hadn't yet met Count
Alexander Kolowrat, one of the most colourful and extraordinary
Austrians. Born in America but son of one of the richest and
oldest families in the Habsburg Empire (they possessed large
estates in Bohemia and the count's father had married the heiress
of the tobacco-king Upman) Count Alexander had two passions:
films and motor-racing. He, too, had visited the Pathé Studios in
Paris; not, as young Alex Korda, a penniless, starving dreamer,
but as a rich amateur who wanted to learn something about this
strange new invention. Known as Sascha to all his friends and
associates, he was a gargantuan figure who seldom managed to
reduce his weight below 22 stones, however hard he tried. He
was happiest either behind the wheel of a fast car or bending
over a kitchen stove.

Count Kolowrat had started to make documentary films in
1909, ran the Austrian newsreel units during the first world war

and made his first feature pictures in 1916. Though Sascha Films wasn't registered until September 1918, he had produced twelve long films in 1917, nine in 1918 and seven in 1919. Considering Austria's economic and political situation, this was a remarkable achievement. When Korda reached Vienna, the Austrian capital was in the throes of a terrible inflation—almost as bad as the subsequent German disaster. Austria, having lost almost three-quarters of her territory and population, was like a water-headed baby—the metropolis of Vienna had no *hinterland*, very little industry and a sadly-disorganized agriculture. The savings of the middle-class had been wiped out; the cafés were full of *Schieber* who trafficked in foreign currency, in gold or in often imaginary goods. All this did not deter Count Kolowrat. He believed in films and though he had to sell a few forests or a castle or two in Bohemia, in order to finance his hobby, he went on producing films through the most disheartening years of Austria's history.

The two Alexanders, Korda and Kolowrat, took to each other from the first moment. Even so, it wasn't until June, seven months after his arrival, that Alex started his first picture—an elaborate and carefully-planned film version of Mark Twain's *The Prince and the Pauper*. Count Kolowrat gave Korda *carte blanche*—and then almost wrecked the picture himself.

'The Prince and the Pauper' was set in the reign of Edward VI, the Boy King, and aimed to reproduce the whole pomp and circumstance of the rich Tudor period. Korda told his assistant, Karl Hartl, to find a dwarf for the important rôle of the court jester. After a long search, Hartl came up with the perfect man —a Viennese engineer to whom Nature had given a tiny body and a large head. It wasn't easy to persuade the intelligent young man to take the part—but Korda's charm worked the usual miracle. After a week's rehearsals they were ready to shoot the scenes in which he appeared. On the first day Count Kolowrat visited the studio. He was wildly enthusiastic about Hartl's discovery. He liked the little man so much that he invited him to the studio canteen where they had a long and animated private conversation.

The next day the 'court jester' had disappeared without a trace and the film had to stop.

It took three whole days before the mystery was solved and the diminutive actor could return to work. Count Sascha was training for the famous Semmering Race in which only small sports cars were to take part. He was determined to win it. The rules prescribed 'a driver and an adult passenger' for each car. Count Kolowrat alone weighed almost 300 lb. First he tried to reduce the weight of the car—he had the seats and the whole superstructure removed so that only the chassis remained. Then he mounted two bamboo chairs on it. Even this wasn't sufficient —until he saw the dwarf and had a brainwave. The little engineer was, beyond doubt, an adult. So he simply kidnapped the little actor without telling Korda or Hartl. He won the race.

Korda was furious. By now he could swear in German with admirable fluency though with a strong Hungarian accent. When the dwarf appeared on the floor, he was still a nervous wreck. He had spent the worst hours of his life in that bamboo seat, doing penance for all the sins he had ever committed or was going to commit. Shaken and battered, driven at a mad pace over the hairpin curves of the Semmering—it was awful! It took all the combined persuasive talent of Korda and Hartl to make the little man go through with his rôle. He said that he had had enough for a lifetime of motor-racing, films and everything else with which Count Sascha was even remotely connected.

The Mark Twain story starred Master Tibor Lubinszky, Hungary's Jackie Cooper. Korda's old Budapest paper, the *Ciné-Weekly*, reported proudly in October 1920 that according to the preliminary reports Korda's first Austrian picture was 'perfection itself'. In the Christmas issue of the weekly, Korda stated:

> "After 'The Prince and the Pauper' I started last week preparing my new film. Its title: 'The Venice of Dreams'. The stars are my wife and Alberto Capozzi. The interiors

will be shot here in Vienna, the location sequences in Venice, where I plan to begin after Christmas. After that I'm doing another film for Sascha; the Italian picture is for the Doremi Studios in Rome. For my Sascha picture I intend to choose the locations next October in Naples, Terra del Greco, Taormina and Tripoli. If anybody else made this trip, *I* would be most envious. I have no further plans. Perhaps I'll stay in Vienna, perhaps I won't. I had offers to work in Rome and Berlin but it's a little difficult to get used to such a gipsy existence. For the time being I have no intention to come home. Not yet.

I send warmest greetings to *Ciné-Weekly* and its readers. Please, don't forget your former editor and when you see a picture of mine, believe me, your opinion is the most important to me—just as if I had made it in Budapest . . ."

When he sent this message, Korda was whistling in the dark. 'The Prince and the Pauper' was an excellent picture; but both Kolowrat and Korda had forgotten that Mark Twain's works were still copyright. Another version of the same novel had actually been filmed in America and there were long, complex negotiations until the matter was settled. It was settled finally very much to Korda's credit and advantage for the American version was withdrawn and the Austrian shown all over the States. Later there was a dispute as to Korda's percentage in the profits; this was settled by arbitration and he received a substantial amount.

All this was still in the future when Alexander Incze, on his way to the United States, spent New Year's Eve 1920/21 with the Kordas in Vienna. He found his old friend a little subdued. The film 'The Venice of Dreams' was never made. For almost a year Alexander Korda was unemployed.

* * * *

Maria Corda had made a film in Italy soon after Korda began work in Vienna. In 1921 the birth of their son, Peter Vincent, had kept her out of films but by the end of the year she was ready to resume her career. Her husband accompanied her to Rome.

Maria was still working in Italy when Korda decided to return to Vienna to discuss his future plans with Count Kolowrat. As he boarded the train, he ran into Lajos Biro.

The two men had known each other in Budapest but not intimately. Biro was thirteen years Korda's senior and a writer of international reputation. Eight years before their accidental meeting he had written an autobiographical note for an anthology of short stories published in Budapest. He said:

> "I am thirty-three years old. I became a journalist at eighteen and still follow the same profession. I have written a few thousand articles, a few hundred short stories, a dozen novels and plays. At twenty-five I got married; my wife is the finest human being I know; I adore my little daughter. My life's desire is to retire with them to a big house in green County Gomor and write novels. That's all I can tell you about myself."

These few lines more or less sum up Lajos Biro. A man of great modesty, of liberal, even radical sympathies; a most prolific writer who could turn his hand to any form of literature; a family man whose 'life's wish' was to retire from the hurly-burly with his family and devote all his time to his books.

During the short-lived liberal régime of Count Michael Karolyi, Biro had entered politics for the first and last time in his life. He became Under Secretary of State for Cultural Affairs. He left Hungary in 1919 because he was in total opposition to Bela Kun's Communist régime. Later he returned for several visits but never again settled in his country. His books and plays had been translated into many languages and he had no difficulty in establishing himself abroad. He had started to work for films at an early stage of his career and became one of the finest craftsmen in the new medium.

For Korda, the chance meeting at Rome station was providential. Here was a man who spoke his language—both literally and intellectually—who had wide connections, a mature judgment. For the next thirty years, with a few brief interruptions, they were to work together. In a way Biro replaced the father Korda had lost so early in his life.

Biro had written a novel called *Serpolette*. It was based on the tragic story of the Habsburg Archduke John Nepomuk Salvator, who fell in love with a commoner, resigned his rank and adopted the name of John Orth. He was a passionate sailor and in 1890 set out on his yacht to circumnavigate the globe. Legend had it that the woman for whom he had sacrificed so much deceived him with one of his sailors, whereupon he disappeared without trace.

Biro fashioned a taut, dramatic book from the somewhat melodramatic material. The film rights were sold first to a Hungarian company and in turn acquired by Sascha Films. It wasn't difficult for Korda to make arrangements that his new friend's story should be assigned to him. Later Alex bought a story from Ernest Vajda, called *Masters of the Sea* and the preparations for these two pictures took up most of the next twelve months.

In the meantime, with short intervals, Maria Corda continued filming in Italy. In the spring of 1920 Mrs. Kellner and Zoltan Korda had joined Alex in Vienna. Vincent was still working in the artists' colonies of Kecskemét and Nagybánya.

Family feeling was always strong in Central Europeans; but in Korda had it was a deep, basic need. He had never forgotten how valiantly his mother had struggled to keep the family together and provide a home for her three orphaned sons. He was deeply attached to her and though his financial resources were far from ample, he did everything to make her happy in her new home. Unfortunately, no long after her arrival, Mrs. Korda became seriously ill. Alex provided for her with loving care; she was taken to the famous Loew Sanatorium, the nursing home of kings and millionaires which had an international reputation. But the specialists could do nothing and, late in 1921, not long after her grandson's birth she died. Alex was heartbroken and for a long time a prey to deep melancholy. He had needed his mother's courage and wisdom more than ever at the threshold of his international career. Zoltan was at his side, working as a film-editor and the two brothers grew even closer to each other.

* * * *

For his two pictures—Biro's *Serpolette* was re-titled 'Eine Versunkene Welt' (A Vanished World)—Korda assembled a first-class cast.

John Orth's leading rôle was entrusted to Alberto Capozzi, one of the most popular Italian stars. Highly temperamental and hot-blooded, he had his own very decided ideas of an actor's importance. Once he had refused the rôle of St. Paul because he "couldn't disfigure his face with a beard". He invented a new acting style—called 'the languid one'—which was practically slow-motion and ensured one important thing: a great deal of footage on the screen. He was supported by Victor Varconi, Paul Lucas, the child-star Tibor Lubinszky and several leading actors of the Vienna Burgtheater. Maria Corda was co-starred with Capozzi.

The weather on the beautiful Dalmatian coast was perfect and though there were some difficulties, Korda's patience and skill turned both pictures into exciting and original cinema. They had a considerable international success ('A Vanished World' won a gold medal in Italy) and brought Sascha Films a fair profit.

The second film, 'Masters of the Sea', was a big action story, somewhat in the manner of Jules Verne's *20,000 Leagues Under the Sea*, a tale of pirates who used the most up-to-date technical methods—including submarines—for their war on society.

Part of the picture was made in the lovely walled town of Ragusa. Karl Hartl arrived first in Dalmatia as production-manager, with a large assortment of daggers, rifles and revolvers. A few hours later he was arrested as a spy. He stayed in jail two days until experts arrived and established that all this armament represented no danger for the safety of Yugoslavia. Later, when they filmed a sequence in which the pirate ship was set on fire, Hartl was left behind by mistake on the burning boat and was rescued in the nick of time. He certainly showed a remarkable loyalty to Korda to endure all these tribulations!

But Korda, as usual, didn't feel happy unless he was his own master. He liked the gargantuan Count Kolowrat, whose tastes and hobbies he partly shared. But when a Hungarian distributor, Dr. Szucs, who had founded Vita Films in Vienna, offered him a chance, he parted from Sascha in a perfectly amicable manner.

A few weeks after finishing the two Dalmatian pictures, he was already at work on his spectacular picture 'Samson and Delilah'. Maria Corda had returned to Vienna and she starred in the double rôle of the Biblical temptress and a modern operatic *prima donna*. The script was by Ernest Vajda and Korda himself.

The climax of the film was the scene in which Samson—played by Alfredo Galaor, formerly a chauffeur and a man of magnificent physique—wrecks the temple. To make this sequence possible, the art director created an ingenious contraption. The roof of the temple, made of lath and canvas, rested on two columns. When these were pressed apart, they would collapse without much effort; the imitation blocks of stone were supposed to fall with a most convincing effect. The great day arrived. Hundreds of extras stood by to be 'buried' under the ruins. Several stunt-men were to perform daring acrobatics. Four cameras were in position to register every detail. Finally Korda gave the signal. The cameras whirred. Samson-Galaor walked majestically through the jeering, shouting crowd towards the two columns. He pressed them apart; they trembled, began to slide, slanted ominously. The extras scattered, screaming, there were clouds of dust—but the columns did not collapse and the cleverly constructed roof remained stubbornly attached to them.

Korda sent for oxen; skilfully camouflaged ropes were fastened to the columns and the big, lumbering animals pulled hard. In vain. They tried lorries—with the same result. And all the time actors, technicians, extras stood by—eating their heads off.

Two whole days passed in futile efforts. During the third night the columns had been partly sawn through—leaving them with just enough strength to stand up. In spite of this the right effect couldn't be achieved. Time was running short; the schedule called for cast and crew to leave that night for the Island of Rugen where a ship had been chartered for the next sequence. Tired of the long, futile experiments, the staff went to lunch rather late. As Korda, calm as usual, entered the studio canteen, there was a deep rumble followed by a tremendous crash outside. The temple had collapsed—on its own account—and nobody was present, no camera had turned. Two of his assistants, shaking in their shoes, hurried up to Korda.

"What are we to do?" asked Hartl.

Alex didn't remove the cigar from his mouth but replied in his accented German:

"Rebuild whole set. Got plenty of time until I come back from Rugen."

And that's how it was done.

The German and Austrian papers were full of praise for the film. True to his preferences, Korda had gathered a technical staff which was largely Hungarian—one of his cameramen and his art director, the brilliant Alexander Ferenczy, were his compatriots. The picture made a handsome profit and prepared the way for Korda's next move—to Berlin.

★　　　★　　　★　　　★

In 1923 Germany seemed to be a far from ideal place for a young, ambitious film-maker. In January, French and Belgian

troops had occupied the Ruhr as the Germans had fallen behind
with their reparation payments. The long, bitter struggle began
and one of its first consequences was the most devastating
inflation the world had ever seen. Before it ended, money was
worth less than the paper it was printed on and a newspaper cost
several milliard marks. It took many months before Germany's
economic recovery began.

Berlin, just like Vienna—but on a far vaster scale—became the
happy hunting ground of the black marketeer, the illicit dealer
in foreign currency and precious metals, of stock exchange mani-
pulators and get-rich-overnight crooks. All morality had disinteg-
rated; everything and everybody was for sale.

Yet in the midst of this feverish dance of death, literature and
the arts had a strange, morbid renaissance. And Korda saw the
difficulties—the film industry had to live from hand-to-mouth
very much like the unfortunate middle class, selling a piece of
furniture one week, a cherished painting or small article of
jewellery the next. But this was also the chance to experiment,
to be bold. And boldness Korda never lacked.

With Dr. Gabriel Schwarz, another Hungarian financier, he
founded in February 1923 the Alexander Korda Film Company
Ltd., with a capital of one million marks. In the same month he
began his new picture called 'Das Unbekannte Morgen' (The
Unknown Tomorrow) in which Maria Corda co-starred with
Werner Krauss, one of Germany's leading actors. Krauss, today
still a prominent member of the Vienna Burgtheater, was much
impressed by Korda as a director. He found that the young
Hungarian did not try to force an actor into the mould of his own
ideas, to dominate them. He gave free rein to the player's
imagination—if such existed.

Because of the ever-growing inflation, the production had
a tough time. In April 1923 the German trade papers published
a news item that 'The Unknown Tomorrow' was living up to
its title and would be abandoned. Before the picture passed
the German board of censors, almost eight months elapsed and

another three went by before it was presented at the Marmorhaus, Berlin. This, however, had the advantage that while the picture was produced with inflation marks, it earned stabilized gold currency. The press called it interesting, full of suspense with excellent acting, grandiose and effective sets. In Austria it was shown under the title 'The Crystal Ball'.

Korda, however, had to look for new finance as his partner no longer had sufficient resources to back him. He found it in another Hungarian, a Viennese banker called Imre Gross.

Alex had planned for several years to do a film about the Mayerling tragedy. This was obviously impossible while the Habsburg Monarchy existed. Now Lajos Biro wrote another script and the biggest German company, Hansa-Ufa, undertook to distribute it. Once again Korda gathered several of his fellow-countrymen to help him: Marcel Vértes, the Hungarian painter and illustrator, designed the costumes; Maria Corda was cast as the star-crossed, unhappy Baroness Vetsera; Koloman Zatony was Crown Prince Rudolf; Emil Fenyvessy the Emperor Francis Joseph; and the fat, jovial Puffy Huszar was also given a supporting part. Karl Hartl, ever-faithful, was production manager.

The picture was shot mostly in Berlin, starting in October 1923, but later the unit moved to Vienna for location shots at the Imperial Palace, the Prater Park and Schönbrunn.

The Mayerling film was first shown in Berlin on May 30, 1924. A South German paper wrote: "It is mile-high above the earlier pictures of a similar *genre*. It succeeds in making its characters human beings, instead of the stiff puppets of history. With the tragic destiny of the star-crossed lovers in the foreground, it shows a masterly technique." The Berlin critics were equally flattering: "A magnificent achievement by Korda," wrote one of them. "We prophesy a gigantic success."

The success, though not gigantic, was solid enough; but Imre Gross, the financial backer, still lost a good deal of money— mainly because Korda did not stint the production and the crazy inflation made the dollar-contracts cost astronomic sums in marks. 'Tragedy in the House of Habsburg' cost about $80,000 and only half of this sum was recovered. Twelve or fifteen years later Gross, a ruined man, came to London where Korda—by then head of London Films—repaid most of his losses and gave him a new start.

Late in 1923 Korda joined FIHAG, a large international production and distribution organization with five German companies, one French and one Hungarian associate, acting as clearing house and general banker for them.

When the inflation was halted and the 'Gold-Mark' established, many of these companies got into difficulties. What this conversion meant, can be illustrated by a simple figure: in November 1923 the copy of a film trade paper sold for 30 milliard marks in Berlin; a week later for 20 gold pfennigs. Soon FIHAG itself was in trouble. After long and complex negotiations it went into liquidation. The profits of Korda's first picture were lost in the general débâcle for which he was in no way responsible.

In 1924 Korda began his association with another compatriot, Joseph Somlo.

Somlo, born in 1884, is still happily and busily active in films. As head of the Vienna branch of Projectograph—the distribution firm for which Korda worked—he knew Alex as a young journalist. "Always penniless," Somlo described his friend at the start of his career, "but always smoking a big cigar. His pockets were bulging with three or four books he had just bought or borrowed. His eyes were red-rimmed from endless reading."

In 1919 Somlo settled in Berlin and became head of the foreign department of UFA, at the same time founding his own production and distribution firm with Mr. Fellner.

When the FIHAG troubles started, Korda went to Somlo. His scale of living hadn't changed; his expenditure seldom bore any relation to his income and Maria loved luxury befitting a famous star. Alex needed money. He had taken a thirteen-room apartment on the Kurfürstendamm, perhaps the most elegant of

Berlin's downtown streets. For several months only three rooms were furnished—but he kept open house and no Hungarian actor, writer, journalist or artist was ever turned away from his hospitable home.

Somlo and Fellner arranged for him to do a picture in co-operation with UFA and the Dreamland Studios in Vienna. "We simply stole the idea of *Pygmalion*," Somlo told me, "with the important difference that our Professor Higgins was married."

Maria Corda was the Galathea of the film called 'Everybody's Woman'. Pygmalion's wife was played by Maie Hanbury, then wife of the late Jeffrey Bernard, managing director of the Stoll Film Company. Miss Hanbury, whose first film part this was, thought it great fun to act under Korda's direction. The leading man didn't speak a word of English; she didn't know a word of German—but somehow they got by. The film tears of Maria she found especially amusing. Her dresser would stand by, ready for the signal to hurry forward and drop glycerine on her cheeks.

In Alex she discovered a highly intelligent, very reserved man, with far more culture and vision than many others she had met at that time in the film industry. He had a deep love for English literature and especially for the plays of Shaw. He spoke of *The Devil's Disciple* and how much he would have liked to make a film of it. As a director he was always courteous and patient though very sure of what he wanted.

When the film was finished, Maie Hanbury frankly thought it dreadful. Joseph Somlo and his partners, however, were pleased with 'Everybody's Woman', and when it had its première, first in Berlin and later in Munich, the critics also praised it. One of them waxed lyrical about Maria Corda's 'lovely shoulders'; the film had a bath-tub scene which was straight out of *Pygmalion*, though the scrubbing of the waif Galathea was done by two maids looking like nurses in a particularly severe women's prison.

A little later Korda took a motoring holiday in Italy with his wife and brother Zoltan. He certainly deserved it for he had been working hard and Joseph Somlo was glad to advance him some money. But letters and telegrams reached Berlin from different Italian cities, asking for more. The first three or four times Somlo cabled various sums. Then he felt he had done his part—and did not answer any more S O S messages. He never knew how Alex got back to Berlin in the end—probably on three wheels, having had to sell the fourth to pay for the petrol.

But there were no hard feelings; Korda's next two pictures were again made for 'Felsom', the Fellner & Somlo distribution firm. He started the first in April 1925, finishing it by the end of June—a rather fast pace for him. Yet it wasn't exactly a cheap picture. The unit went to Paris, where it rained all the time and no shooting could be done, so that in the end the exteriors had to be filmed in Berlin. At least one German critic remarked that 'My Wife's Dancer' (which was released in England as 'Dance Mad') proved a remarkable fact: Paris cars carried Berlin number plates and the Berlin ABOAG bus company was apparently operating in the French capital! Otherwise, however, he had no faults to find and praised the 'wonderful pace' of the direction. The film did excellent business in Germany and abroad. It was scripted by Adolph Lantz; Maria Corda starred again; her partners were Willi Fritsch, then at the start of his successful career, with Livio Pavanelli, Lea Seidl, Hermann Thimig and Korda's old friend Victor Varconi supporting her in the lively, frothy comedy.

Then came Korda's most ambitious and perhaps most successful German picture: 'A Modern Dubarry'.

In 1925 Lajos Biro had gone to America; two of his plays were running on Broadway with considerable success. When he returned after three months, Korda asked him for an original story. In four weeks Biro turned out 'A Modern Dubarry', which was also published in book and serial form in Germany and Hungary. A romantic, somewhat melodramatic story, it provided excellent spectacle and strong dramatic parts. Maria Corda played 'Toinette, a modern Dubarry'; King Sandor the

monarch of 'Astoria' was Jean Bradin, a French star whose career
ended rather early. Hans Albers, still one of Germany's most
popular stage and film actors, played Toinette's first lover.
Maria Corda received 30,000 marks for her part—at the same
time a young actress was paid 300 for her bit. Her name was
Marlene Dietrich.

The film started in March 1926 at the UFA studios in Tempelhof. Everything went well and by June it was completed. But
one day when Somlo went out to the studios, he found Biro and
Korda walking up and down between the stages, deep in a
friendly argument. Korda kept on pulling bits of paper from his
pocket, making notes. When Somlo joined them, they explained
that in their view the picture needed something extra—a revolution. Part of a street set was standing on the back lot and Korda
thought he could use it with very little change. Somlo's arrangement with UFA was that as producer he received a percentage
of the production cost—so he had no objection to the extra
expenditure. As a matter of fact, that little revolution Biro and
Korda tagged on to the picture, cost 60,000 marks. Having seen
the film, I don't think it improved it noticeably—but it made
them both happier.

'A Modern Dubarry' and 'Dance Mad' were distributed in
England by C. M. Woolf's W. & F. Film Service. For the first
time Alexander Korda's name appeared in a London paper. The
Daily Express, reviewing 'A Modern Dubarry' in December
1926, wrote: 'The producer Alexander Korda, an old hand
at the game, combines continuity and spectacle with wonderful
skill.'

★　　★　　★　　★

The recovery of European currencies could only be maintained
by strict regulations of foreign exchange transactions. In most
countries the earnings of American film companies were frozen.
If they wanted to recover these often substantial amounts, they

had to produce pictures in Europe. In the silent film era this wasn't particularly difficult; sub-titles could be done at small cost in any number of languages.

Fox Film Productions set up a European branch. In Germany it was headed by Julius Aussenberg. In August 1926 Fox bought the film rights of Clement Vautel's French novel, *Madame ne veut pas d'enfants*. It was a saucy, sexy story, in the style of Margueritte's *La Garçonne* and similar French novels of the twenties. Maria Corda (who spelled her name with a 'C' perhaps to dissociate herself from her husband's growing reputation) was signed for the title part. The script was written by Adolph Lantz and Bela Balazs (who later became the leading Communist theoretician of the cinema). Karl Hartl was associate producer and his assistant was Rudolf Sieber, Marlene Dietrich's husband. The cast included Harry Liedtke, who had been for fifteen years a leading romantic actor in German pictures; the pretty Dina Gralla; and Trude Hesterberg, a musical comedy star. Korda was now able to attract the best box-office names and the finest talent in Germany.

There were two unknowns in the same film. A young British officer who had served on the Allied Control Commission in Berlin; his job had now come to an end and he was puzzled as to how to make a living. A friend advised him to try and get into pictures. He went to see Korda at his Tempelhof offices. Alex sat behind a large desk, smoking a big cigar. They both spoke German—both with a strong accent, only Korda's was Hungarian and his visitor's English. Alex told the young man to forget his idea; films were a mug's game. Rather depressed, the ex-officer thanked him and turned to go. He was already at the door when Korda asked him whether he had a dress suit—tails or a dinner jacket. The young man swung round and said yes, he still had a pretty good wardrobe. Alex scribbled a line and sent him down the corridor. That's how John Loder became an *edelcomparse*, a dress extra. It kept him going—and started him on his career.

The other 'dress extra' who was to become famous was Marlene Dietrich.

When he tackled this picture, Korda had two problems. He had to make it quickly and he had to earn a large sum of money in a hurry. For this was to be his last film in Germany.

In April 1921, Alexander Incze, on his way back from Hollywood, had met Korda in Vienna and given him Adolf Zukor's visiting card. Zukor, head of Paramount, had seen 'The Prince and the Pauper' and sent word to 'look him up' if he ever came to America. Now, five years later, Korda was about to cross the Atlantic.

He wanted to go to Hollywood, which was the goal of all European film-makers. In February 1926 Lajos Biro had gone to the States for the second time with an optional contract from Paramount; his family joined him in June. Korda's close friend and collaborator achieved speedy success with the screen-adaptation of 'Hotel Imperial' (which was filmed four times, the last version being 'Five Graves to Cairo') and wrote the screen-plays for the first two Jannings films, 'The Way of all Flesh' and 'The Last Command'. He prepared the way for the Kordas; both Maria and Alex were engaged by First National. The contracts were signed in October 1926; their starting date was February 1927.

'Madame Doesn't Want Children' was made in thirteen actual shooting days; not since the early days in Transylvania had Korda worked so fast. There was a boat to catch—and he didn't want to miss it.

*   *   *   *

Korda's capacity for enduring friendship was proverbial throughout his career. He was always surrounded by a crowd—and if some were hangers-on, the kind of parasites every success-ful man attracts, the majority were friends and companions he liked and needed. Once, much later, an old friend told him that there were a good many people in his organization who didn't pull their weight. Why didn't he get rid of them? "Because I like them," replied Alex. "I'd much rather live and work among good-looking, well-mannered people who are not so efficient than among ugly and surly robots and experts."

His loyalty to his friends was fantastic. Those he had found in Vienna and Berlin he kept for many years and some of them played important parts in his later career. He never forgot a good turn, and usually repaid it a hundredfold. After the second world war he brought Karl Hartl to London to produce 'The Angel with the Trumpet' and 'The Wonder Kid', and Hartl provided advice and help in the making of 'The Third Man'. Biro was his close collaborator until the writer's untimely death. Victor Varconi worked with him in Hollywood; so did Ernest Vajda.When Joseph Somlo, escaping from Hitler's Germany with a few hundred marks, reached Paris and, later, London—Korda immediately brought him together with Victor Savile and C. M. Woolf and helped him to launch his own production company. Almost thirty years after the Mayerling picture, Koloman Zatony arrived in England and Korda offered help and advice to him and his family. Joseph Aussenberg became Korda's German representative after the second world war. The two 'dress extras', John Loder and Marlene Dietrich, were starred in later Korda pictures. No doubt as he grew older he found a special delight (and sometimes solace) in these enduring friendships.

★   ★   ★   ★

Korda's contract with First National was for $350 a week. He asked Heinrich Fraenkel, First National's German chief of publicity, whether he would be able to live on it in Hollywood.

"It depends *how* you want to live," Fraenkel replied.

"Well," replied Korda in his soft, heavily accented German, "here in Europe I usually live at the Adlon or the Grand in Vienna; I eat at Sacher's or Fouquet's in Paris; my tailor is Knicze." (Knicze was the best tailor in Berlin.) "If I can't afford the same in America—I think I'll come back . . ."

CHAPTER V

YEARS OF THE LOCUST

WHEN I arrived in California, a battle-scarred veteran of the film industry told me: "It is a grave mistake to get to Hollywood too early in your life. Once you've reached the Pacific Ocean there's no place left to go to." In 1950 Los Angeles had two and a half million inhabitants, out of which only about 30,000 were engaged in film-making—and by no means all of them full time. In 1926 when Korda started work there, the proportion was about the same. But to this handful of people, surrounded by comparative sanity, celluloid was the only reason for living. Whether it was prohibition or nuclear warfare, they always judged everything from one point of view. What my old-timer friend meant was that Hollywood was the ultimate goal for anybody in pictures. Films were made elsewhere but they did not really count; you could have a fabulous success in Stockholm, Berlin or Paris—what mattered was the review in *Variety* or the *Hollywood Reporter*. Beyond the Pacific there was the rest of the world—and it was of no importance. Once you got to Hollywood you should never want to leave it. If you did, you were a renegade and as quickly forgotten as if you had never existed.

Today this *Weltanschauung* is somewhat weakened as Hollywood's business has become global; it has set up branches in Elstree and Geiselgasteig, in Cinécitta and Nice, in Tokyo and Toronto. But in Korda's days it was still dominant. A contract with one of the major studios was the yardstick of solid success.

Yet it was a false yardstick. To many Hollywood gave a fair chance; to others it denied even a start. In some ways Korda's years in California resembled the first years of our present decade.

In 1950–51 the film industry was assailed by Senator McCarthy and his investigations; always pathologically sensitive to public criticism, Hollywood was decimating the ranks of its best creative artists, blacklisting scores of them. At the same time the threat of television was creeping upon the sunny scene like the smog, blanketing the plain between the sea and the Sierras. The number of movie-goers was dropping; the critical faculties of audiences seemed more acute. It was a period of uneasy transition which led to the break-up of the vast film-empires or their transformation into television film factories.

In the years 1927 to 1930 there was an even more serious crisis. The Wall Street crash of 1929 wiped out the fortunes of several film-moguls and weakened the financial backing of the studios. Their shares changed hands rapidly; new executives appeared almost every month if not every week, adding to the general confusion. In a way, a greater menace—though Hollywood's ultimate salvation—was the coming of the talkies. It was a far greater revolution than the one twenty-five years later brought about by the adoption of various technical gimmicks, from 3-D to Cinerama or Todd-AO. In the fifties the studios were forced to adopt these in order to lure back the audiences into the emptying cinemas—and they were all willing to try the experiment. In 1928 when Warner Brothers, on the edge of bankruptcy, took the plunge and made the first semi-talkie, 'The Jazz Singer', most of the other studios resisted the innovation. Clive Brook, who starred in the first *real* talkie, told me that all the bigwigs used to come round and look at the 'rushes', the daily takes. One of them kept asking him anxiously:

"D'you think Ronnie Colman can *talk*? Do you think Anna Steen can *talk*?"

The late Mr. Colman proved in scores of films that he could talk very well indeed; but of Hollywood's stars about half spoke broken or heavily accented English. Some of them had none at all. Quite apart from the cost of capital investment, sound-proof stages, new cameras and the rest, producers had spent huge amounts building up these stars—who now became a dead loss. No wonder that when a newspaper proclaimed: 'THE TALKIES WON'T LAST OUT THE YEAR!' many wishful-thinkers applauded. Directors, too, were affected—it was quite different directing a silent picture from piloting a film through the difficult stages of an often experimental new technique, dealing with nervous actors, unsure technicians. The headline in the American paper was proved wrong—before long it became evident that talkies were here to stay. The depression of the 'silents' was not short-lived.

All this militated strongly against Korda. No wonder he was unhappy. To be blunt, he loathed Hollywood. Some years later, in an interview, he made it clear: "I found working in Hollywood rather difficult. They talk too much shop. Shop, shop, shop, from daybreak to sunset and on to daybreak again. There are very few people out there who are possessed of any general culture."

Korda, the avid reader, the scholar—Clive Brook was much surprised when I told him how little formal schooling his old friend had had, as he found Alex remarkably well-versed in the classics—couldn't help feeling uncomfortable in the average Hollywood setting. Once, not long after his arrival, he found himself the centre of a fascinated group. He was talking—not shop but about pre-Columbian art. A studio executive, half-drunk, lurched into the room. Most of the guests were gathered around the tall, slim Hungarian, and scarcely noticed his arrival. He raised his voice in a querulous complaint: "What's that guy got that they lap it all up? He hasn't made one big-grosser yet—and he thinks he's wonderful!"

Korda took no notice; but the executive became really furious. He tried to crash into the group—and fell flat on his face. For several years he was Korda's sworn enemy—but in the end they became friends. Somehow the film-magnate had discovered that 'the guy' could also make successful pictures—but he still thought that excessive book-learning was a hindrance rather than a help to a film director.

It wasn't so much the individuals Alex hated in Hollywood—though in some cases he had plenty of cause—but the system. By and large he had little choice as to the pictures he directed; he *had* to do them and do them quickly and cheaply. As in Transylvania or Berlin, he disliked being an employee. This drive to be independent, his own boss, the master of his soul, was perhaps the strongest individual trait of his character. His basic complaint during these Hollywood years was that no one understood him, nobody had any idea of what he was trying to do. This wasn't the self-pitying protest of the 'misunderstood genius'; it was the well-founded complaint of the man who felt that his talent was being wasted.

⋆   ⋆   ⋆   ⋆

When Korda arrived in Hollywood, he must have puzzled and even repelled some of his new associates. He spoke very little English and was given a Hungarian assistant—today one of the most distinguished American directors, Charles Vidor—so that he could communicate with his crew. In six months he spoke better English than Vidor! He would sit for hours in a corner with a book of English grammar and by talking to himself, soak up the language.

He hated the American method of starting work early. He would appear grumpily on the set, looking like his own father; unshaven, with a drooping moustache and a monocle. His monocles were thick, in the German style, without a ribbon. He was constantly dropping and breaking them. His crew used to joke about how many gross he must have brought from Germany.

Instead of the usual nine o'clock starting hour, Alex did not seem to function as a director until about eleven. But then he came to life with a vengeance. He had a wonderful eye for detail and used his photographic memory to the best effect. On the other hand, he must have been a terrible actor—at least in

English. Whenever he tried to show an actor how to portray a scene, it always resulted in the crew becoming hysterical—though they were careful to hide their merriment to avoid hurting his feelings.

He smoked so many cigars that it was impossible to carry a day's supply in his pockets so Vidor carried some of them. Years later when Korda was knighted, his former assistant sent him a congratulatory cable and signed it 'The Keeper of the Cigars'. Although many years had passed since their association, Alex recognized immediately who had sent the cable to him.

He always had the extraordinary ability to capture attention and his charm helped him over the early, difficult months. There were many gatherings with perhaps forty or fifty people divided into several groups. One by one, as though drawn by a magnet, they ended by completely surrounding Korda and he, in broken English, kept them amused and entertained.

It took some time before he could avoid the pitfalls English represents for beginners. On one occasion, in the projection room, he was looking at a rough-cut with his cutter, Harold Young. He turned to Young and said: "Now, my boy, in this place we will have a time *collapse*"—meaning a 'lapse'. And when he was preparing another picture, he took his staff to the women's wardrobe to see Jane Winton try on some costumes. Alex wanted to tell her what she should wear for a sequence at a hunting lodge. "You wear a jacket which fits the shoulders, so . . . a skirt which comes above the boots, so . . . and in your hand you have a little crap . . ." Everybody hooted with laughter—and Young had to explain to him the difference between a riding crop and the word he had used.

*　　*　　*　　*

When the Kordas reached Hollywood, Lajos Biro was just about to return to Europe. His wife had to undergo an operation and preferred Hungarian surgeons. After a few months Biro again joined his friend in California. When his contract with Paramount expired, he went to First National and they worked together on several pictures. But in 1928 Biro was called to Berlin by Universal and with the exception of a short, unrewarding period in 1930, did not spend any length of time in Hollywood again.

During these months of separation Korda wrote a number of letters to his paternal friend. In his life story these are unique documents. For one thing, he typed them himself instead of dictating them; they expressed his most private thoughts and feelings. To his old comrade he did not have to pretend or gloss over things. They provide a remarkable backstage picture of Hollywood in the years of crisis—together with a summary of the dreams, hopes, disappointments and agonies of a creative spirit. They were written in Hungarian, with here and there an English sentence or expression. I am reproducing them here in a faithful translation; the English passages of the originals are marked in italics. To avoid cumbersome footnotes, I have added a brief glossary at the end of each letter.

The first of these is dated July 31, 1928.

"My dear Mr. Biro, many thanks for both your letters. The Garrett affair was settled in the end: Toncsi isn't going to London to do this film. They only wanted to give a three weeks' guarantee; it wouldn't have been worth while for such a short time and in any case, we still haven't started the Sills picture here. We've put together quite a good story for him (the co-authors are Birinszky and Dr. Laszlo) and we're going on the floor on August 20th. Toncsi is playing the extremely good feminine lead. I hope it'll go well.

I don't know whether you've heard of the great changes that have taken place here. One day after his beautiful speeches and declarations, Howley departed. He was replaced as supreme lord and master by Joseph Kennedy who arrived in Hollywood three weeks ago. (Do you know who Kennedy is? The owner of F.B.O., President of Pathé, Keith Albee, Vice-President of the Radio Corporation of America etc.) For two weeks all was fear and trembling on the lot. Rockett, whose contract Howley had taken to New York for signature, was in despair. He was certain that he would be fired. Of course, this would have meant a very bad outlook for me, too. It was quite certain that Rowland would be sacked. The air was full of a thorough change in our régime. Then after two weeks of 'suspense' the matter was settled in the following way. Rowland is to go. Rockett remains as sole boss in Burbank. A whole lot of people were kicked out. (For instance, Thompson.) Those who used to belong to the Rothacker clique. Kennedy is enthroned up in the clouds. No one sees him. He's here with a large staff but until yesterday he wouldn't talk to anybody—of course, with the exception of Rockett and once a five-minute audience when he received the supervisers (sic!) all together. No directors. Yesterday, however, my phone rang: Mr. Joseph Kennedy. At first I thought someone was playing a joke but then Rockett came on the phone and told me to wait a minute, Kennedy wanted to speak to me. And at last, really: '*I want congratulate you to the Night Watch. I recognize on the handling a masterly hand. I am sorry I had no opportunity to have a chat with you until now. I hear: Madame is very unhappy. I am Wednesday at First National. I will brighten up your and her affairs.*'

You can imagine what this meant for me: to hear about a raise in my salary and about Toncsi's contract all at the same time, out of the blue. It seems that all (that is, a few) problems of my life will be settled by these two things—and it looks as if they will be settled together. Toncsi will be engaged not only for First National but also for F.B.O. and Pathé at the same time. And I have been promised $2,000 a week. (You are right—I'm going to save!)

With this I've also reported about *Night Watch*. It has turned out to be quite a good film though there is nothing of a *masterly hand* about it—but I always say, it isn't worthwhile to make a better film than I'm making. You need luck.

Otherwise—there's a *talkie*-madness in Hollywood. It's awful to consider what horrors the Hollywood producers will get '*talked*'. But what does it matter? I'd like to scratch those few hundred thousand dollars together, with or without *talkies*—and then, I, too, would like to sit down a little and spend forty or fifty more years completely uneventfully, in wealth and youthful health. It's a good plan, isn't it?

So my next film is this Sills picture. Then comes the *Squall*. I haven't read the treatment yet but Szekely and Rockett both like it very much. They want me to do it in a Hungarian setting. What would you say—the whole thing on a Hungarian farm, at the time of the harvest and threshing? Of course, it will have *talkie* and *sound* in it. Hungarian songs. (Brahms, Liszt as musical background.) 'Tosca' has also been assigned to me as F. is probably leaving here.

It is terrible how much I write about myself. But since you've left, there's hardly anybody to talk to.

So: no special news. Slowly but surely I am being bored to death. I begin to realize that apart from a raise nothing in the world interests me.

You can imagine how much I envy you for Switzerland and Austria. You can imagine how much I miss you. What could we do to get together again? First National is always open for you! How could something be arranged for single films?

Please—if you don't decide to stay in London or Berlin—wouldn't it be wise to sign a contract here, for three or four months every year, for one or two screenplays? You would be given the subjects in advance, come over here for a few weeks—I think you'd make as much as in a whole year in

Europe. And so your whole year or at least the greater part
of it would be yours. Please, write about these ideas . . .''

Maria Corda had received an offer to make some pictures in
London but evidently the terms weren't good enough. Sills was
Milton Sills, then a well-known American star. Dr. Laszlo was
one of Korda's Hungarian friends, a lawyer who was his house-
guest and who fancied himself as a writer; Howley one of the First
National executives. Joseph Kennedy, the American diplomat
and businessman, had taken up films after amassing a fortune in
banking and shipbuilding; in Britain he was best-known as U.S.
Ambassador (1937-40). He was, indeed, a very important man.
Al Rockett was Korda's producer under whom he worked;
Richard Rowland another producer and Thompson the studio
manager. 'Night Watch' had been one of the Biro screenplays.
The letter gives a striking example of the 'psychosis of waiting'
so many creative artists have to endure in Hollywood—the
uncertainty, fear and tension. Burbank was the site of the First
National studios; 'The Squall' was another Biro story. Mr.
Szekely, a film executive, was an early Biro associate.

Six weeks later, on September 2nd, 1928, Korda wrote to Biro
again:

"My dear, kind Mr. Biro:
I postponed writing as I had no news—until now when I
have a very sad item to report: poor Dr. Szekely died
Sunday dawn. About ten days ago he went down with
pneumonia and his heart, his weakened physique couldn't
stand it. The funeral was yesterday—he was, by his own
wish cremated without any religious ceremony. It is really
tragic: poor man, he wanted to retire at the end of the year,
he was full of plans about Europe, Nice, a good life which
he could have bought on the money he had saved. The
whole Hungarian colony is very sad.
At First National there is much excitement. After a reign

of four weeks Kennedy is out. We don't know yet who succeeds him; but Rockett is staying on.

A few days ago I read in Louella Parsons' column that Billie Dove's next picture is 'The 30th Day of October', written by you and *me*. I'm sure it's unnecessary for me to say that I wasn't responsible for claiming credit where no credit was due. Rockett's attitude is that you wrote this screenplay during your contract time at First National. You undertook to deliver four originals and this was one of them. (He seems to remember that some time ago I came to him with a similar idea.) I don't think it's worthwhile to argue with Rockett over it. He's always happy to work with you —even at long distance—if you have some idea or want to write another story. There's a good chance that 'Birth of Love' will be bought and I'll make it as a *special* next season. Have you any other ideas for Dove? Sills? (Toncsi?) Barthelmess? We have no writers, no screenplays, one could do a deal within a week.

But are you at all interested in deals? Maybe among the mountains of Pertisau and Switzerland one loses one's taste for *business*. I wish I'd reached that state.

Dr. Laszlo and Birinszky have finished the next screenplay for me. (Sills and Toncsi; *start* October 1.) A difficult birth.

Otherwise—boredom, sky-high.

With great affection. I miss you—indescribably.

Korda."

The great man who was going to do such wonderful things for him had departed after four weeks—and all was uncertainty again. Otherwise, this letter is pretty well self-explanatory. I wonder when he reported on his friend Szekely's death, whether Korda had an inkling how his own ambitions of retirement and well-earned rest would be equally frustrated thirty years later?

The next letter was dated September 7, 1928. In the meantime Biro had evidently dropped the formality in their relationship; after six years' friendship they had progressed to first names.

"My dear Lajos, how much good your letter did in this hermit's life I'm leading under a flood of external complications, I can only tell you one day face to face—if at all! I'm so unused to the tone of true friendship, to kind words that if I'd been given this unasked by anyone, it would have been a boon. But that it came from you, not only did me a world of good but made me happy and proud. Something happened to me that's rare enough these days: after your letter I was in a bright mood all day. Please, tell your wife: I am most grateful to her because I feel in the letter not only your friendship but hers, too. Among my plans of saving money one ambition is growing stronger and stronger—to acquire somehow a 'neighbouring estate'. It will be hard but I'll fight for it.

In the meantime you must have got my latest news about Kennedy. There was also some talk here about Warner Brothers—who are doing now fabulously well because of Vitaphone—buying First National. (The Warner shares rose within four weeks from $28 to $120.) Thank God, this isn't true. As you can see from the enclosed cutting, Rockett has been firmly established here, his position is very important. Yesterday I discussed my contract with him (as Kennedy's departure postponed the matter) and I'm signing it today. Two years guaranteed, without options, at $2,150 a week— the third year is optional at $2,750. It's a good feeling even to put these figures on paper. I'll guard every dollar with tooth and nail because after two years, even with the craziest way of living, I should have at least $120,000. And then nothing can happen to me. Rockett is behaving most generously. And it looks as if with a little luck these two years can bring me great achievements.

Yesterday I talked a great deal about you with Rockett. He is going to New York to-morrow and wants to cable you from there an offer for three films. The first would be '*The Squall*' and the third '*The Miracle*' which you must do alone—as I persuaded him to drop the idea of an American continuity-writer. I think if you came over for three or four months, maybe five, you could easily do three *scripts* and this would still be more comfortable than work a whole year for some European studio. Quite apart from the fact that financially, I think, it would be far more advantageous; for the three scripts they ought to pay you at least $40–$50,000. And if you're here, there's a good chance of selling some of your other stories. Your reputation here is excellent. In my opinion even if you came here without a contract, you wouldn't be without a job for a week. I know that it isn't pleasant even to spend four months here—though, after all, Hollywood is still considerably better than the Siberian lead-mines. True: the lead-mines are the only places that are worse. Except for the Hungarians—who bore me to death—we see nobody.

As for your *mystery* story, I wouldn't write it if I were you —not after 'The 30th of October'. You have discharged your moral obligation with your other story.

What else is there to say? Outside Hollywood the whole world has ceased to exist for me. Here, for the time being, there is a craze about *sound* and *talkie*. One can't tell what the result will be. For the time being they all believe madly in it here. A *sound stage* is being built on our lot, too; it'll be ready in four weeks.

'To be a more important personage'—God knows, it would do me a little good. Here, whenever I go to the barber, I decide never to get a shave again. Whatever for? You can imagine how bored I am with these truly kind people—when even our *lorum* games have stopped. There's one thing left: I read a lot. And I smoke good cigars which is a great consolation. Otherwise, do not think that I've grown melancholy. Only it's a terribly empty feeling to be without a single human being to whom I can talk—and who can talk to me. My *entourage*—not only the immediate circle but my friends, too—consider me a necessary, even useful, fool. Maybe they're right. *Anyway*: the main thing's to get the money together. With money everything else becomes possible.

Thanks for what you wrote about *The Squall*. I hope you'll do the *continuity*. I'm very much interested in the genuine Hungarian atmosphere. A farm—like the one on which I was raised. I'd like to set the whole thing during harvest-time. But as there's no harvest in November, I'll make it the threshing. I've already ordered wheat and flails. I think it'll be interesting and original.

I'm just beginning to realize how long this letter is. But you see: it gave me greater pleasure to write than you can possibly have in reading it. I won't even re-read it. I hope that you'll feel among these confused lines my sincere and very grateful affection. I embrace you with sincere friendship,

Alexander Korda."

Biro always dreamt about a modest little estate to which he could retire. Korda's dream was to own the 'neighbouring' one. Korda's 'fears' about Warner Brothers buying First National were completely justified; in spite of his hopeful predictions, the newly-prosperous Warners acquired First National in October 1928. He was trying to persuade his friend to join him in Hollywood; every word of the letter showed how great his need was for this companionship. 'To be a more important personage' was a quote from Biro's daughter, Vera, who at the age of six, declared primly: "After all, it is better to be a more important personage . . ." when she was given a treat or granted some privilege. Korda's ideas about 'The Squall' came to nothing. In spite of the flails and the wheat, the picture was finally made in a

Spanish, not a Hungarian setting. '*Lorum*' is a Hungarian card-game Korda loved.

He wrote again, a month later. His plans of getting Biro to Hollywood had failed.

"My dear friend,

I waited with great impatience for your letter which you had announced in your cable. Rockett was no longer here and I couldn't understand how the negotiations which seemed to be completely settled, could have been upset. Rockett returned a week ago after great new changes of which I'll write later—and now, after your letter and Rockett's informations I'm able to form a clear picture. Unfortunately, neither he nor I can now do anything in this business; you can imagine how this hurt me. But Rockett is just as sorry. In my opinion the whole matter was wrecked by E's extremely clumsy cable and methods of negotiation. Rockett's attitude was as follows: because of his friendship with you, he released you from your contract six months before it expired. So if you want to come over again and for *only* six months, he would simply revive your old agreement. But if you're willing to come for a *longer* time, then he could make you a better offer on a long-term contract (for instance, six months a year). In my opinion if the matter had been handled not from New York but here and I had conducted the negotiations, it would have all been settled long ago. After all, E. ought to be familiar enough with your intentions to make a counter-proposal himself, without your verbal instructions. If, for instance, E. had told Rockett: 'Biro doesn't want to be paid when he isn't working; he doesn't want a weekly salary but only a firm assignment for two, three, four, five or any number of *stories, treatments, continuities,*' Rockett would have been glad to pay $12,000–$15,000 for each job and given an undertaking even for six of them. You know that if E.'s offer had been based on the argument:

Biro is taking the chance on a *continuity* needing maybe more
time: this is a language R. would have immediately understood. From his point of view the offer he made was *fair*. For
a larger salary he wanted to have some *bonus*—in this case, a
longer commitment on your part.

But now, at least for the time being (I hope) all this is
pointless. I wish you enjoyable work and much success. I
envy you for Europe, for Berlin.

With us, as you may have read already, there is again a
change. Warners have bought us lock-stock-and-barrel,
just while Rockett was in New York. Now we're waiting
for developments. *Talkie* does tremendous business everywhere—and for *the time being*—it is the only business.
Luckily for me, Rockett signed my contract on the last day
before the Warner *deal*. (This showed considerable good will.
If he had wanted to, he could have dragged it out.) It's a
little less good than I wrote earlier but even so, excellent.
$1,750—for the first year, $2,250—the second, $2,500—the
third. But the '*feature*' of the contract is that the *first two
years* are firmly set, not optional. So if Warners don't like
me, you know what they can do. They must pay the two
years and the total is $208,000, out of which I am going to
save at least $120,000. This is the 'little dream'. In the worst
case, it is sufficient.

Otherwise there's no news. Everything's the same as
before.

I know I don't have to ask you yet I mention it—if you
can arrange something for Zoli, please, do. It seems he had
no great inclination to come over here and would like to
have another *chance* in Berlin. Couldn't some help be given
to him? If *not*, please persuade him to come here. I'm sure I
can find a place for him somehow.

Do write sometimes. It is a very great joy for me.
Affectionately,

Korda."

The negotiations between Biro and First National had fallen through and Korda blamed Biro's agent for the failure. (He was also his and Maria's agent.) The 'little dream' was a favourite Biro expression about saving a comfortable competence and retiring on it. Apparently Korda had the same dream—one that Hollywood certainly never fulfilled. Zoltan Korda was still in Berlin (most of the time seriously ill) and reluctant to go to America. As a matter of fact, he had a boat ticket for almost a year in his pocket before he decided to use it. Alex, of course, felt a deep fraternal anxiety for his tough and independent-minded brother's welfare.

On December 28, 1928, he wrote to Biro again:

"My dear Lajos:

I was on a picture, working like a horse: I didn't have a quiet half-hour to write to you. Now I've finished my film and I thought I'd have a few weeks' vacation; but man proposes, Warner Bros. dispose and after four days' rest I must start *The Squall. Story:* awful. *Cast:* awful (Nubi: Myrna Loy). Eighty per cent *talkie* and the screenplay itself is terrible. But Wednesday is lovely. I'm saving money. And everything else is unimportant.

I miss you very much. There's not a soul to whom I could say a single word. These brave Hungarians are without exception Martians for me and their greatest fault is that they aren't living on Mars. My life passes as usual. I read it in Swift, at the beginning of one of the Gulliver chapters: '*Having been condemned by nature and fortune to an active and restless life* . . .' And in this accursedly *active* and even more accursedly *restless* life, you can imagine in what terrible loneliness I'm living. I haven't even a family. But I have plans: the great dream, the little dream. A motor tour in Europe and life somewhere on the Mediterranean—after all, that is the real world, the rest is just colonies. Maybe I'll succeed.

You're telling me you're thinking of producing a picture

Family portrait: from L. to R. (*standing*) Zoltan, Henrik Kellner; (*sitting*) Vincent, Mrs. Kellner, Alex

Korda and his favourite cameraman, Georges Perinal

Twenty-one years: the Korda brothers at the coming-of-age party of London Films
Left to right: Vincent, Alexander and Zoltan

The third wedding: Alexa, General Corniglion-Molinier, and Alex, *and right,* Korda
the yachtsman

yourself. Just as I'd like to be your neighbouring squire somewhere, anywhere—you must know how happy I'd be if I could work with you in the future. If you find something or have some serious combination: think of me. In a year or eighteen months I'd be happy to return to Europe if we could make a picture or two together every year.

How is your work at Universal? How are you satisfied with Berlin? Maybe now the *talkie* will kill the silent *film* here; and European production will be resurrected. In any case, neither this year nor next can it be expected that more than a quarter of the average, exportable pictures will be produced—compared to last year. *Talkies* without *talk* can't be sold even to a dog; though here the instructions are: *don't worry about the silent version*! So—if the Europeans are clever, here's a great *chance*! How are Fellner & Somlo? Pommer? There's no professional news here. Or rather: every day there's so much news that no one can make sense of it. I believe no one knows anything. Not even Schulberg or Zukor.

Please, my dear Lajos, tell me frankly: what's happening to Zoli? And if he can't get on over there at all, please, persuade him to come here. Here he'll learn about *talkies*, special effects, model shots; and if later we do something and he can't find a good job here, I'm sure he'll become an outstanding associate of ours.

How much more I'd like to write, to tell you, to ask you! It can't be done in a letter. Please, write sometimes. It is always a great joy and consolation to recognize your hand-writing on an envelope.

Your sincere friend,

Korda."

'The Squall' was Biro's original story which had been long delayed because of the switch-over from silent to talking films. 'Lovely Wednesday' was the usual pay-day in Hollywood.

Fellner & Somlo we have met in Berlin. Erich Pommer, the German producer, was Korda's Berlin acquaintance with whom he later became associated in Britain. Schulberg and Adolf Zukor were the top executives of Paramount.

Zoltan Korda was still in Berlin and Alex's anxiety was growing about him. Vincent was in Paris, painting happily, not even dreaming of films. He was beginning to acquire a considerable reputation and many of his pictures were bought by Scandinavian collectors.

This early letter held the germs of London Films, of the Korda-Biro collaboration, the 'little' and 'big dreams'. About nine months later Zoltan Korda did arrive in Hollywood and in due course became his brother's most trusted and important associate, director of a dozen successful films.

*   *   *   *

The first picture Alex directed in Hollywood was called 'The Stolen Bride'. As the tale goes, he was called into a conference and asked:

"You are Hungarian, aren't you? Well, we're going to make a Hungarian picture—all about gipsies. There's a butler in it and we think he ought to wear a military uniform and click his heels and bow. Is that right?"

Again legend has it that Korda said yes and got the job. The star was Billie Dove. To add a touch of verisimilitude, Korda had the butler kneel and kiss her feet.

Si non è vero . . . If this ever happened, the First National executives must have considered it a 'masterly touch'. And Alex was quite capable of doing such a thing—with his tongue in his cheek.

He was in good company. In 1926 and 1927 First National had quite a roster of stars. Norma Talmadge and her sister Constance, Colleen More, Richard Barthelmess, Billie Dove, Milton Sills, Harry Langdon, Johnny Hines and Ken Maynard were featured in the company's publicity. Richard A. Rowland, who had signed Maria and Alex, was the first vice-president and general manager. Jack Okey, who later helped to build Denham studios, was studio manager; Ned Marin, the Western Sales Manager, and Al Rockett (Korda's boss and friend) one of the production supervisors.

After a short spell of hotel-life, the Kordas settled down on North Rodeo Drive, one of the pleasant streets of Beverly Hills. It was a big, well-appointed house. Korda, as Clive Brook told me, had simple enough tastes—but *show* was part of his life and character. He never had much money; but he still smoked his big cigars, kept his house and a whole host of hangers-on and had a huge foreign car. There was no ostentation, nothing *nouveau riche* about all this; luxury, good living seemed to belong to him, were considered his birthright.

Following 'The Stolen Bride', Korda went to work on 'The Private Life of Helen of Troy'. John Erskine's amusing and irreverent book had become a best-seller; its style and philosophy were very much to Korda's taste—as so many of his later pictures showed. Of course, the sly wit and deliberate anachronisms were not exactly easy to transpose to the silent screen. The picture starred Maria Corda, Lewis Stone and Ricardo Cortez; it was first presented at the Globe, New York, on December 9, 1927. The reviews were favourable, but when the critics were polled at the end of the year, 'Helen' only received 21 votes. (The winner, 'Lilac Time', got 88.)

The editor of the Erskine picture was Harold Young, whose collaboration with Alex was to last many years. Young also shot some background material in Toulon for 'Night Watch' while he was on his way to England on a job. Apparently there were other cutters at the studio who were due for pictures before he was—but none of them wanted to work with Alex. They called him, with a little geographical confusion, 'that crazy German'. Probably, as Korda was used to editing his own films, the American cutters resented his methods. Young himself took on the first picture as a favour to the chief editor, who was a friend of his. Pretty soon he discovered that the 'crazy German', in spite of his individual taste in clothes, beards and monocles, knew what he was doing.

⋆   ⋆   ⋆   ⋆

Nineteen twenty eight started for Korda with the film version of Biro's play 'Yellow Lily'.

Clive Brook was anxious to play the male lead but Alex was doubtful. Brook asked him to let him make some wardrobe tests—the costumes were dazzling Hungarian uniforms—and when the director saw him, he smiled and said: "You are right, you will be very good."

This was a small but really excellent picture. His actors and technicians were finding out that Alex had a genius for 'making things look good'. He ordered some half-pillars for the biggest set, put in an imitation tapestry (sacking, daubed over), a few large candelabra and floor-covering made up to look like Persian carpets—and it resulted in the most luxurious-looking room. Everybody who saw the picture thought that Alex must have spent a million dollars—which, of course, he could never have afforded.

With Clive Brook, 'Yellow Lily' starred Billie Dove. Ned Marin was the producer. Alex chose the same editor and the same cameraman to work with him as on 'Helen'. He liked to create a team and usually managed to establish a team-spirit where there wasn't one before.

Yet he didn't find it easy. The trouble with him was that he kept so much ahead of his time. With 'Helen' he anticipated the light, satirical treatment of history. But this satire didn't find the right echo with the public of the late twenties, who were mostly used to spectacles and Westerns; comedy had to be the knock-about, Mack Sennett type, excellent in its own style but by no means without alternative.

'Yellow Lily' was followed by 'Night Watch', the picture in

which Joseph Kennedy found a 'masterly handling'. Again, it was a Ned Marin production, starring Billie Dove, and the scenario was Biro's work. Paul Lucas and Milton Sills co-starred with her and Korda managed to give no less than five of his Hungarian friends supporting parts.

In 1929, his last year with First National, Korda directed three pictures. As before, these made no great impact; once again, he received only an honourable mention by the critics among the top directors. In the meantime Maria had made two trips to Europe, once to star in a German picture and the second time to make 'Tessa', a spy story, with Victor Savile in London. But the three 1929 pictures brought at least some new, interesting friends for Korda. In 'Her Private Life', released in August 1929, Billie Dove starred again but the cast included a whole galaxy of present or future stars—Walter Pidgeon, Montague Lowe, Roland Young and ZaSu Pitts among them. The film was based on a Zoë Akins novel and had a certain amount of dialogue though basically it was still a silent picture.

Walter Pidgeon and Roland Young became Korda's lifelong friends; Young came to England several times to star for London Films.

Before the Zoë Akins film, Korda directed 'Love and the Devil' (originally called 'Comedy of Life'), in which Maria Corda and Milton Sills were co-starred. This was the story to which Korda referred in his letters as being scripted by his friends, Dr. Joseph Laszlo and Leo Birinsky. It was entirely silent.

Between 'Love and the Devil' and 'Her Private Life' he made 'The Squall'. It starred Alice Joye and Myrna Loy with ZaSu Pitts and Loretta Young in supporting parts. It was released in 1929. After the third film he decided not to renew his First National contract for a third year. Ned Marin, his producer, had gone to Fox and Korda signed a three-year agreement with the same studio.

★   ★   ★   ★

In these two years, 1929 to 1930, Hollywood made the complete change-over from silent pictures to talkies. The capital investment involved was about 500 million dollars. In April, 1930, the whole industry was shaken by the fall of William Fox, one of the pioneer giants who had been manœuvred out of his position by the Wall Street bankers—and a few of his closest associates. (It was Fox who introduced the 70 mm. wide film, created the modern Fox-Movietone; in 1929 he came within an ace of gaining control of M-G-M.) Korda's fellow directors at Fox—there were twenty-one listed—formed an impressive group with Frank Borzage, John Ford, W. K. Howard, Henry King, Frank Lloyd, William Cameron Menzies, Leo McCarey, Guthrie McClintie and Raoul Walsh the most prominent among them. After Fox departed, W. K. Sheehan became head of the studio and Sol M. Wurtzel was appointed General Superintendent, in charge of production.

Even before Fox's ejection, Korda felt uneasy in Hollywood. In 1930 he had paid a short visit to Europe, glad to escape for a few weeks' holiday. His nostalgia for Europe, a burning homesickness, was increasing, and though the trip was costly, he enjoyed it. He saw some of his friends, got the 'feel' of Continental film production and then returned to the grindstone.

Now he cabled his old friend Andor Zsoldos, who was working in Berlin. The cable said:

"Gladly direct German picture stop look around stop European contract would be important also because of private affairs stop would like to do your old story private dress rehearsal stop careful no publicity yet stop letter sent affectionately Alex."

Zsoldos knew what was the background of the cable. Alex wrote to him regularly every three months or so and had already indicated in several letters that he had serious family troubles— and was committing equally serious blunders in his professional work. His divorce suit had already started; whatever money he had was being spent on it. He also wrote about the senselessness of wasting time on silent pictures—for the talkies were killing the old methods.

Three days later Zsoldos sent Alex a contract offer from the Berlin Greenbaum Company to direct 'Rakoczi March', a screen play which Zsoldos had written with Laszlo Vajda, based on a famous Hungarian play. Paul Abraham, the well-known Hungarian composer of 'Ball in the Savoy', had composed the music. But Korda found the financial conditions unacceptable —indeed, they would have been far below his usual fees. The film was later made in German and Hungarian versions and became most successful. Zsoldos, however, had a feeling that Alex would not stay long in Hollywood.

It was in the spring of 1930 that Korda directed his first picture for Fox. By then his brother Zoltan had joined him; though he was still convalescent, he worked on the story of 'Women Everywhere'. Lajos Biro did the script in collaboration with George Grossmith—someone who was destined to play an important part in Korda's life. When Alex first saw Grossmith, a cultured Englishman of over sixty, with a smile that revealed teeth like a piano keyboard, he didn't know that the smile and the teeth were famous wherever Englishmen gathered. For Korda had still been in his teens when Grossmith made all England sing: 'Yip-I-Addy-I-Ay!'

At the end of the first day's work in the studio when Korda looked at the rushes, he turned to Biro and said: "That man! I shall never be able to do anything with him!"

He changed his mind soon enough—for G.G. contributed so much to the picture that he was given a screen-credit on the script. And Korda became his close friend. They had long talks in the studio canteen or in Korda's home. "England ought to be making the best pictures in the world," Korda told Grossmith.

"We—ell," replied G.G., displaying his teeth and sucking in air at the corners of his mouth in the Grossmith manner, "why can't we three—you and Biro and I—go to England and make them?"

It was one of those conversations which never lead to anything
—except that in this case it did. Korda finished 'Women Everywhere'; but it didn't set the Thames—or the Pacific—on fire. It
was released in June 1930. Shortly before that, Biro had returned to
Berlin, where his daughter Vera had fallen ill. In September Korda
wrote to Biro who was holidaying with his family in Hungary:

"My dear Lajos, forgive me not writing for such a long
time but I've had so much trouble since I returned to this
accursed Hollywood that I couldn't find a quiet hour.

Conditions are very bad here now. The awful films are
coming home to roost. All the companies, with the exception of M-G-M. are in very serious trouble. Warners' haven't
paid a dividend; their shares have fallen to 26 and it's said
that the Brothers are losing control. Everywhere there are
tremendous economies; as usual, they're throwing out the
casting sofa and reorganizing. At Paramount it looks like
Wanger becoming *boss* again, over Schulberg. In our studio
all *supervisors* have been sacked, only Rockett remains
and Sheehan with Wurtzel will be controlling the whole
production. As you know, I was to direct 'Basquerie' but
they gave me such an awful script you can't even imagine.
I told them so—whereupon there was a terrific row. If I
hadn't a contract, they'd have kicked me out. Even so,
Louella Parsons already said in her column that I'd been
dismissed. But then, everything was straightened out.
Wurtzel told *me* to bring a subject. Five minutes later *he* gave
me one. I worked on it for three days; then they decided I
was to do 'The Princess and the Plumber'. From the fire into
the frying pan! But Myron Selznick warned me against
doing anything foolish now; so I'm starting the picture next
Monday. Don't care a damn. I'm busting my guts with the
so-called writer who's a former *gagman*. Once more, for the
last time, blast them all. Marin's no longer here. He's been
kicked out within half an hour and has already left.

I'm fed up to the teeth with Hollywood. I'm working very seriously on a plan—i.e. to get some money together ($250,000) and start in Europe. I'm convinced that the European market is a good one and is going to get better. And to earn real money, to save, is only possible through independent production. I'd be very glad if you gave me your opinion about this.

I've talked to Selznick about your affairs, too. The studios start at full steam in October again; he is convinced he can do something for you. Of course, if my European plan succeeds, I'd like to include you. Warner-First National isn't producing any pictures now; they're loaning out all their writers and directors until the end of January.

Europe didn't do me any good. It was too beautiful, too pleasant. It is difficult to get used to this place again. Of course, I'll let you know at once if there's any change here.

Reinitz wrote to me, asking for $600. It's very difficult for me to send him such a sum now. The stock exchange is awful. I'm losing a lot. Conditions are madly uncertain. I'm sending him $300—in three instalments. If you see him, please explain to him, why. If in the meantime I'm doing better, I'll send him the rest.

Dear Lajos, with all my affection,

Laci."

By this time Korda knew he wouldn't stay long in Hollywood, even though he had no idea what troubles lay in store for him. Wanger was Walter Wanger, the producer and director, still active in Hollywood—just as Louella Parsons is still the all-powerful American film columnist. Myron Selznick was Korda's agent. Reinitz was Bela Reinitz, one of Hungary's foremost composers of *Lieder*, a man of great talent and constant poverty whom Korda supported for years.

Two months later Korda wrote his last letter from Hollywood to Biro—dated late November. In the meantime he had finished the 'accursed' 'Princess and the Plumber'. This was based on a story by Alice Duer Miller; the screen-play was by Howard J. Green, whom Alex evidently did not like. But his cast was excellent—Charles Farrell, Maureen O'Sullivan and the veteran H.B. Warner headed it. The film was reviewed—not unfavourably —on November 20, and released a month later.

By then Korda was no longer with Fox nor with any other company in Hollywood.

"My dear Lajos" (he wrote in November), "how is it when bad luck climbs on your back? That's how it is with me now. Not only the divorce and the European trip which took most of my money, not only the state of the stock market (A.T. & T. is 186 today; I refused to sell when it was 310!)—but there's also the outrageous, swinish behaviour of my studio. The reason—or rather, the row—doesn't matter; the fact is that Mr. Wurtzel cancelled my contract for alleged 'disobedience' and they refuse to pay the rest of my salary, about $30,000. Of course, they simply want to bully me into a compromise—still, it's a loathsome business, unpleasant and means a considerable financial loss. In the meantime? My agent's optimistic, I'm pessimistic. There's an ugly mood here. You hardly meet the famous American optimism, except in the newspapers and Hoover's statements. But *we* know official optimism too well to put much faith in it. Of course, the momentary hysterical pessimism is just as groundless as the *bull* optimism. *For the long run*—I wish you and myself that we owned only a hundred thousand dollars worth of good stocks at the present prices. In five years they'll be worth five times as much.

As I say, I'm a pessimist about myself; that's the reason behind the two cables I sent you. I cannot start afresh here, at a lower salary. Nor do I want to. As far as one can see it from such a distance, in my opinion (1) you can make a great deal of money in Europe with a good picture; (2) a good

English-speaking film has a tremendous market over here; (3) if one makes a good picture in Europe, one can get a new contract in America just as easily as if one made it here; And finally: (4) if one earns good money in Europe, why the hell should one come back to this accursed Hollywood?

Of course, it is impossible to negotiate from here or even seek business contacts on general lines. I am only waiting for my suit against Fox to be settled and then intend to start for Berlin. In the meantime this is my conception of the business side:

If you could come to some agreement with UFA or any of the firms mentioned in my cables to make three or four films a year, I could get French and British *release*, perhaps participation, too. In my view the inferiority of Hollywood film production is so marked to-day that a half-way decent European (English-speaking) picture which fulfils certain American requirements, starts with a tremendous chance on the American market, too. But this is a more distant problem. What is immediate—a film in Europe must earn enough money to provide a sufficient income for the director-writer-*producer* group. Of course, I'm not thinking of expensive productions; with all the experience I gained here I want to make films quickly, cheaply, over there. And to finish the German *version* first, then cut it, *preview* it—and only then, so to speak, copy it in English and French. You know—one shoots 100 per cent more film than the final *cut*. Why do this with every version?

Of course, all this depends on what you think of it. Can you see the possibility of somebody investing a year's work in such an enterprise as working capital? Has it any future? Doesn't the political situation threaten with an imminent explosion?

Here I lead a rather boring life. I'm at home all day. I read. I sleep. I wait . . .

   ★ ★ ★ ★ Laci."

What had happened?

One Sunday morning Mr. Sol Wurtzel ordered a private showing of the recently finished 'Princess and the Plumber'. Al Rockett was present and so was, of course, Korda. Wurtzel brought along his eleven-year-old son, presumably for a Sunday treat.

When the show ended, they all emerged into the blinding white Californian sunshine, Korda towering above the rather short Wurtzel. He asked the question every director, writer or actor must ask when the Olympian powers are silent.

"How did you like it, Mr. Wurtzel?"

Mr. Wurtzel removed his cigar and pointed at his son.

"Why don't you ask him?"

Korda turned to the small boy with a pleasant smile.

"Well?"

The younger Wurtzel twisted his small face into a grimace of distaste.

"It stinks," he said, briefly.

Korda seldom lost his self-control; but it was difficult to know what to say or do in such a situation. So he looked at Wurtzel again.

"You heard him," the production chief said. Then, as he turned away, he added: "You're fired."

Mr. Wurtzel knew very well that he couldn't fire a director who had a long-term contract. But he also knew that in Hollywood—as indeed, anywhere else—there were means and ways to break a cast-iron agreement if you had enough ill-will to apply.

There is a story that still goes the rounds of Hollywood, a classic. Perhaps it is just a legend though its elements are real enough.

A writer fell foul of a producer. The producer was the mighty studio head who could make and break people with the greatest of ease. The writer had a five-year contract at a very large salary and no options—that is, his employment was quite safe. They had wanted him very badly at that time and he had a good agent.

After consulting his lawyers, the studio head decided to apply the heat. He put the writer to work with the most cantankerous director. Somewhat to his dismay, the writer won the director's friendship and they worked in perfect harmony. Within a week or so the victim of the persecution campaign found himself in the story department. Every morning three books or plays were put on his desk; every evening three full synopses were to be ready. The writer seemed delighted. For years he had only written and never read; and though the stuff he had to read now was poor material, he did not mind. He was still drawing his big salary every Wednesday—while the ordinary drudges in the story department were paid fifty or a hundred dollars for the same work.

Finally, after trying every unpleasant trick, the Great Man gave the writer the most despised, lowliest job—that of studio guide. It was his duty to shepherd the rubberneck visitors from Kansas and Iowa over the lot, explain to them the secrets of film-making and keep them away from the more temperamental stars. The writer clocked in every day at eight-thirty and worked his full schedule; still cheerful, still drawing the big money.

Then one day a group of three men arrived and asked to be shown over the studio. The writer did his usual cheerful, efficient job. The visitors seemed to be much taken with him. At the end of the tour they tipped him generously and one of them asked:

"You seem to be a bright young man. Wouldn't you like to improve yourself—get a better job?"

"No, thank you," said the writer. "I like this one. I meet people—most of the time I'm in the fresh air, too. And I'm well paid."

"Are you?" the second man seemed curious. "What is your salary?"

"Three thousand five hundred dollars a week."

The visitors gaped. They happened to be bankers—heads of the three banks financing the studio. The rest of the story they found out quickly enough. Twenty-four hours later the writer was back in his private office—and the studio chief was *out*.

But Korda wasn't the legendary writer and Sol Wurtzel wasn't the big bad wolf in the story—his actions were worse. On Monday morning when Alex arrived at the studio, he found his staff—Miss Fisher, his faithful secretary, Eddie Marin, his assistant—standing in the corridor outside his office. He was already suspecting the worst as he had had great difficulty in getting past the gate in his Chrysler.

A workman was removing his name-plate and putting up another. Miss Fisher and Marin, who hadn't been at the Sunday showing, were puzzled and shocked. Alex explained quickly what had happened and then hurried over to the executive wing. But Mr. Wurtzel was 'in conference'.

He drove to his agent, who reassured him; this must be some misunderstanding, a temporary cloud, it would pass. But it didn't. Certainly, Mr. Wurtzel said, Mr. Korda was still employed by the studio. If he would like to take up his allotted place in the story department, his contract would be honoured. Of course, if he didn't like to be in the dog-house, prepare synopses like any other honest, hard-working reader, this would be considered 'disobedience' and a breach of contract.

There were various intrigues and hostile influences behind all this. One of Korda's fellow-countrymen for whom he had found a job, turned, in typical Hollywood fashion, against his benefactor and did everything to make him unpopular with the bosses. Slowly he undermined the confidence of the Fox executives in Alex until even Al Rockett, his friend and first producer, had forsaken him.

Korda decided to fight back. He wasn't going into the dog-house, whoever built it—even though his personal problems were pressing enough.

His marriage had been breaking up for some time. Korda was a man of great self-control, gentleness and patience. Maria was everything that belonged to the tradition of the great silent film-stars: tempestuous, with quickly changing moods and strong passions. Perhaps the break-up was hastened by the fact that her

own career, like that of so many silent stars, was being interrupted, perhaps ended, by the coming of the talkies. She spoke
several languages but all of them with an accent. They separated
in 1930—Korda set up a generous trust-fund for her in America
—and in 1931 they were divorced.

A few days after the Sunday screening, Alex spent a hot afternoon at Clive Brook's cottage on Malibu Beach. There, lying in
the sand, he told his friends—Clive Brook, Ronald Colman and
Warner Baxter—that Hollywood no longer wanted him and
that there was nothing left but to go back to Europe and start
all over again.

In the meantime he had nothing to do but wait. An agent
came to him and said that he had a contract in his pocket, all
signed and ready to start when Alex was free of his present
commitments; he couldn't tell him the name of the studio but
it was a far better agreement than the present one had been.
Korda believed him—until the agent, (today one of Hollywood's
most prosperous producers) also became 'unavailable' whenever he wanted to pin him down about that wonderful new
job.

It soon became evident that his case would be difficult to win.
For one reason, in Hollywood (at least in those days) Justice was
usually on the side of the 'big battalions'—the men in power.
No agent would risk quarrelling with a top executive, however
important his client's interests. Litigation was costly and took a
long time. In the end, under pressure of his advisers, Korda agreed
to a compromise. He was paid about one third of his claim. Most
of this money was already 'spoken for'—as usual he had debts
and heavy responsibilities.

It was about this time that one of his old Hungarian friends
arrived in Hollywood. He found Alex unemployed. "Something
must be done," the friend said. "I'll arrange a party . . ."

"What good would that do?" demanded Korda. "I've been
fired—and I haven't any other job in sight . . ."

"Exactly!" cried his friend. "We'll invite the top executives, give them a wonderful time—and before the party's over, I'm sure one of them will come up with an offer . . ."

Somewhat reluctantly, Korda agreed to the idea. His friend took all the arrangements upon himself. Champagne, caviar, a gipsy band, flowers—the house in North Rodeo Drive was transformed into a glittering *boîte de nuit*. And the 'big brass' came —the top executives, the men in charge of the various studios. They brought their girl friends and wives. Korda's own intimates, the stars who had worked with him, rallied around to give him support.

One of the most important guests was an inveterate gambler. He insisted on making up a school of poker. Alex had to sit in though he had little enthusiasm in his present state of mind. The gipsies fiddled, the champagne flowed, everybody had a wonderful time. Except the big executive who was losing heavily. It was his habit never to quit a game until at least he had regained his original stake. And so the poker school didn't break up until seven o'clock in the morning. By that time most of the others had departed, thanking Korda for a most wonderful party. At seven the great executive himself staggered off, having finished with a few hundred dollars to the good. Every time Korda said good-bye to one of his important guests, he waited for the magic words: "Come and see me . . ." or "Give me a call soon . . ." One of them actually spoke these magic words—though not very warmly. At half past seven he stood in the middle of the wreckage, surveying the debris of the party. He had spent several thousand dollars— and he had one slender hope left.

Next day he went round to the studio chief. He was kept waiting two hours—and then sent away with a lame excuse. He realized that he had been blacklisted. All his powerful enemy had to do was to lift the phone and tell his colleagues: "I don't want Korda to be employed." No one had any intention of offering him a job; he was unemployable.

Years later he visited the same studio where he had been kept cooling his heels. All the doors opened as if by magic; flunkeys

and secretaries wafted him to the inner sanctum of the Big Chief.
Korda smiled a little bitterly but he said nothing.

Now, a week or two after the party, he left for Berlin. He had
very little money—he had to borrow some to pay his current
tax without which he could not leave the States—and no prospects. Nothing except his ideas, his talent and his faith in his own
future.

CHAPTER VI

THE MAKING OF LONDON FILMS

KORDA'S first stop in Europe was Berlin. His friend Biro
was working there and had plans for him.

In 1930 Max Reinhardt was still the uncrowned
king of the German theatre. Of Hungarian origin, the great
German director and producer owned a number of theatres in
Berlin and Vienna. He had been thinking for a long time of
entering films, to exploit the outstanding actors he had under
contract and the many plays in which he owned screen rights.

Reinhardt discussed his plans with Lajos Biro and Gabriel
Pascal—another Hungarian. In England Pascal later became
famous as the man who persuaded G. B. Shaw to permit
screen versions of his plays. But Pascal had been long active in
Vienna and Berlin—with varied success but immense drive and
optimism, befitting his flamboyant personality—and had produced highly lucrative films.

Koda arrived in Berlin and Biro took him to Reinhardt. The
theatrical producer had his own ideas as to what pictures he
wanted to make. Korda thought these totally impracticable.
And once again he would have been obliged to work under
somebody else's authority which he was most reluctant to do.
The negotiations petered out.

Nor did the discussions with Pascal lead to anything. Pascal
wanted Alex to direct Emerich Kalman's 'Countess Maritza', a
very successful musical comedy. His offer was unusual: 50 per
cent of the profits, a suite in the Hotel Adlon with full board—
but no cash. Korda turned it down. Later Hans Oswald directed
the picture on the same terms and made a great deal of money.

There wasn't very much love lost between Korda and Pascal though later Alex helped his fellow-countryman in his English productions and found him amusing if a trifle trying. "This Pascal has such a loud voice," Korda once told Steven Pallos, "as if the talkies had been invented expressly for him . . ."

After a brief stay in the German capital, Korda went to Paris. There he installed himself at the Hotel Raphael, which remained his favourite 'home from home', and began to look around. He soon discovered that Paramount had almost as many frozen francs as German marks and that they intended to go into production. Robert Kane, head of their Paris office, was an old acquaintance. Korda's Hollywood friends got in touch with Adolph Zukor and Korda was given a contract to direct a number of pictures. Soon Lajos Biro joined him.

Steven Pallos, to-day a well-known British producer, began to work in films in Austria after the first world war and was a director of a well-established French firm of distributors at the time of Korda's return to Europe. He had a deep affection, almost a feeling of hero-worship for Korda; he urged him to settle in England, start his own company and produce pictures with Anglo-French finance. Biro had already been called to London several times to work on various scripts for British Gaumont. In the summer of 1931 he was also signed by the French Paramount company.

Korda directed three films in France and Biro was associated with all of them. These were 'Marius', 'Rive Gauche' and 'The Girl from Maxim's', which was made both in French and English.

These films gave Korda the opportunity to work together with some well-known French authors, among them Marcel Pagnol and Marcel Achard. Both of these eminent writers were beginners in the film business and most suspicious of its pitfalls. Slowly it dawned on them that these unusual foreigners, Korda and Biro, knew quite a bit and that each of them had first-rate talent in his own sphere. Achard, introducing Biro to a particularly dense distributor, said to him: "You know, he's an author, honestly, old boy, just like me!"

Marcel Pagnol, only 37 at the time, had three or four successful plays to his credit, of which 'Topaze' was the triumph of 1930. He had begun his Marseilles trilogy with 'Marius' in 1929. A few months before Korda's arrival in Paris he had become interested in the possibilities of the cinema. He founded two companies for production and distribution. He was also responsible for the start of the famous '*Cahiers du film*', in which he expressed his ideas on the function and art of the cinema.

Korda had already directed 'Rive Gauche' when he was told by Robert Kane that Paramount had bought 'Marius' and wanted him to do the film version. Kane also suggested a number of well-known French stars to appear in the picture.

At that time Korda had heard neither of Pagnol nor of 'Marius'. The play had already finished its run; but through Steven Pallos a special performance was arranged—for an audience consisting of Korda alone. The scattered cast was gathered together and Alex sat in the darkened theatre, completely enthralled. No wonder—for 'Marius' was played by such brilliant actors as Raimu and Pierre Fresnay, both comparative unknowns then.

Korda went back to Robert Kane and insisted that the original stage cast should be kept for the film. Apart from the demands of film technique, 'Marius' was photographed almost straight. The French were amazed by the ability of a Hungarian to catch the rich, racy atmosphere of Marseilles. Korda seemed to have a deep understanding for the typically Latin or Mediterranean setting and the down-to-earth, half-sentimental, half-cynical characters of Pagnol's play. The picture was much enhanced by Vincent Korda's settings. Vincent, most reluctantly, had yielded to his brother's persuasion and did the set designs—the first in his long and distinguished career. When 'Marius' was re-issued in London eighteen years after its original production it was chosen by several critics as one of the ten best films of 1950!

Pagnol's meeting with Korda was a happy event for both of

them; they remained life-long friends. 'Marius' was actually made in three versions—with Korda directing both the French and German and a Swedish director working on a Swedish one. Harold Young came over from Hollywood to edit the picture and stayed on with Alex until 1935.

★   ★   ★   ★

Once the Pagnol picture was finished, Steven Pallos renewed his suggestion to form an independent company. A somewhat tentative agreement was made by Korda, Biro and Pallos himself to work together on films in the future. Pallos had obtained a distribution arrangement from Pathé. The three partners invested enough to start a firm which was called Pallas Films Ltd.— named after the Greek goddess rather than the third partner. It acquired several story properties—some of them were re-sold at a profit—but its actual operation was postponed by Korda's and Biro's commitments for Paramount.

In the autumn of 1931 Paramount executives arrived in Paris from Hollywood. They were dissatisfied with the British production of the company and decided to send Biro and Korda to London to take charge.

Korda was sorry to leave Paris. He loved the life of the boulevards; his French had become fluent and idiomatic though not always grammatical; and he had made many friends. He was still short of money—his divorce and the subsequent financial settlement had been very costly—but as usual, he was living in the style of a *grandseigneur*, and he had some forebodings about settling in London.

Korda landed in England in November, 1931. He had a contract to direct two pictures for British Paramount but no other prospects or financial backers. Characteristically, he took offices in Grosvenor Street, Mayfair. At first, as he said himself, he did little "except worry about bills". But soon he went to work. And he had friends.

John Loder, back in England for a visit, remembered the man who gave him his start in pictures. He introduced Alex to his brother-in-law, a wealthy and influential gentleman, head of a large brewery. In his house Korda met for the first time such prominent Englishmen as Lord Birkenhead and Winston Churchill.

Victor Savile, the veteran director, had worked with Maria Corda who starred in his silent picture 'Tessa'. Later Savile had gone to Hollywood, where he became a good friend of the Kordas. Now, back in England, with British Gaumont, he introduced Alex to C. M. Woolf, deputy chairman and managing director of his company.

Michael Balcon had first met Korda in Berlin when Alex was making 'A Modern Dubarry'. It was he who arranged a distribution contract for the first London Film production, 'Wedding Rehearsal'.

But before he got so far, Korda had to direct two films for British Paramount. In February 1932, Zoltan and Vincent joined him in London. Vincent as we have seen, had made his entry into films by designing the sets of 'Marius', though his brother hadn't found it easy to lure him from his painting. Zoltan had stayed behind in Hollywood for more than a year, recovering from an illness. Now the three brothers were together, ready to storm the citadels of the British cinema.

The first of Korda's British Paramount films was 'Service for Ladies', a slight and charming comedy. It was mainly notable because it introduced to the British screen a former bank clerk called Leslie Stainer—who was to become famous as Leslie Howard. He and his director hit it off very well. "I found myself in perfect accord with Alexander Korda," Howard told an American reporter a year later. "We think alike, agree upon the same things, work the same way. He would make a scene, then throw the whole thing in the ashbin because he did not like it, and do it over again quite differently and very much better. That is why his work is so good. I would certainly like to do more work with him . . ."

The chance was to come before very long. 'Service for Ladies' had a considerable success both in Britain and America.

'Women Who Play', the second contract-picture Korda directed, was a more sombre film—it dealt with prostitutes. It was made at the British & Dominions Studio, Elstree. In the same place and at the same time Harry Lackman was shooting Frederick Lonsdale's 'Aren't We All', a comedy of high society.

The job of the casting department was to find extras for both pictures. Tough and sexy types for Alex; refined and elegant people for Lackman.

The candidates waited in two different large dressing-rooms to be inspected by the producers. Unfortunately, the third assistant director made a slight mistake—he conducted Harry Lackman to the room in which Korda's prospective 'crowd artistes' waited. Harry, always a quick-tempered man, exploded with a roar: "D'you expect me to use these tramps? Get them out of here!" It took quite a while to explain to him that impeccable types were waiting in the next room.

Among these 'impeccable types' was a girl registered by the casting department as Merle O'Brien. A day or two later she was lunching in the studio canteen. Maria Corda, visiting her ex-husband, noticed her dark, exotic beauty. "Look, Alex!" she said, "what a striking face that girl has!"

Alex looked and grunted non-committally. But then he looked again. Later that day he wandered on the set of 'Aren't We All?' where Miss O'Brien stood, wearing a smart evening gown. He asked her name. She told him—though she didn't know him from Adam.

"Well, Miss O'Brien," Korda said, "I want to see if there's anything behind this face of yours. Would you care to make a test for me?"

She was puzzled by his Hungarian accent, his grave courtesy. She also thought he was joking.

But she took the tests which Alex directed himself. Nothing happened.

The original file card of Miss O'Brien has been preserved. She was born in India, daughter of an English railway official. A former officer of the Indian army told me how Merle and a girl-friend used to play the piano and give song recitals in the Railway Institute at Lahore. Then she came to England to make a career. She was called Queenie Thompson O'Brien. For a while she was a dance hostess at the Café de Paris; a shy, sweet, very popular girl. When she started film work, she changed her name to Merle O'Brien.

The file card gave her name, her address, her height, her colour, her type ("smart crowd; promising"), her age, her ward-robe and then added, under the heading 'experience': "*In good demand for special crowd work. A.K. interested.*"

How "interested" A.K. was became evident before many months passed.

★　　★　　★　　★

While 'Service for Ladies' was a success, 'Women Who Play' didn't make much of a splash. The Paramount contract came to an end. It was a difficult and confused period in Korda's life.

Then a solicitor introduced him to Leopold Sutro, the banker. Sutro liked Korda's global ideas; he agreed to back him and the first pictures were partly made in Paris.

Korda and his associates cast around for a name for the company —nobody liked Pallas Productions. And so, in February 1932, they founded London Films; strangely enough, no British company was using this name. It was Korda's idea to choose Big Ben for the symbol and trade-mark. This choice was deliberate, a monument known to all the world. Once Alex was asked why Big Ben always struck eleven in his pictures?

"That was when the sun happened to come out," he replied. "We'd waited three hours to get the shot!"

Big Ben haunted him later, during the time he was in hospital not far from the Houses of Parliament. Every quarter of an hour his room reverberated with the chimes. Perhaps he wished he hadn't chosen it for his symbol—or had chosen another hospital!

The directors of the company were George Grossmith, chairman, Lord Lurgan, Lajos Biro, J. S. Cerf, J. R. Sutro, Alexander Korda and Captain A. S. N. Dixie.

Grossmith had returned from Hollywood; Korda remembered his kindness in the dark days, the talks they had about working together; he loved the Edwardian gusto, the Bohemian high spirits of the fine actor who was also delightful company. J. S. Cerf was a Frenchman, connected with Pathé; John Sutro represented his father's interests. The new company had its offices at 22 Grosvenor Street. Its director of publicity was a young and enthusiastic journalist, John B. Myers; its casting director and location manager, George Grossmith junior.

In those early days London Films was a happy family party. Alex and his two brothers, George Grossmith, his son and his son-in-law, Harry George (secretary of the company), and a number of enthusiastic young men who had only recently left school or university. Time meant nothing and they often worked round the clock. The first year of the infant London Films was a pretty precarious one and sometimes they had to forgo their pay packets; but Korda inspired and sustained them all.

There was an occasion when Korda had to meet a number of bank managers who were a little unhappy about the overdraft. These gentlemen were kept waiting for some time in the Grosvenor Street office while Alex was on his way from the studio. At last he arrived, profuse with apologies; he wished everybody a very good morning, there was a pause and one of the bankers rose: "Mr. Korda, we realize that we have to make allowances for the artistic temperament but . . ."

Alex broke in with a smile and his charmingly broken English: "Gentlemen, the only artistic temperament I have ever experienced has come from bankers . . ." The tension was broken, everybody laughed—and Korda got the money.

Most people seem to think that the career of London Films

began with the fabulous 'Private Life of Henry VIII'. Actually, the company made seven films before 'Henry'.

In 1928 the Quota Act was introduced in Britain. This was a measure to stimulate and protect production and was badly needed. In 1923 only 10 per cent of the films shown in Britain were made in the country. By 1926 the proportion had dropped to 5 per cent. The first Quota Act made it compulsory for cinemas to devote an increasing percentage of their screentime to British films, beginning with 5 per cent. This was called the Exhibitors' Quota. At the same time the distributors (or renters) of films were also obliged to include a rising percentage of British films in their programme, beginning with $7\frac{1}{2}$ per cent. This was the Renters' Quota; it was hoped that the all-powerful American renters would sponsor a number of British pictures.

The first Quota Act laid the foundations of the modern British film industry but the initial effects were far from happy. The cinemas, to comply with the law, would show British pictures in the morning, to almost empty seats, even warning their patrons that the 'real programme' would start later. The 'Quota Quickies' made cheaply to comply with the Renters' Quota gave British films a bad name which it took many years to live down.

The Quota Act proved how easily a bad law could be evaded. It is still in force though with some modifications; it is still basically bad for it can be contravened. The penalties for breaking it are ridiculously mild; any exhibitor can easily pay the small fines from the profits of his American pictures. Except, of course, that British pictures—thanks to Korda, Rank and a few others— are a great deal better and often excellent box office. Today about 50 per cent of the screen time in British cinemas is taken up by the home product though a certain proportion of this is Anglo-American in finance and conception.

The pictures which Korda made in 1932–33 were 'quota quickies' for the Renters' Quota. Mr. Graham, head of Paramount in Britain, gave him a distribution contract; the films were delivered at a fixed price. Graham's daughter, Dorothy,

worked in the scenario department of London Films. The pictures
had to be made reasonably cheaply and quickly. But Korda
attempted something better than the tasteless and shabby product.
For one thing, he introduced completely new faces and provided
an excellent training for a whole generation of future stars.

The first of these films was 'Wedding Rehearsal', based on a
story by the future Lord Castlerosse, columnist, man-about-
town and lover of life who became one of Korda's early British
friends. Michael Balcon liked it so much that he persuaded
C. M. Woolf to provide distribution through 'Ideal Films', one
of the B. & D. subsidiaries. Though it was fairly widely shown
in the States, in Britain the distribution wasn't well handled; or
perhaps the story was too light-hearted, even cynical. Yet two or
three years later the same film would have been a sensation—if
only because of its cast. George Grossmith and Lady Tree headed
it; the young ladies included Wendy Barrie, Joan Gardner (the
future Mrs. Zoltan Korda) and Diana Napier. In a small part
Merle O'Brien—now re-baptized Merle Oberon—got her first
chance; those tests had paid off, even if she had had to wait a
couple of months. The men were headed by Roland Young,
whom Alex brought over from Hollywood; John Loder and
Maurice Evans played the juvenile leads.

'Men of Tomorrow' was a picture with a university background. A large part of it was shot in Oxford. A young stage
actor named Robert Donat made his début in it; another, called
Emlyn Williams, played his second screen rôle. Joan Gardner
and Merle Oberon (in a somewhat larger part than in 'Wedding
Rehearsal') shared the leads.

The four young stars didn't see much of Korda, who left the
direction tactfully to Leontine Sagan. Miss Sagan had become
famous through her direction of 'Mädchen in Uniform'. Perhaps
she and Korda had decided between them that if Miss Sagan
knew little about Oxford, Alex knew even less.

Donat, Williams, with the Misses Gardner and Oberon, were
young, high-spirited and (of course) disrespectful to their elders

behind their backs. The fact that nepotism was so disarmingly obvious in the Hungarian camp—not *two* Korda brothers but *three*! (Zoltan was production supervisor; Vincent had designed the sets)—gave rise to a game the four of them started during the interminable waits between shots. How many Kordas *were* there and what were their real names? They were doing splendidly, Merle and Robert and Emlyn—Con Korda, Dis Korda, Miseri Korda, Umbilical Korda were some of the names they came up with—when a soft Hungarian voice behind them said:

"And have you not forgotten, children, the best-loved of all, the Lost Korda?"

It was about the only time Donat and Williams met Alex during the entire film. And Emlyn Williams told me that he thought of that story in November, 1956, when Vincent Korda's son Michael (with his own son Alan) was missing in Budapest for several crucial fighting days—a lost Korda indeed!

★   ★   ★   ★

Next came 'Bright Lights of London', with Robert Donat and Pearl Argyle; then 'Strange Evidence' with Frank Vosper, Leslie Banks and Diana Napier. 'Counsel's Opinion' was later remade on a much more lavish scale as 'The Divorce of Lady X.' It starred Binnie Barnes, Cyril Maude, Laurence Grossmith and Francis Lister; the cast included Harry Tate (in a brief cameo as a taxi-driver), Ronald Simpson, Henry Kendall and Hay Petrie.

The last of the seven was 'Cash', directed by Zoltan Korda. It was one of the first 'crazy comedies', starring Edmund Gwenn with Wendy Barrie and Robert Donat; the script was by Anthony Gibbs and Arthur Wimperis.

Though all these pictures were released in America, they did not get a truly fair showing in Britain. Their fate hardened Korda's resolve to fight for a proper distribution of his pictures. As he told me, years later: "Suppose we'd been making sausages. I wouldn't expect from any rival sausage factory to sell my goods in its shops—if it had shops. So the answer is to get your own shops—or, alternately, to make your sausages so good that even your rival has to stock them. The first is costly, the second is difficult—that's why I'd like to try them both at the same time . . ."

★   ★   ★   ★

There are at least half-a-dozen versions of how 'The Private Life of Henry VIII' came to be born. Somewhat mischievously, Korda himself delighted in telling a different story every time he was asked how it all began.

According to one version, Alex was in a London cab when he heard the driver sing 'I am 'Enery the Heighth, I am'. He asked what the song was about and then decided that a king, still being sung about four centuries after his death, would make a wonderful subject for a film. So he set to work with Lajos Biro and Philip Lindsay, the historical novelist, to prepare a script.

Version Number Two starts with a conference in Korda's Dorchester Hotel suite to discuss the possibility of Alex directing Charles Laughton in 'Ready Money'. Those present were Korda, Laughton, the Hon. Richard Norton (later Lord Grantley), then in charge of British United Artists production, and Lawrence Howard, Laughton's agent. Howard noticed a statuette of Henry VIII on the mantelpiece which Korda had just bought. He picked it up and remarked that it looked very like Charles Laughton. And so the idea was born—with Lajos Biro roughing out the outline that very night.

The third version was given by Laughton himself in an interview, in February 1935:

"I met Korda in Paris one day and we dined and talked about my season at the Old Vic. From this dinner there emerged an audacious plan, that of producing a costume picture based on the life of Henry VIII, the film to be made on a co-operative basis, with no salaries to be paid and everyone to share in the profits or losses. We returned to London and assembled a cast. The actors, at first dubious, finally said: '*If Korda and Laughton are crazy, we might as well be, too.*' "

Years later when I talked to Charles Laughton, he was positive that the idea of 'Henry VIII' originated with Korda, though he helped with research and suggestions himself.

Whatever the truth about any of these three or several other versions, nobody except its originators was enthusiastic about it. Korda took it to C. M. Woolf, who thought it was crazy and politely kicked him out. The Sutro interests couldn't provide the money—or not all of it. Korda therefore started the picture without knowing how he would ever finish it. He gathered a magnificent group of players for his venture. The five wives (for Catherine of Aragon did not appear) were played by Elsa Lanchester, Binnie Barnes, Merle Oberon, Wendy Barrie and Everley Gregg. Culpepper, Catherine Howard's unhappy lover, was Robert Donat; Cromwell was Franklin Diall, and Cranmer was Lawrence Hanray. Every small part was given to an experienced, hand-picked actor. But money kept running out. "During the making of the film," Charles Laughton said, "we were often apprehensive that while we were saying our lines the sets would collapse and smother us. We finished the picture in five weeks, one of the least expensive big productions ever made. We were fairly satisfied with it but never for a moment did we think it would be the great financial success that it was. We would have sold it to the first bidder. But there were no bidders . . ."

Almost every actor who appeared in the picture had a story to tell about it. John Loder recalled how one day King George V came to visit the studio and was told by Alex that there were a dozen beautiful English girls in the cast. The King smiled and asked: "Are there that many?"

Gibb McLaughlin played the part of the French executioner.

On his first day at work he had a scene with the late Sam Livesey. He was busy sharpening his blade and Alex said he would like McLaughlin to whistle a tune—to show that he was happy at his work. The first tune that came to the actor's mind was one of the dances from 'Henry VIII' by Edward German. But Alex stopped him, saying that wouldn't be right—it was a modern tune and nothing to do with the subject. So McLaughlin just whistled a tune of his own making. It struck him, rather forcibly, that here was a Hungarian who obviously knew that he was wrong— who knew enough about music and history to put him right. An actor, of course, could always tell at once when he was being directed—and Korda not only knew his job—he already knew more about England and English music than an Englishman.

Wally Patch, the Cockney comedian, was originally engaged to play the British executioner.

"Can you speak bad French?" Korda asked him.

"I can't even speak good English," replied Wally. "Cor knows what my French is like!"

"Well, what sort of muscles have you?"

"Oh, they're O.K.," said Wally confidently. But then, the film was behind schedule and he had to cancel the engagement.

"Never mind," said George Grossmith jr., the casting director, "are you good at carving?"

"Well, I used to be a bookmaker," said Wally—and took the smaller part of the Carver at the royal banquet.

This banquet was memorable in more ways than one. Charles Laughton demonstrated Tudor table manners, which were any-thing but genteel. And Binnie Barnes almost gave up acting because of it. She was very young, a night-club singer, when Alex gave her a contract—at fifteen pounds a week. "I hadn't much idea what was going on," Miss Barnes told me, "I learned my lines and whatever acting I did was more by the grace of God than by conscious effort."

She certainly had to make a considerable effort to last through the banqueting sequence. It was real food, of course; every day the chickens and boar's head and the rest were freshly prepared and sent up from the Savoy. And the actors really had to eat. Day after day, Miss Barnes felt herself getting plumper and plumper—and still it went on. She was choking with food and couldn't stand it any more. So she went to Alex and told him she couldn't go on. He looked at her and said: "You've jolly well got to . . ." She cried and protested but he repeated: "You've got to, Binnie—we've all got to do it . . ." She was still protesting; Korda took out his watch and threw it on the floor. It was an expensive watch and it broke. "You see," Alex said. Binnie Barnes didn't. "But it's simple," he explained. "I dropped my watch, so it broke. There was nothing I could do about it. I can do just as little about this scene—it's got to be shot and you've got to go on eating . . ." So she did.

'Henry' was the first British film of Georges Perinal, the brilliant French cameraman who had worked on René Clair's classic 'Sous Les Toits de Paris', 'Le Million' and 'A Nous La Liberté'. Perinal saw everything from the point of view of his camera—and he was always steeped in the deepest pessimism. Before making 'Henry' Korda took him to Hampton Court, giving a glowingly enthusiastic lecture about the palace, the grounds, the maze. Perinal listened to it silently, sunk in his usual gloom. At the very end he said: "It will all come out black . . ." Actually, as Laughton told me, they had to give up the idea of using Hampton Court—they couldn't line up a single camera shot that would have produced a purely Tudor result. The great palace had been rebuilt and altered so many times that the styles and periods were inextricably mixed.

When Korda shot the scene in which Laurence Hanray, as Cranmer, told Henry VIII about the infidelity of Katherine Howard, the set was cleared of all but the essential technicians. It was a moving scene and Perinal, having lit the set, huddled near the camera, watching Laughton and Hanray going through it. Korda himself was touched by the performance; when he turned round, he noticed that there were tears in Perinal's eyes.

Charles Laughton as Henry VIII and Merle Oberon as Anne Boleyn

Valerie Hobson and Sabu in 'The Drum'

Korda with Deborah Kerr and Glynis Johns on the set of 'Perfect Strangers'

Conversation piece: Korda, Orson Welles, Vivien Leigh and Julien Duvivier on the set of 'Anna Karenina'

"Why, Georges," he whispered, "you are crying!"

"Yes," whispered back Perinal, "isn't it terrible? There was a mike shadow—we have to do it all over again!"

The city finance which Alex had obtained ran out, and still the film wasn't finished. Then an angel appeared—in the portly person of Signor Ludovico Toeplitz de Grand Ry, son of an Italian banker. He provided the necessary money so that 'Henry' could be completed. With his Falstaffian figure and beard it was unavoidable that he should be nicknamed 'Henry IX'. He stayed briefly in Korda's life; when 'Henry' was finished, Toeplitz insisted that in the future he should have a say not only in financial but also in artistic matters. This Korda very firmly refused and the two men parted. Toeplitz was actually given the choice whether, as part of the settlement, he should take 'Henry' or 'The Girl from Maxim's', which had been completed not long before. He chose the second picture as the more certain box-office property, which showed a little lack of judgment. Later Toeplitz formed his own company and made a film called 'The Dictator', with Clive Brook—which, unfortunately, wasn't a success. It was he who brought Filippo Del Giudice, one of the most colourful and forceful personalities, into British films.

Even when 'Henry' emerged from the cutting rooms, there was no one who really wanted it. Korda showed it to British Gaumont. The executives declared that 'the public would never stand for it'. Charles Laughton as a lover, a royal profligate—now, if it had been 'The Ghoul', a juicy horror picture—that was an entirely different matter. Fox and Paramount were equally unenthusiastic. Even United Artists refused at first, until Murray Silverstone, sparked by Richard Norton's glowing report, agreed to distribute it.

'The Private Life of Henry VIII' was presented on October 12, 1933, at the Radio City Music Hall, New York City. It was an astute move on Korda's part to insist on an American première. If the Americans didn't like the picture, he could keep silent about

E

it—but if they did, the London presentation, a fortnight later, would benefit greatly by the New York success.

The Americans liked 'Henry'—very much. The press was almost unanimously eulogistic; serious and popular critics alike brought out their most flattering adjectives. But in spite of the excellent American reviews, Korda and his associates were still anxious about the British reaction. 'Henry' was presented on October 24th at the Leicester Square Theatre by Jack Buchanan, who was then the managing director of the West End cinema. It was a glittering première and the reaction of the audience was encouraging. Korda and his friends stayed up all night, waiting for the morning papers, just as actors do after a Broadway or West End première. And suddenly they found themselves famous, praised sky-high for a picture which the wise men of Wardour Street wouldn't touch. It wasn't the first or the last time in the history of show business—but perhaps never before had one man's wisdom and faith found such vindication.

'Greatest British Film Triumph!' proclaimed the *Daily Mail*'s four-column headline. 'A picture in a thousand,' wrote the *Daily Telegraph*. 'Korda deserves all the congratulations that have been showered on him,' said the *Sunday Express*. 'It puts British films two or three years forward in one bound . . . it will make British history . . . a complete triumph!' the chorus of praise swelled.

The estimates of 'Henry's' final cost ranged from £50,000 to £80,000. During its first world run it made more than £500,000 —in its first week in New York it took only £100 less than the world record figure for any film at any single theatre up to that date. In 1953 it was still making £10,000 a year and it started a new, lucrative career on television in 1957.

But it did more than that. It established Lajos Biro as one of the leading screenwriters of the world; his collaborator, Arthur Wimperis, responsible for the impish wit of the dialogue, won equal fame. For Laughton it meant, if not the climax, at least one of the peaks of his distinguished and triumphant career. Every one of his 'wives' ended up in Hollywood. Merle Oberon's part of Anne Boleyn was only a couple of pages—but she studied it with such enthusiasm and concentration that her performance brought her more praise than all the leads she had played in the earlier, small pictures. Elsa Lanchester also triumphed in the sly and fascinating cameo she made of Anne of Cleves. Robert Donat soon went on to even better and bigger things—Korda lent him to Hollywood for the title part in 'The Count of Monte Cristo'.

With all this paean of praise, this rags-to-riches success story, it seems almost sacrilege to ask whether 'The Private Life of Henry VIII' is truly a great picture? It has, of course, no 'message' and no 'plot' in the usual sense. Some critics attacked it for small lapses in historical accuracy. Others claimed that it wasn't history at all. But then, Korda had no intention of presenting a broad canvas. When Francis Hackett, the author of a colourful and romantic but carefully researched Henry VIII biography, sued London Films, alleging plagiarism, Korda replied: "In all the film there is not one incident, not one line or phrase, borrowed from Mr. Hackett. If by any chance there are minor similarities—and I am not aware of any—that is because we both borrowed from history." The case was withdrawn.

Korda was not concerned with the presentation of Tudor politics; financial means made it impossible to show such glittering pageantry as the Field of Cloth of Gold. Perhaps the greatest personal achievement in the film was that of Vincent Korda who, on a comparatively small stage, worked a miracle in re-creating Tudor pomp and pageant. A reluctant recruit to films, Vincent's contribution to 'Henry' and scores of other pictures has never been truly appreciated except by those who worked with him. Charles Laughton had especially warm words of praise for his work; and so had dozens of producers, directors, actors and exhibitors to whom I spoke.

'Henry' was new, daring and different—and a success. It established Korda as a leading British director and producer. There were, of course, people within and outside the industry who resented this. English history, they said, was being vulgarized and desecrated by this 'coffee-drinking Hungarian'. He didn't understand English traditions, he wasn't fit to handle such subjects.

Korda replied that just because he was a foreigner he could bring a fresh approach, a new viewpoint to these subjects. In art and literature, in music and films there was a long tradition of outsiders tackling English themes—and some with conspicuous success. The critics—only a few of whom were motivated by envy or jealousy—were soon silenced.

*   *   *   *

The two or three hundred people to whom I talked about Alexander Korda had two things in common. Stars, directors, producers, technicians, secretaries or bankers—they all tried to imitate his accent and they all spoke of his charm.

The actors did it rather well—the soft voice, the Continental vowels, the startling expletives that proved what a command of English barrack-room language this Hungarian possessed. But even if the others only produced a pale imitation of the original, they proved what a lasting impression it made on them.

"Tremendous charm . . . fantastic charm . . . a snakecharmer's magic . . . he could turn it on at will . . . it was his essence . . ." Like a vast chorus, it was the same word again and again, sometimes used as a compliment, sometimes with a little envy, even with hostility.

Whatever it was, it worked. And above all, it could arouse a deep loyalty, create enduring affection. Great men and little people alike fell under his sway. He took a deep interest in the personal problems of his staff; he not only played but lived the part of a fairy godfather. Many quarrelled with him—but almost no one could remain his enemy.

Very quickly he gathered a kind of Pretorian guard around himself. Sir David Cunynghame, his first production manager;

George Grossmith jr., his casting director; Dorothy Holloway, his casting secretary; Ernest Bailey, his chauffeur—they stayed with him for years if not decades; a shining testimonial to his qualities as an employer.

John Myers did more than anybody else to make the world 'Korda-conscious'. He was in charge of publicity at British Gaumont when Korda beckoned, and left his job with hardly a moment's hesitation.

Though Myers considered himself an experienced publicity man, Alex taught him a great deal. "He not only knew all about publicity," Myers told me, "he was a creative genius in the field."

Korda wasn't particularly interested in personal publicity— but he was quite willing for Myers to 'build him up' in the cause of London Films and his specific plans. Columnists and critics always found him accessible; as a former newspaperman, he talked their language and he always gave them good copy.

> "Within our organization I would say that he liked yes-men," Myers recalled, "but they had to be intelligent. One executive soon realized this. We would have a story conference and Alex would suggest an idea. Most of us would applaud it—because, with few exceptions, they were original and excellent ideas. But this particular gentleman would say: 'Alex, let me think it over—I haven't made up my mind.' Then he would go off, occupy himself with his own work, never giving the slightest thought to the problem in hand. But a day or two later he would go back to Korda and tell him: 'Remember that idea? I've turned it over in my mind—I think it's wonderful. You're a genius!' And Alex would say to the rest of us: 'See—he isn't just a yes-man, he thinks!' "

Korda liked to bring entirely new people into films—both on the executive and artistic side. He had hardly founded London

Films when he assembled a group of young players and began to build them into a sort of repertory company. Merle Oberon, Binnie Barnes, Wendy Barrie, Joan Gardner, Pearl Argyle, Robert Donat—in the office they were known as the 'little unknowns'. Wardour Street called them 'Korda's Follies'. But with very few exceptions his discoveries became stars of the first magnitude. Wardour Street was wrong.

At one time he was employing the sons of three past or future British Prime Ministers—Oliver Stanley (later Lord Baldwin), Anthony Asquith and Randolph Churchill. Some accused him of snobbery or a deliberate seeking of influence. But Myers and others maintain that he liked these men and enjoyed working with them.

He had immense tolerance. One day there was a rather violent argument in the office. Korda kept his Olympian calm. When his visitor left, Myers told him: "Alex, this man is a crook . . ." Korda spread his hands: "I know, John—but he's such a nice crook . . ."

When I met him, John Myers took off his wrist-watch and handed it to me. It was a fine watch, apparently of gun-metal. I turned it over. It bore a warm, affectionate inscription of gratitude from Korda. The date was 1933. I was about to give it back to Myers when he said:

"This is perhaps my most characteristic souvenir of Alex. He gave it to me about a year after I'd joined him. I was very touched but he waved aside my thanks. When I went into the Air Force in 1939, I got in a man to value my effects so that I could make a will. He looked at the watch and told me I ought to insure it. Why? I asked him. It's a nice watch—but not particularly valuable. He gave me a curious look. 'Don't you know?' he asked. 'It's solid platinum!' It was just like Alex to give me a most valuable present—and never call my attention to its value!"

CHAPTER VII

THE MAN FROM THE PRU

'HENRY' was a success. London Films became a hive of industry. Great plans were announced weekly. Korda, tired of hotel life, bought himself a home in Avenue Road, St. John's Wood. It was an open house for his friends and associates where he loved to entertain for breakfast or dinner. The breakfasts became just as famous as the card-games —mostly bridge—that often went on until the small hours of the morning.

One of the main problems was to find a cook. The one the faithful Miss Fisher hired turned out to be a failure. Korda phoned Budapest and asked his friend Incze to get him a real Hungarian one. Incze duly dispatched a lady. Alex invited his brothers and Steven Pallos to dinner. The meal turned out to be a disaster. Excuses were made for the new arrival—maybe she was tired out by the journey, wasn't used to English weights and measures—or perhaps she had stage fright. But a second and third meal was equally bad. Korda told his secretary to pay the cook off and send her home. It was only later that he discovered: the would-be cook was a young Hungarian actress who had chosen this way to break into pictures. As Alex didn't even see her, her ambitions were thoroughly frustrated. Finally Incze did produce a cook who had no show business ambitions but had a wonderful way with goulash and stuffed cabbage.

*　　*　　*　　*

Money in London Films was still scarce; for it is one of the mysteries of film production that you can have a triumph on your hands and still be forced to live on credit. The returns of 'Henry' were considerable—but they took time in collection. And there were creditors to be paid, investors to be satisfied.

Korda's successor to 'Henry' was perhaps an even more ambitious picture. He had offered his contract with Elisabeth Bergner to Paramount if they backed 'Henry'; they had refused the deal. He still had the contract and the services of Miss Bergner and her director-husband, Dr. Paul Czinner.

This was 1933 and Hitler's chilling shadow was over Germany. Scores of artists, writers, directors had to flee from Nazidom. Many of them came to England and Korda was only too ready to help them. Wardour Street had suddenly a German accent. Josef Somlo came, first to Paris, then to London, with his wife and daughters, a few hundred marks in his pocket. Screenwriters like Emeric Pressburger and Wolfgang Wilhelm, producers like Erich Pommer—they represented a new element in British films.

Among them was Professor Eugene Robert, the Hungarian-born theatrical producer who wanted to continue his career in London as a stage producer. He decided to present his first play at His Majesty's Theatre. He asked Melchior Lengyel and Lajos Biro to speak to Korda and persuade him to be his 'angel'. Korda invested £10,000 which he could ill afford at the time. It was a gala première—and a complete flop. The entire £10,000 was lost. Korda never reproached his friends.

In spite of the financial difficulties, 'Catherine the Great' got under way in the spring of 1934. It was based on the play 'The Czarina' by Lengyel (who became later world-famous as the author of 'Ninotchka') and Biro. After 'Henry', Korda had no difficulty in assembling an outstanding cast. For Peter, the half-crazy Czar, he decided on a piece of really 'offbeat' casting. He chose Douglas Fairbanks jr.

They had known each other, though rather casually, during Korda's early years in Hollywood. Then they met again in England in the course of the delicate and confidential negotiations over Alex's partnership in United Artists. But it was in 'Catherine' that Fairbanks worked with him for the first time as an actor.

Paul Czinner, the director, and Elisabeth Bergner both had their very decided ideas of what they wanted and how they wanted it. Alex, quite often, had other ideas. As a producer he itched to be a director and this unavoidably led to clashes. Douglas Fairbanks jr., who was a born diplomat, had to serve as a sort of general peace-maker, soothing over the difficulties. "In spite of all the trouble," Mr. Fairbanks told me, "it turned out to be a fine, sensitive picture. It hadn't the financial success it deserved but I still think it one of Korda's major achievements."

As Elizabeth, the Dowager Empress, a comparative newcomer appeared in the picture. It was Charles Laughton who interested Korda in Flora Robson and he gave her the rôle when she was quite unknown.

"But he was good at bolstering people with a sex inferiority complex," Miss Robson wrote to me. "I had elderly lovers in 'Catherine the Great' and felt a sight in a pale blue wig. He used to kneel at my feet before a 'take' and say: 'My Greta Garbo!' in his delicious foreign accent, which made me laugh and feel better. Charles Laughton said he gave him the same confidence. I think he had tremendous charm and kindness.

A year later, after my Old Vic season, he gave me a film contract and he was the first to give me good publicity. I was four years under contract before I got another film but he let me out to the theatre and asked bigger salaries, so I can say he put me on the map. He backed one play for me, 'Mary Read', at Her Majesty's; Robert Donat played with me then. We lost money as it was a big production and although we both made successes, our names were not big enough to fill the theatre.

After that play he sent me away for my best holiday before I did Queen Elizabeth in 'Fire Over England'. He

had made money on my contract and gave it all back on
the holiday in Egypt . . ."

'Catherine the Great' also featured Sir Gerald du Maurier,
Irene Vanbrugh, and Lawrence Hanray in a distinguished cast.
There were Korda's 'young ladies', Joan Gardner and Diana
Napier, and a whole host of names who later became much
better known: Griffith Jones, Dorothy Hale, Ralph Truman,
Bruce Belfrage, Hilda Sims and Harold Warrender among them.
    In a way this film was a direct challenge to Hollywood. Korda
knew that Paramount also planned a film about the 'Semiramis
of the North'. Hollywood's Catherine was Marlene Dietrich,
directed by Joseph von Sternberg; the Paramount picture was
far more spectacular and sexy. While Bergner's Catherine was a
woman of intellect for whom her lovers were of secondary
importance, Marlene was simply the glittering courtesan on the
throne. The Czar of Douglas Fairbanks jr. was a weakling with
great charm who could awaken pity; Sam Jaffe's Paul was pure
monster. Comparing the two pictures, a Continental film critic
wrote: "London has a far higher historical culture than Hollywood—especially when aided by Hungarian screenwriters and
Hungarian directors!"
    Strangely enough, this was one Korda picture liked far more
by the trade press—the shrewd judges of box-office potentialities
—than by the regular critics. Korda was discovering that nothing
was more difficult than to follow up a great success.

*   *   *   *

He also realized a more important thing: his present financial
backing was quite inadequate to carry out the sort of programme
in which he believed; to pay for a whole series of films instead
of trying to scrape together enough money to do them singly.
His quota films had taught him a lesson about British distribution;
he knew he had to create global markets. All this needed money

—more than the Sutros or the Toeplitzes were able or willing to provide.

Money also meant security. When he had achieved his success with 'Henry', there were some among his associates who tried to wrest control of his achievement from him. The double-cross has a long and dishonourable tradition in show business and the price of staying on top is, like liberty's, eternal vigilance.

Zoltan Korda was shooting 'Sanders of the River' on location in darkest Africa, putting the colour and excitement of native dances and tribal customs on celluloid. After many weeks he and his technicians emerged from the bush, arriving at a small town which was their rendezvous with another unit and with the unit manager. Zoltan's group was the first to arrive. They found stacks of mail awaiting them. In this pile there was supposed to be an important letter—containing a cheque, for they had run out of money.

The letter was discovered; it was addressed to the 'Unit Manager' of London Films, with no name indicated. After waiting another day in vain, Zoltan Korda decided to open the envelope. It contained the cheque all right—with a personal letter.

". . . The information you have sent about Z. K. is most useful. Send us some more and we'll soon be able make it hot for A. K. . . ."

At this point Zoltan stopped reading. He called in his cameraman and his assistant and made them sign a statement that he had opened the letter and under what circumstances; then he read the rest of it—aloud. The absent unit manager was being congratulated on providing 'damaging information' about the 'extravagance and inefficiency' of the Kordas; information that was to be presented to the financial backers of London Films.

When the well-paid informer arrived two days later, Zoltan confronted him with the proof of his duplicity. The man went white and admitted everything. He offered to return to London at once; but Zoltan kept him until shooting was finished. In England he reported to his brother about the strange incident. Alex already knew of the various intrigues but said nothing. Even now he settled the whole business gently and discreetly. Some people resigned; others discovered suddenly that they had always believed in Alexander Korda. Nothing more was heard of the matter.

Korda never talked of his 'lucky star'; but he must have believed in Providence or the fortunate accident that had operated again and again in his life. If he hadn't been in the Café New York when Janovics came to look for a director; if he hadn't met Lajos Biro by accident at Rome railway station; if he hadn't given a job to John Loder in Berlin or made friends with George Grossmith in Hollywood; if . . . there had been a whole series of comparatively small incidents which had the most important consequences for his career.

And now an Australian named Montague Marks arrived in London from New York.

'Monty' Marks, as everybody called him, was by all standards a remarkable man. He had started life as a painter—and a successful one. In the first World War he joined the Royal Flying Corps and was one of the three survivors of his gallant squadron. Then, returning to America where he had lived for some time and where his wife was much sought after as a miniature painter, he entered business. His salary was an office-boy's; within two years he had made a small fortune, representing his firm in Japan.

He had become interested in films through his connections with Westinghouse and was associated with some Americans who had produced a film of 'Pagliacci', using actors who mimed while the sound was dubbed in—the voices of famous opera-singers.

Marks was asked to take the film to Britain and interest a producer in it. He had a letter of introduction to the London head of Western Electric.

"I know the very man for you," the executive said. "Alexander Korda. I'm going to call him right away."

He did and Marks could hear every word Alex was saying at the other end of the telephone as he faced the Western Electric manager. It was obvious that Korda didn't want to see him and used every possible excuse. He was too busy, he wasn't interested in 'Pagliacci' or any other American picture; he suggested others who might be better qualified—and so on. In the end he became quite angry and cursed both Marks and his sponsor. But the Western Electric director was insistent; Marks' letter of intro-duction was couched in very warm terms. So in the end Alex suddenly switched round and said: "All right, tell him to come to dinner tonight at half past eight. But I still don't want that blasted film . . ."

That night Montague Marks went round to Avenue Road. He was shown into the living-room and left to amuse himself. Korda was late. When he came in, he was full of apologies. Having been put in the wrong, he now put himself out to be the charming host. He and Marks talked until 3 a.m. By the time Monty left, he had become part of the Korda organization. Whether 'Pagliacci' ever came up in the conversation, he couldn't even remember.

It was evident that London Films needed capital—a substantial amount on a long-term investment. Some months earlier, Marks had brought a piece of business to the Prudential. He knew they had to invest their large capital at a certain monthly or annual rate—but he hadn't the faintest idea whether they would be interested in films. So he went to them and explained Korda's plans. Of course, by then the success of 'Henry' had put Alex very much on the map. Still, the Prudential executive whom he saw, said: "This sounds interesting—but we don't know anything about films. Most of our investments have been in bricks and mortar—and we can draw on past experience there. But we have an expert who knows all about films. I'll arrange a meeting; you put your proposition to him and if he thinks it is a sound one, we'll consider the matter seriously!"

A week later this meeting took place. The Prudential executive

introduced Marks to Sir Connop Guthrie, then left them alone
to discuss the matter.

"I'm certainly happy to deal with someone who knows all
about films," Marks began.

"Eh?" Sir Connop looked startled. "Films? *I* don't know
anything about them . . ."

"B—but . . ." Marks was taken aback, "I was told you were
an expert."

"Not me. I once arranged a loan for a group of cinemas—but
that's the nearest I got to pictures . . ."

"For heaven's sake, don't tell that to the Pru," Marks begged
him. "At least, listen to my proposition . . ."

Sir Connop listened and he approved. He told the Prudential
board that Korda was an up-and-coming young man and that
British films had a fine chance of competing with Hollywood.

There were a number of meetings and conferences; the lawyers
had to have their innings. But finally the deal was signed; for the
first time, Prudential had agreed to back British film production.

Montague Marks was handed the first cheque—for £250,000
—and took it down to Grosvenor Street. The board of London
Films was waiting with understandable excitement. Alex hadn't
really believed that Marks would pull it off—though he was an
optimist as far as his own plans went, he remained a sceptic in
financial matters until the money was actually in the bank. The
cheque passed from hand to hand, was inspected, fingered,
admired. Then the whole board performed a kind of Red
Indian dance of triumph. They were just like ten-year-old kids
—and Marks, as he admitted to me, danced with them.

Of course, the 'man from the Pru' wanted suitable security.
The insurance company was given all the preferred shares in
London Films and had a lien on all the pictures made or to be
made in the future. Marks himself was made General Manager of
the company with a very handsome salary.

Korda, however, had another concern. He wanted to secure
American distribution for his films. That was when the nego-

tiations with United Artists began—the long and delicate talks to which Douglas Fairbanks jr. referred.

At this time United Artists had a large and costly distribution organization but its members—Charles Chaplin, Mary Pickford and Douglas Fairbanks sr.—could not provide it with sufficient product to cover the overheads. They needed pictures badly. Korda, in a way, seemed an answer to their prayers.

It was Douglas Fairbanks sr. who sponsored the 'new boy'. It was a difficult deal—because Korda was to be given a partnership without actually paying for it.

The older Fairbanks had a great affection for Alex. "I have unbounded faith in him and look forward to being directed by Korda in future films," he said in an interview after 'The Private Life of Don Juan' had been finished. His son told me: "My father was amused and fascinated by Alex. He was considerably older but Alex had the ability of turning himself into a father-figure, behaving in any company as if he were the oldest present."

The negotiations started shortly after the phenomenal success of 'Henry VIII' and were successfully concluded before the end of 1933. On January 1, 1934, it was announced that Douglas Fairbanks sr. had joined the board of London Films. This was followed by a statement from Joseph M. Schenck that closer co-operation between United Artists and London Films was to be established.

The story of Korda's relationship with United Artists is a very interesting though somewhat chequered one.

Another giant of the cinema became associated with him in 1935 when Sam Goldwyn made arrangements to borrow Merle Oberon from Alex for 'The Dark Angel'. This led to a business partnership from which was born the idea of buying control of United Artists. In June, 1937, Korda announced that arrangements for this deal were virtually completed; he had just returned from Hollywood with Murray Silverstone, head of United Artists in Britain. The plan was for Korda and Goldwyn to buy out Douglas Fairbanks sr., Mary Pickford and Charles Chaplin at £400,000 each, with Korda sharing in the profits and distribution possibilities of the company. Korda expressed his hope that fourteen of his films would be shown in thousands of U.S. cinemas.

This meant, in theory, that British films had at last obtained an entry into the American market. Lord Strabolgi, chairman of the British Film Advancement Council, made it clear in October, 1937, how important an achievement this was:

> "As for the more serious and expensive pictures made in Britain between 1934 and 1937, they have in many cases simply copied the Hollywood technique. The Americans being under no obligation to show these spectacular British pictures in their own theatres, ignored them for the most part. A few highly successful British pictures of a specialized kind, such as 'The Private Life of Henry VIII' and 'The Ghost Goes West' did well in the U.S.A. but on the whole the American companies who control large numbers of the American cinemas felt no inducement to displace their own products by British pictures. *Only Korda, by his arrangement with United Artists, was able to break this boycott.*" (My italics.)

In November 1937 Goldwyn confirmed that he and Korda would take up an option of buying the 60 per cent remaining interest of Fairbanks, Mary Pickford and Goldwyn. (They were already holding 20 per cent each.) This would cost £900,000 and the two future owners would end up by holding 50 per cent each though Fairbanks and Miss Pickford had agreed to leave £300,000 worth of their shares in the company.

It was now a question of finding the money. The £900,000— or Korda's share of it—was to be guaranteed by a British group, headed by Oscar Deutsch, who had created the Odeon cinema circuit and who wanted American films for his own theatres. There was a report that Prudential would advance the money but Mr. E. H. Lever, on behalf of the company, declared that they would supply only a very small proportion of the capital. On November 15, the *Financial Times* reported that the negotiations had been successfully concluded but final action was being deferred until the legal advisers of the interested parties had examined the proposed details.

Pending the final contract, United Artists announced that it would show twenty-one new British films throughout America. Murray Silverstone said the success of the Korda films had been so great in all countries that his company had resolved to make the world-wide distribution of British films a permanent policy.

But then difficulties arose. In December 1937 the three owners of United Artists held a meeting to decide whether Korda would be permitted to produce pictures for release *not* by United Artists. In the few weeks between November and Christmas, 1937, Goldwyn and Korda decided not to take up their option for buying out Fairbanks, Mary Pickford and Chaplin—though keeping their 20 per cent shares. Korda asked that in order to keep Denham Studios running at a profit he should be allowed to make films for outside release while giving United Artists about three pictures a year. There was a serious difference of opinion between Miss Pickford, Douglas Fairbanks sr. and Chaplin on this point. In January 1938 Korda made a statement.

"Samuel Goldwyn and I did not go on with our scheme to buy United Artists in equal shares because, owing to the change in world conditions since we first took up our options to buy the shares of Charles Chaplin, Mary Pickford and Douglas Fairbanks for £1,200,000, it did not look like a good investment. It would have cost too much to borrow the money." But though the original plan was abandoned, a new policy emerged from the discussions which would enable British independent producers to market their films through United Artists at greatly reduced costs and to receive a share in the profits. "All this is due to one man," a daily paper wrote, "Alexander Korda."

In May 1938 Korda returned from New York, where he had

settled the final details of the United Artists agreement in its modified form. Certainly he was responsible for opening the gates to British films which had been closed until then. The trouble was that United Artists did not own any cinemas in America and the biggest, most numerous picture-houses belonged to exhibitors owned or partly owned by the big Hollywood studios. Once again the simile of the sausage-manufacturer not selling somebody else's sausages in his shops became applicable. Yet even so, Korda's films earned more money in the States than any British films had done before—or since.

Korda kept his shares in United Artists until 1944. Then he sold them for £250,000—and paid one million dollars into the British Treasury, a comparatively small but still very welcome windfall for dollar-starved Britain.

*   *   *   *

To return to 1934, Korda had obtained his financial backing, enough for a truly ambitious programme, and had secured American, even global distribution. He still lacked one thing—his own studios.

With the Prudential backing, London Films had taken a lease of Isleworth Studios at £35,000 a year. The place was far from ideal, cramped and old-fashioned—and it cost a lot of money.

It was Monty Marks who pointed out to Korda that it would be far more economical to build his own studios; he worked out estimates according to which the interest on the capital involved would only amount to £10,000—obviously a considerable saving compared to the rent paid at Isleworth. Korda agreed and gave Marks authority to look for a suitable site. As he was going abroad, Marks was left in charge of the scheme.

He began to scout around, having a list of properties for sale. The first place he inspected was Iver, where a big house and its adjoining acres were for sale. But the price was high: £50,000.

Marks went on to the next place on his list—a small Buckingham-
shire village called Denham. He knew at once that this was what
they needed. He immediately took an option on it; then phoned
Alex on the Continent. Korda, feeling that things were going
too fast, was furious and told Marks to cancel the deal. Marks
pretended that he had done so—but when Alex returned, took
him to Denham. It was winter and the site looked forlorn and
unattractive. But Korda became enthusiastic—and then depressed
at the thought that he had lost the property because of the
instructions he had given Marks.

As they drove back to London, Marks confessed his little
deception. He still had the option and the price had come down
from £25,000 to £15,000. Alex became so excited and jubilant
that he hugged his general manager. Then, as they got back to the
office, he immediately started to sketch out a rough plan—his
ideal studio.

By the summer of 1934 all contracts had been signed and Korda
sent for his old Hollywood friend, Jack Okey, who had built
some of America's most important studios, including Paramount
and Warner Brothers First National in Hollywood.

The actual building started in the early summer of 1935 and
was completed by May 1936. Denham was to be the most up-
to-date and best-equipped sound film studio in Europe, if not the
world. The buildings covered 28 acres and the total area of the
lot was 165 acres. For 1½ miles the River Colne wound through
the estate, sufficiently wide in part for any screen water scene.
The 'old house'—formerly the residence on the Denham estate
—was kept intact. Gardens, dense woodland, meadows were all
included in the property to be used for exteriors.

Initially there were to be three large stages but their number
was increased to seven; four of them were air-conditioned so
that shooting could go on even in the thickest fog; all were completely sound-proofed. There were two projection theatres,
many individual dressing rooms; the studio had its own water
supply (enough for a city the size of York) and the largest electric

power plant used by any private concern in Britain—with a
power output of 4,500 kilowatts. This cost £100,000 extra
because the plans were based on the remote possibility of all
stages needing full power at the same time. Actually, they never
did. But at least Denham was independent of the grid system.
There were machine shops, a foundry, metal, blacksmith's, turn-
smith's and plumbing shops, a woodworking mill, modeller's
studio, ornamental plasterer's shops, various workshops for
electrical and camera repairs, a large property building, make-up
and hairdressing shop, even a first aid post. There were eighteen
cutting rooms and of course, ample space for administrative
offices. Korda's own large office, designed in pastel greys and
blues, with simple but comfortable furniture, faced the road in
the front of the main building.

Long before the studio was finished, the grounds were in use
for various Korda productions. 'Moscow Nights' and 'The Ghost
Goes West' were the first films for which exteriors were shot in
the Denham woods and fields. Glourie Castle was built and the
battle of Culloden fought there. In July 1935 the large-scale
location sequences of 'The Shape of Things to Come' started at
Denham; there was one particular spot for ever known as 'the
City Square'. 'The Man Who Could Work Miracles' also went
to Denham for its exteriors.

In January 1936 Korda told Caroline Lejeune:

> "Denham is a marvellous place. You will admire it far
> more than any of our pictures. But please remember, we
> have built it only now because we are ready for it now.
> A studio without a 100 per cent staff is nothing but an
> empty shell. For three years we have been collecting our
> staff, getting them used to working together, sometimes
> apparently doing nothing with them but training them and
> waiting. Now we have about two hundred experts, fully
> trained for their jobs. From the minute we take over Den-
> ham, we shall be able to work at full pressure."

At last the great moment came. Denham was ready for full-scale operation. It was decided to let an independent producer go in first with a musical—to 'warm up the place'.

This 'warming-up' occurred in a somewhat unexpected manner. On the morning before the official opening, Monty Marks was called urgently—the studio was on fire! He rushed to the spot and found one of the stages in flames. Korda, summoned by Marks, arrived at breakneck speed. In spite of the efforts of the firemen, the stage was completely burned out. The fire was probably caused by the blow-lamp of a workman left under the flooring; the real cause was never established.

Prudential found itself in the somewhat farcical situation of having to pay as an insurance company for the damage that its film company had suffered. The respectable sum of £45,000 was involved and duly paid. The damage was quickly repaired; the first picture actually finished at Denham was Korda's greatest, most striking film, 'Rembrandt'.

★   ★   ★   ★

The glory of Denham lasted only three years—but while it was being built and while it was in operation, Korda produced some of his finest and most successful pictures.

Either at Denham, or at British-and-Dominion studios, Sound City, 'The Private Life of Don Juan,' 'The Scarlet Pimpernel', 'Rembrandt', 'Men Are Not Gods', 'Sanders of the River', 'The Ghost Goes West,' 'The Shape of Things to Come', 'The Man Who Could Work Miracles', and 'Elephant Boy' were made in the years 1934–36—a list of which any producer could be proud.

'Don Juan' was based on a play by Henri Bataille, the popular French writer. For the script Korda called in that most urbane and witty British playwright, Freddy Lonsdale. Though this was their only collaboration, they became very fond of each other and remained friends for many years.

Lonsdale, whose philosophy was to extract the maximum

enjoyment from life with the minimum effort, once told Korda:
"Alex, you're wasting yourself in England. You're not really a
financier. You're a creative artist. Why don't you go to America
and accept one of those offers from the big companies that you're
always turning down, and make a fortune for yourself? You
could be one of the greatest directors in the world if you chose,
and a rich man inside a couple of years. You could then retire—
enjoy yourself—and do all the things you've always wanted
to do."

Korda smiled and shook his head.

"Freddie," he said, "I don't want to be a rich man. I don't
want to retire. And as for what I've always wanted to do—why,
I'm doing it now. I've been working and waiting for years, to
have my own studios, the right people to work for me and a
free hand in the films I make and the way I make them. If I were
to give up now it would be a kind of treachery to myself and to
the people who have helped me in England. No, Freddie, I'm
not going to America to finish my career. I'm going to stay just
where I am—and begin . . ."

'Don Juan' was in the tradition of 'Henry', 'Catherine' and
'Helen of Troy'. It used the device of a play within a play—
including a sequence in a theatre where a comedy about Don
Juan was being presented with Owen Nares and Heather Thatcher
acting it, until the real Don Juan—Douglas Fairbanks sr.—leapt
on the stage, interrupting the performance. Merle Oberon was
Antonita, the ageing Don Juan's fickle love; Melville Cooper
played Leporello, the Don's faithful and cynical servant. Benita
Hume had an important part; of Korda's 'Young Ladies', Joan
Gardner, Binnie Barnes (in a charming cameo of a mercenary
barmaid), Patricia Hilliard and Diana Napier appeared. Douglas
Fairbanks sr. pointed out that in Korda's pictures there was always
an undercurrent of satire—he could no more help pulling Don
Juan's leg about his loves than Henry's about his wives or the
Tsar of Russia's about his mistresses. "Satire," as Fairbanks main-
tained, "is Korda's charm, his chief characteristic, his métier."

'Don Juan' also marked the rather frustrating start of another great star's career in pictures.

"Alex was my first employer in motion pictures," James Mason wrote to me. "Being a friend of Laughton, he frequented the Old Vic during the 1933–34 season, was impressed by my performance in 'Love for Love' and offered me a good part in 'Don Juan'. I was vastly impressed by my prowess and went to work for him. I was somewhat irked by his directorial manners. He arrived on the set at about 11 a.m. and sank into his canvas chair, lit up his cigar and sheltered behind *The Times* for about half an hour without audible comment. He gave me little or no direction and I could not convincingly tell myself that I was shimmering with the bright comedy that the part called for. After three or four days David Cunynghame took me aside and said that Alex had decided I was 'mis-cast' in the part and that my services in it were no longer required; they were cognisant of the fact that I had been guaranteed ten days' work and they would therefore find me something later in the picture. Knowing the script, I could see no very interesting prospect for me there, so I let them forget about the balance of the ten days . . ."

Several people told me the story how Korda took Sir Connop Guthrie to the première of 'Don Juan' at the London Pavilion. If the film went over well, he was reasonably sure of obtaining support from the Prudential. Unluckily, the film was not a success and the audience laughed in a number of wrong places. But Korda's lucky star was still shining, for Prudential eventually decided to back him . . .

Montague Marks denies this story absolutely. The arrangements with Prudential, he told me, were complete before 'Don Juan' was shown to the public. True, the executives of the great insurance company attended the première. The film was received with polite applause. Korda and Marks knew that it wasn't the great success they had hoped for—their guests, however, liked it and were unaware of the cool reception. Korda took his party to the Savoy—for a celebration supper. He had laid on caviar and champagne. "I want a kipper and beer," protested his chief guest, the septuagenarian chairman of the company. It was a painful evening, Marks recalled, but there was never any question of the big deal falling through. Actually, the press was highly complimentary. Yet the picture did not do well with the audiences. Looking back at it with the sense of proportion provided by the years, one can see the reason. It was the star himself. Douglas Fairbanks sr. had triumphed in many a swashbuckling action-packed picture. But here he had to do a great deal more than vault over balustrades, climb balconies or fight duels. His rasping voice with the strong American accent was incongruous and unsuitable for the suave Spanish lover. And because he failed (or failed in part) the picture itself was a failure.

But Korda had many other irons in the fire and now began a whole group of productions, all of which started at Isleworth with some going on location in the Denham grounds and others being finished at the new studios.

Alex had always wanted to make a film of 'The Scarlet Pimpernel'. He had read Baroness Orczy's novel as a young boy and was greatly attracted to the character of the perfect English gentleman who pretended to be a fool. And in Leslie Howard he found the ideal Pimpernel. "Alexander Korda runs a one-man show," Howard said when the picture was finished. "It is splendid working with him, however. His methods would amaze Hollywood. He doesn't even appear to have heard of a shooting schedule and it is entirely refreshing."

Some people tried to dissuade Korda, pointing out that this was a very old story and wouldn't lend itself to screen adaptation. But Alex replied that five million copies of the book had been sold in a score of languages—and there was his ready-made audience. He turned out to be right.

At first there were many difficulties. The original director, an American, tried to turn the film into a gory, heavy-handed melo-drama instead of the light-hearted though suspenseful conception Korda had in mind. In the end he had to be replaced and Harold Young, the Hollywood film-editor who had worked on a number of Korda's pictures, took over under Alex's close supervision.

Merle Oberon was cast as Lady Blakeney; as Chauvelin, Ray-mond Massey played the villain with great distinction. This was the first of a whole series of rôles which the Canadian star did for Korda. Nigel Bruce (who became later well-known as Dr. Watson in the Sherlock Holmes films) was the Prince of Wales; of Korda's 'repertory company' Joan Gardner, Gertrude Musgrove and Derrick de Marney appeared. Ernest Milton was Robespierre, Bruce Belfrage, Pitt; Lawrence Hanray, Burke and Alfred Wellesley, Fox. James Mason had a small bit-part—without a word of dialogue.

During the production, Korda addressed his crowd artistes before an important scene.

"I want plenty of noise and shouting," he declared. "Yell and scream, you're a revolutionary mob!" He then took the scene to the accompaniment of loud and realistically blood-curdling sound-effects. "Cut!" he cried at the end of it. "O.K.?"

"O.K. for camera," said Harold Rosson, the director of photography.

"O.K. for sound," said the sound-engineer, "but what goddam revolutionary shouted 'whoopee!'?"

A strange fact about 'Pimpernel' was that originally Alex had announced Charles Laughton for Sir Percy Blakeney. But soon after the press announcement, an avalanche of letters descended upon him. Readers all over the world protested hotly that Mr. Laughton, however great an actor, did not conform to their ideas of the romantic Sir Percy. And Alex, always the astute showman, bowed to the public's wishes. He persuaded Leslie Howard to return from Hollywood to star in the picture.

The film was an unqualified success. It cost £81,000 and grossed £420,000, of which the foreign earnings were £270,000. It broke all house records at the Leicester Square Theatre, which was becoming Korda's special 'shop-window'. The press was unanimously enthusiastic though one American critic objected to 'the royalist white-washing of the nobility while the revolutionaries were all presented as ugly, villainous fanatics'.

This was balanced by what happened to 'Pimpernel' in France. The film was evidently considered dangerous to French morale. (After all, the Pimpernel did confound those 'Frenchies'.) So it was dubbed into French but the dialogue switched in dubbing, making the actual villain a hero and the actual hero a villain. Thus the French liked it—and smiled. The story might be a slight exaggeration—but certainly 'Pimpernel' had a triumphant career in all five continents.

For one important director 'Pimpernel' was the start of a long-enduring collaboration with Korda. It was a strange and abortive encounter—but at the same time a highly characteristic one for Alex.

In 1935 Korda sent for Carol Reed, who had done a few small pictures. He was very young and thrilled to meet the great man. Korda told him that he had seen his pictures and thought highly of them. Anxious to get his views on his work, Reed asked him which ones he had seen.

"Oh, I can't remember the titles," Alex said with a wave of those eloquent hands. "But they were pretty good . . ."

Carol Reed knew then that Korda hadn't seen any of them; but it didn't matter. The main thing was that Korda wanted him—to direct 'The Scarlet Pimpernel'. As this was one of the most interesting and important jobs going, the young director was dazed with delight. He stammered his thanks; Korda waved them away and said that terms would be discussed with his agent. Then, as Reed was about to leave, he said: "By the way—we're having script trouble with *Pimpernel*, so it'll take a little time before we're ready. How would you like to do a few smaller pictures in the meantime—with Elsa Lanchester?"

Carol Reed knew that he was being tricked; but he didn't mind. He realized that Alex wouldn't trust him yet with such a costly and big film; 'Pimpernel' had been merely used as bait. He was deeply disappointed—but had fallen under Korda's spell, the famous charm had done its work.

"Yes, of course, I'd love to . . ." he said.

He never heard of those 'smaller pictures' again. Much later, when he had become Korda's star director with three or four international hits to his credit, he reminded Alex of their first meeting. Korda had forgotten it—but when Reed explained his own feelings at the time, he roared with laughter. Again and again, at a reception or story conference, he would say to Carol Reed: "Tell them about the time I wanted to double-cross you!" It became a favourite party piece.

*   *   *   *

Jeffrey Dell was introduced to Korda by Charles Laughton, who had appeared in 'Payment Deferred', which Dell had adapted for the stage. It took weeks before he was able to see Alex and when he did he had a somewhat frustrating time. Then he was offered a three-year contract and put to work on various scripts, few of which came to fruition.

I don't think the Korda charm worked on Dell; he was puzzled and sometimes exasperated by Alex yet at the same time fascinated by the Korda brothers. He was assigned to 'Sanders of the River', to work with Zoltan Korda.

"In my simplicity," Dell said in an interview, "I imagined that those who make African pictures were men of robust and massive physique with iron constitutions and a 'bring-them-back-alive' manner. But when I met Zoltan, or Zolly as he is usually known, I had a first class surprise. Picture

for yourself a small size in satyrs, remove the horns and the
points of the ears and add a kindly humorous twinkle to the
eyes. Imagine, too, a quiet voice speaking a limited but
extremely colourful comic vocabulary of broken English
and you have a slight idea of Zolly Korda. He has genuinely
simple tastes, and early in our association, confided to me
that his real ambition was to sit all day on the edge of a
cornfield in his beloved Hungary and, as he himself expressed it, 'smoke a pipe vit my feets in the veet'."

For the time being there was little prospect of Zoltan Korda
achieving this wishdream. (He never smoked a pipe, anyhow,
and he never achieved it.) 'Sanders of the River' took eighteen
months to shoot. It was the first of Zoltan Korda's love affairs
with Africa and the world East of Suez—love affairs whose off-
springs were such distinguished pictures as 'Four Feathers', 'The
Drum', 'Elephant Boy', 'Jungle Book' or 'Cry the Beloved
Country'. The script of 'Sanders' was written by Lajos Biro
and Jeffrey Dell; Arthur Wimperis helped with the dialogue
and wrote the lyrics of the songs.

Two units were sent to Africa and the story goes that these not
only lost touch with each other but at least on one occasion a
plaintive cable arrived in London from the second unit director,
saying: "Where am I?"

Zoltan Korda was especially fascinated with the native dances
on which he had spent thousands of feet of celluloid. Sometimes
he would sit in the projection room for a whole day, looking at
them, listening to the savage rhythm, the chanting and shouting.
Yet these dances were instrumental in persuading Paul Robeson,
the magnificent American singer, to take the part of Bosambo.
When Zoltan Korda ran the dancing sequences for him, Robeson,
who had been doubtful about his rôle, was so impressed with the
music that he agreed at once.

Sanders was played by Leslie Banks (Korda had wanted Ralph
Richardson for the part but Richardson was in a play and couldn't

do it) and the enchanting Nina Mae McKinney had the feminine lead. The cast-list proudly announced that members of the Acholi, Sesi, Tefik, Juruba, Mendi and Kroo tribes took part in the picture with their various chiefs. One of the most unusual actors in the film was the Marquis de Portago, Korda's personal friend, who played an Italian. The Marquis used to arrive at the studio in a most expensive racing car and collect a sum at the end of the week which barely covered the cost of the petrol. He did it for fun—just as he had been adviser on Spanish settings of 'Don Juan'.

The African tribes could not be transported to Isleworth—so a whole trainload of Cardiff Negro dockers from Tiger Bay arrived for the studio scenes. Luckily these belonged to some of the same tribes as their African brethren. It was an exciting and fantastic period for the studio; and when the picture was finished, it proved a very solid success. It had a longer life than almost any other Korda picture. When it was shown on British television in November 1957, it was still called one of the greatest films ever made. It also drew a strong protest from Mr. Matthew Mbu, the Commissioner for Nigeria in London. He said that 'Sanders' brought 'disgrace and disrepute' to his country, creating ill-feeling against Nigerians in the United Kingdom. (When the picture was originally released in New York, there were Communist demonstrations against it. Robeson had to apologize for appearing in it!) But the Lagos correspondent of the *Manchester Guardian* reported that Mr. Mbu's fellow-countrymen had a different view. Twenty-two years after it was produced, 'Sanders' was still going the rounds in Nigeria and was highly popular. It was shown at three Lagos cinemas in a single week and the audiences never tired of Paul Robeson's voice, tending to overlook any 'offensive' parts in the interests of entertainment.

This wasn't the last attack on Korda for his 'jingoism'. Perhaps it was strange for a Hungarian to be a staunch champion of the British Empire and the White Man's Burden—as if he had been brought up on Kipling instead of the Hungarian classics. There was a good deal of resentment that a 'foreigner' should choose subjects like 'Sanders', 'Four Feathers', 'Fire Over England' or 'The Drum'. I think Korda believed in what he was doing; partly because from an early age he had been an anglophile, if not an anglo-maniac; and partly because he thought that a British film-producer should serve his adopted country to the best of his ability. He felt that, with the rise of the dictators, the Pax Britannica should be presented on the screen as perhaps the greatest bulwark against them. In this, indeed, he proved a remarkable 'prophet.' And after all, even Hollywood was making pictures like 'The Life of a Bengal Lancer' which waved the Union Jack most heartily.

Alex had also been a great fan of H. G. Wells, having read his books in translation as a young journalist. Now they met and Wells put his signature on a penny post-card, agreeing to write the story of 'The Shape of Things to Come'.

Work on the script had started in 1934. In February, 1935, Wells said:

"There is one thing in the making of my film which I particularly want to avoid, and that is the impression that we are representing some sort of imaginative utopia, an ideal but impracticable existence. I want to convey the effect that the condition of life shown on the screen is a practicable objective; in fact the only sane objective for a reasonable man. Our only hope of achieving a planned world is to get people to realize in the first place that such a thing is possible."

These were wise words; but they had little direct bearing on the making of films. No wonder that Korda himself told John Betjeman in an interview: "This is the most difficult film to make I've ever come across."

Korda always knew how to guide writers; but he was over-awed by the eminence of Wells. In any case, the contract stated that not a word was to be changed without the author's permission. Wells was a world-famous novelist, a social reformer and a provocative thinker. He wasn't a screenwriter; nor did he stop to consider that *ideas*, abstract thoughts, are almost impossible to present through a film—except by action, character, incident; certainly not through dialogue alone. I translated two of Wells' scripts ('The Man Who Could Work Miracles' and the never-filmed 'Modern Faust') and found that he expected the impossible from actor and director alike. There was far too much talk and not enough movement in his script. Lajos Biro warned Korda about it in a long, detailed memorandum; he told his friend that the camera could make many things acceptable but the special effects of the trick department weren't all-powerful. And he pointed out that apart from some minor details, the whole story could have been just as well set in 1934 as in 2054. Wells was so preoccupied with ideas that for once his imagination was crippled by them.

Perhaps Korda saw this but he did little about it. He brought over William Cameron Menzies, for many years one of Hollywood's leading art directors, to direct the picture. The cast was brilliant: Raymond Massey, Ralph Richardson, Sophie Stewart, Margaretta Scott, Ann Todd gave outstanding performances. All this did not save the picture from being an expensive and not entirely successful experiment.

Ann Todd was 'hired' by Korda at Le Touquet, where he saw her at the Casino. "I want you to come to London and play in my most important picture," he told her.

"Wonderful," she said. "When do I start?"

"In a week's time."

"What about wardrobe fittings?"

"Oh, don't worry about that. We'll fix you up," Korda reassured her.

It wasn't until she got to the studio that she discovered her costume consisted of tattered rags so that she certainly did not need elaborate fittings.

"I loved him dearly," Ann Todd told me about Korda. "He was a magnificent director, drawing the best out of any player. But he could be wicked, too . . ."

Miss Todd appeared in a play which was a great success; so was her performance. The management received an offer for the film rights; Korda told Ann not to worry as he would certainly make the picture. Then it turned out that he had bought the play —but proposed to star another actress in it. Furious, Ann Todd stormed into his office.

"But darling . . ." Korda tried to stop her angry reproaches.

"Don't put on the charm, Alex," she said. "This was a wicked thing to do! You've deceived me . . . you're a horrible man!"

Korda smiled at her. "But you'll forgive me, won't you?" he said softly.

She did.

Perhaps it was poetic justice that in the end the film was never made.

Margaretta Scott spent most of the time during the shooting of 'Things to Come' on horseback. She wasn't a very experienced horsewoman and the best acting she thought she did in the whole picture was to keep the panic out of her eyes every time she was in the saddle. The technicians nicknamed her 'Bronco'.

The shooting went on for many months, partly at Isleworth, partly in the grounds of Denham. The 'City Square' had a large market where vegetables and fish were displayed. As the film went on, the fish became 'higher and higher' until the actors began to protest that they'd need gas-masks for their scenes.

In those days, as Margaretta Scott told me, actors still looked down on film-work. Many of them thought that a 'rep' season of Shakespeare was far more important than the best-paid film part. Today this attitude has completely changed and Korda was one of the main instruments in changing it. Miss Scott was worried about her contract. It gave the film company full publicity rights—that is, they could, in principle, use her photos for any purpose they wanted; force her to make any personal appearance. She refused to sign it and there was a long argument. Finally Korda sent for her and she explained her fears. He looked at her and said:

"But Peggy, do you think we'll make you take baths in asses' milk?"

She laughed so hard that she laughed all her fears away and signed the contract. And Alex kept his word. There were no publicity photographs of bathing in asses' milk—or any other liquid.

The production went on such a long time that all those involved became one big family. Once when Wells came down to the studio—and he was there practically all the time—he took Margaretta Scott for a walk to explain to her the 'deeper implications' of her rôle. The crew, seeing them promenade in such stately, serious privacy, tied a couple of empty film-bobbins to Miss Scott's long, futuristic tunic. The words of Wells were punctuated by a loud and persistent clatter—until he declared: "This is a madhouse! One should never discuss serious matters in a studio!" By that time Margaretta Scott discovered what had happened and quickly removed the offending appendage—after which H. G. became mollified.

It was John Clements' first picture—the début of a most successful and distinguished career. He was playing at the Embassy Theatre, Swiss Cottage, when Edward Chapman (who also had an important part in 'Things') told him they wanted a bit player. So Clements applied for and got the part. He was told to report to Brooklands Racecourse, where he found the director and Raymond Massey. They explained that he was to be an 'enemy airman', shot down and dying; but before he died, he threw his gasmask to a little girl to save her life. "I died most convincingly," Clements told me, "at least I think so, for not much later Korda gave me another, bigger chance."

When the picture was shown, one of Korda's old friends and

F

pensioners, a chronically unemployed Hungarian journalist, borrowed some money and sent him a cable:

> *"You already know shape of things to come stop I haven't faintest idea how I'll eat tomorrow!"*

Alex understood the not-so-gentle hint and sent him a large enough sum to provide meals for several months.

The film was first shown in the autumn of 1936 and became what is called a '*succès d'estime*'. *The Times* wrote:

> "Mr. Wells's 'Things to Come' was a sign of genuine advance. It was not an imitation of the stage; it attached great importance to impressionistic fact; it made use of that fluidity which the film alone can make available to narrative; it did not hesitate before fantasy and, above all, whatever one's personal views of the ideals that inspired it, it bore the impress of a challenging and interrogative mind."

The Scotsman paid a personal tribute to Korda: "Here is a producer of enterprise and imagination who has already done much to give size and scope to the cinema . . ."

Two years later it was stated that 'Things to Come' was the most expensive film Korda ever made. Some put the cost at £300,000. Yet Alex, when asked if he thought there was any chance of breaking even, replied bravely: "Of course. It was an expensive effort but we're only a few thousands out at the moment."

*　　*　　*　　*

About this time Alex was producing and directing what many considered his finest achievement—the life-story of Rembrandt.

"For 'Rembrandt' I can give the only sincere full-throated cheer I have been able to give to Korda," said Alastair Cooke, then film critic of the B.B.C. " 'Rembrandt', for the sensitive, was an exquisite picture," James Agate concurred. "This is . . . the story of a human soul, in which Laughton as Rembrandt and Alexander Korda as the director have made a superb hit, a real artistic success," wrote Trevor Allen.

A tremendous amount of work went into 'Rembrandt' before these praises could be earned. For the script Korda brought over the eminent German playwright, Carl Zuckmayer. Vincent Korda spent long weeks studying Dutch interiors; the Corporation of Art Dealers in Amsterdam loaned a large collection of antique furniture without charge—which had to be guarded by special detectives. John Armstrong, the costume designer, studied portraits, contemporary records and museums to recreate the dress of the seventeenth century. Muir Mathieson, the musical director, unearthed a number of Dutch folk-songs which Gertrude Lawrence, Elsa Lanchester and Roger Livesey sang in the film. Laughton himself spent weeks in Holland, poring over every one of Rembrandt's sixty-four self-portraits to familiarize himself with the great painter's face. He discovered that Rembrandt's right eye was slightly smaller than the left, and experimented with make-up until he reproduced this 'mismatched' effect. His moustache and hair were carefully styled to give the closest possible resemblance.

Elsa Lanchester gave a moving performance as Hendrikje, Rembrandt's illiterate, warm-hearted, servant-girl love. Korda took Gertrude Lawrence from the musical stage (she had been Noel Coward's favourite partner) and turned her into a dramatic actress of considerable stature. Roger Livesey was given his first chance as an Amsterdam street beggar; among the supporting actors Edward Chapman, Lawrence Hanray, Raymond Huntley, Herbert Lomas, Marius Goring appeared in a very large cast.

Huntley was engaged on the strength of his performance in a play called 'Bees on the Boat Deck'. It had been his first important film and he was a very shy young man, nervous of the great director. On the first day he was 'tarted up' in the make-up room and in the wardrobe until he looked like Robert Donat's handsome brother. When Alex saw the rushes, he said—loudly: "No! no! I want for him to be fonny like in de Boat Deck!" Alas, there was nothing in the script for Huntley to be 'fonny' about.

What Korda was aiming at in this film was to 'paint with light' as Rembrandt had painted with brush and palette. The Dutch interiors, the carefully composed groups had a matchless visual quality.

'Rembrandt' cost about £110,000. The critics loved it; the public was impressed but puzzled by it. No similar film had ever been made for mass audiences. Yet without 'Rembrandt' we would never have seen the Toulouse-Lautrec film ('Moulin Rouge') nor the Van Gogh picture ('Lust for Life'). Korda was truly a pioneer and 'Rembrandt' must prove, I think, his most enduring achievement.

Charles Laughton agreed with this. But he told me that Korda didn't go far enough. "He stopped just this side of true greatness. Even Alex couldn't stomach facts like that of Rembrandt selling his first wife's grave in order to raise money for his wedding with the second one . . . But in spite of this, Korda did his most sensitive and courageous directorial work on the picture . . ."

Star and director had their arguments and rows. Once, during an exterior scene, Laughton walked off the set, across the grass and back to his dressing-room. Alex, in a despairing voice, called out:

"Charles, come back!" Then he added, *sotto voce*: "His bloody watch must be wrong, it isn't lunch-time yet!"

Perhaps it will take some time before audiences—that is, mass audiences—will learn to appreciate 'Rembrandt'. When it was presented in 1936, the *Daily Express* called it 'a thing of great restraint, beauty, like a highly-polished piece of rosewood furniture . . . It is a new experience for filmgoers and whether it is a commercial success or not, it is certainly artistic." The National Film Board of America named it as one of the ten best foreign films of the year. A Glasgow paper said: ". . . for those who can appreciate the exquisite in screen entertainment, the elect few, the film no doubt will be accepted as a thing of beauty and a joy for ever . . ."

The critics forecast 'Rembrandt' as a box office failure. When someone told Alex that it wouldn't recover its cost, he replied: "I know—but it is very beautiful." And in the end the picture actually made a small profit. It is still shown occasionally and has been televised many times.

'Rembrandt' was to be the last film Alexander Korda directed for some years. With Denham in full operation, with a most ambitious programme and immense technical, administrative and financial problems, he realized that he would have to take complete control of a series of films and supervise them from end to end. To be both producer and director was too much for one man. So Alex, not without some heart-searching and with considerable reluctance, gave up what he liked most and did best. He began to build up his own directors and co-producers. Sometimes his fingers still itched to take over—because, in quite a few cases, he knew that he could do much better. There were inevitable clashes and quarrels because of this interference; some of his collaborators thought that he was a far better director than producer. But this period was like the trying transition a man has to endure when he is giving up smoking; it lasted for a while but in the end Korda resigned himself to the rôle of the top executive, the guiding spirit. Some of his friends and artists resented this and left him—but he had little choice. Perhaps it would have been different if Denham had been, according to his original conception, smaller; if it had only three stages instead of the seven which had to be kept filled—but even then London Films became far too complex an organization and there was no one who could take Korda's place on the administrative and financial side.

★   ★   ★   ★

The three other Korda pictures that belong to this period presented fewer problems and were much more 'commercial' propositions.

'The Ghost Goes West' grew out of a magazine story; originally it was to star Charles Laughton but as the script was shaped, it became evident that a younger, more romantic lead was called for. Robert Donat played the double part of the eighteenth and twentieth century heroes; Korda brought over two American stars—Jean Parker and Eugene Pallette—and left the direction in the extremely capable hands of René Clair. The interiors were shot at Isleworth, the exteriors in and around Denham. The film was a gay and irreverent romp with many of the typical Clair touches, and did extremely well both in America and Britain; an annual ballot of the 'Film Weekly' chose it as the best British film of 1936. It was revived several times and played to large audiences in France, Italy and the rest of the Continent.

Yet when the picture was finished, Korda and his associates were in a quandary—they didn't know whether it was really funny or not. (Public reaction is one of the hardest things to pre-judge at any time.) They needed a success badly; the two pictures following 'Henry VIII' had had, as we know, a mixed reception.

The night of the first showing, Korda, Steven Pallos and a few other friends dined at Avenue Road—then they all went off to the Leicester Square Theatre. But Korda wouldn't let them go inside the auditorium.

"You know the scene where Robert Donat looks up at the sky and asks, 'Where am I, father?' If the audience gets it—we have a success. If it doesn't . . ." and he shrugged eloquently.

So they stood at the back of the royal circle and waited. The sound-track could be clearly heard.

Loud, prolonged laughter greeted the sequence to which Korda referred. Alex turned on his heels.

"We can all go home now," he said. "It is a success."

It was.

*   *   *   *

'The Man Who Could Work Miracles' was another H. G. Wells story but it was scripted by Lajos Biro and Wells interfered very little with the development of the story. The picture was shot entirely at Denham. The director was Lothar Mendes, who had had a distinguished career in Germany, Hollywood and Britain; he is still active in British films. He and Alex had a good many fights—but, as Mendes told me, every quarrel seemed to strengthen their friendship. Korda could be 'really bloody-minded and make you hate him'. But when someone stormed into his office to give him a piece of his mind, the angry visitor always ended up by feeling ashamed himself.

Once Mendes went to see Korda, full of furious determination to get some money due to him.

"Lothar," Korda said, "I know I owe you this money . . . but I can't pay it . . ."

"Look here, Alex," protested the director, "we have a contract and . . ."

"You can sue me, of course," Korda went on.

"I'm certainly going to!"

"But you won't!" Alex stated calmly.

"And why shouldn't I?" demanded Mendes.

Korda put his hand on his shoulder and smiled: "Because you are my friend," he said, softly.

This was an argument Mendes couldn't answer. He didn't sue Korda and in time he did get his money.

For 'The Man Who Could Work Miracles' Korda brought his old friend Roland Young from Hollywood to appear for the second time in a London Films production. Ralph Richardson played a peppery old colonel. Sophie Stewart and Joan Gardner shared the feminine leads, with Ernest Thesiger, Wallace Lupino, Edward Chapman, George Zucco and Lawrence Hanray in the most important supporting parts.

"As long as he was alive," Sir Ralph Richardson told me, "I never did films for any other producer but Alex. We never had a contract but I felt I couldn't work for anybody else. Why? Because he was such a wonderful director. Never a tyrant or a dictator. He understood actors. He would ask you: how do you want to do it? what's your idea? He'd listen and unless you were hopelessly wrong, he'd let you do it your own way. He realized that acting was something that couldn't be taught or imposed; that there was a special mysterious quality in the actor's work that had to come from the inside, spontaneously and couldn't be forced."

In his distinguished career Sir Ralph Richardson certainly won his finest triumphs in the whole series of Korda films with which he was associated.

'The Man Who Could Work Miracles' made heavy demands on the trick department, the 'special effects boys'. Ned Mann, Laurence Butler and E. Cohen who were responsible for this work, were all brought to Britain by Korda or trained by him. Until Alex established this branch of film-making, it existed only in a very primitive form in England. In the same way he was responsible for raising the standards of film make-up. Make-up artists still bless him; by paying substantial salaries and giving them chances to train and experiment, he completely changed the old-fashioned and often ridiculous make-up methods.

The last of the three pictures, 'Men Are Not Gods', was written and directed by Walter Reisch, another refugee from Hitler's Germany. Sam Goldwyn lent his star, Miriam Hopkins, for the leading part. Her co-stars were Gertrude Lawrence and Sebastian Shaw; in a second male lead Rex Harrison made his London Films début. A. E. Matthews, the beloved 'Matty', was given an important supporting rôle while Val Gielgud was 'type-cast' as a stage producer.

It was on the set of 'Men Are Not Gods' that Korda introduced Wally Patch to Miriam Hopkins, with the words: 'Here's our commissionaire.' As Wally was in uniform and rarely used make-up, Miriam Hopkins thought he was a commissionaire in real life. After they had run through the scene together very smoothly, she enquired whether there were any other commissionaires attached to the studio who could act as well as he did.

The film was hailed as an 'intelligent picture and a distinct step forward for the British film' in London; while a New York critic called it 'charming, literate and considerably enlivened by the presence of Miriam Hopkins'.

*   *   *   *

"It was Korda's habit," one of his fellow-producers told me, "whenever a rival company announced its programme, to announce three times as many pictures. Half of them were never made—but by that time he had announced another string of them."

This is a somewhat unjust criticism. If one compiled a list of all the films announced *in a single year* and then never heard of again, it would run into hundreds. This is almost an inborn feature of the film industry.

The years 1934–36 were the most productive, the most highly creative in Korda's life. Perhaps he wanted to do too much—but even so the achievements of these years were most impressive. Yet some of his projects never came to fruition.

On January 1, 1935, John Barrymore announced in America that in three months' time he would be going to London to produce and appear in a film for Alexander Korda, probably 'Hamlet'. Nothing came out of this exciting plan.

About the same time Korda bought Romola Nijinsky's biography of the great dancer. He announced that he would make a picture based on it with Laughton as Diaghilev, the famous impresario. This film was never made; just as A. E. W. Mason's *The Broken Road* and *Mary Read* (the play which had starred Flora Robson and Robert Donat in 1934) never reached the screen. A comedy called 'A Bicycle Built For Two' with

Binnie Barnes as the star shared the same fate. A little later Korda stated that he would make a film based on the life of Franz Liszt, starring Conrad Veidt. The composer of so many Hungarian rhapsodies never came to life in the cinemas; neither did Lawrence of Arabia, though Alex had bought *Revolt in the Desert* and acquired the rights to Lawrence's biography for £6,000 and 7½ per cent of the *gross* receipts. Leslie Howard was mentioned as the star and a great deal of money was spent on the project before it was abandoned.

Korda had also put Anthony Gross and Hector Hoppin, the French cartoon-film makers under contract as a result of their charming 'Joie de Vivre' and announced that they would make a series of cartoons for London Films. Unfortunately, these were never completed.

One of the most interesting Korda ideas brought a famous man into films. Nineteen-thirty-five was the year of the Silver Jubilee and Alex decided that he would make a picture called 'Twenty Five Years of the Reign of George V'.

He chose Anthony Asquith to direct it. For his scriptwriter he engaged—Winston Churchill.

Randolph Churchill had been working for some time in the publicity department of London Films. A meeting was arranged with his father in a pub near Isleworth Studios. As a result of this meeting, Alex bought the film-rights of Churchill's 'Marlborough' for a reported £10,000, and the great politician, then 'in the wilderness' because of his unyielding anti-Nazi attitude, agreed to try his hand at a screenplay.

Anthony Asquith told me how he and Lajos Biro went down to Chartwell to work with Churchill. The idea was that they would teach him the art of screenwriting. They found that he had very little to learn; he had an amazingly vivid, visual mind. Asquith and Biro spent a fortnight at Chartwell and though Churchill was writing a book, painting pictures and laying bricks, with his enormous energy and zest he gave them plenty of his valuable time.

"We must have a map of Europe," Churchill sketched out his ideas, "with a skeleton hand tearing through it—to symbolize the beginning of the Great War." And Asquith retained in his memory a truly Churchillian phrase: "We must have a suffragette in the film," Korda's latest scriptwriter said, "Fair and frail—not morally but physically frail—with a delicate integument hiding an indomitable spirit!"

Alas, the picture was never made. By January 1935 Korda had reluctantly decided to abandon it. There are several versions why he came to this decision. One is that under the Cinematograph Films Act of 1927 a film containing incidents of a dramatic nature could not be booked by the cinemas without a trade show. Since there wasn't much chance of making the film, having it trade-shown and then waiting for bookings in competition with the many other pictures, reconstructed purely from newsreels which did not have to be trade-shown, Korda gave up the idea. Another tale has it that some of his fellow-producers resented a 'foreigner' making such a film. They called on Korda and suggested that this should be an 'all-industry picture' to which various producers would each contribute a reel. Korda realized that this would result in an impossible hotch-potch of styles and conceptions. "You go ahead and do it," he said, "I won't."

Another frustrated Korda project was the film version of Rostand's famous *Cyrano de Bergerac*. It was planned as early as January 1936 when photographs of Charles Laughton, wearing different-sized false noses for his part of Cyrano appeared in the film magazines. Korda had placed under contract the eminent English poet Humbert Wolfe, who promised to deliver a rhymed translation of the French play within a month.

"Korda continued to disappoint me," Wolfe said later. "When we first met, he wasn't wearing a hat on the back of his head or a cigar at the back of his mouth. Furthermore, he looked intelligent, and thirdly, he *was* intelligent. He did not seem to know that he ought to open the conversation by calling 'How's tricks?' As I remember, he said: 'I cannot believe that Benes is right in supposing the Germans will go off gold. What do you think?' "

Wolfe completed the translation and spent long evenings with Charles Laughton 'putting the play into training'. Korda was sympathetic and helpful; conferences were called, revisions made, poetry and prose carefully weighed in the critical balance as a medium for 'Cyrano'. Then the whole venture was abandoned.

Many years later Korda sold his rights—at a handsome profit —to Stanley Kramer and Carl Foreman, who made 'Cyrano' with José Ferrer in the title rôle for Columbia Pictures.

In the meantime Korda was becoming a public figure, the most colourful in the British film industry. In 1935 a questionnaire, distributed by Sidney Bernstein through his chain of cinemas, revealed that he had climbed up to the top place in the list of favourite directors, replacing his friend Ernst Lubitsch.

Alex always had a great admiration for craftsmen—Walt Disney was one of them. He called him "one of the major geniuses of the screen". And he believed in *colour* when the technique was in its earliest stages, to be used for dramatic emphasis and greater realism. In 1934 he forecast that it wouldn't be long before black-and-white films would appear as strange as a silent picture in the age of the talkies. In the choice of his subjects he deliberately aimed at the Empire markets. No wonder that less than four years after his arrival in London he was described as 'the British cinema's premier showman'.

Yet he still puzzled many people. They thought him a paradox —a man who disliked personal publicity but was always getting into the limelight; a man who adored leisure but never allowed himself to enjoy it; a man who was extremely receptive of ideas but always had better ones himself. His quiet voice, his uncanny courtesy, his talent for dismissing anybody who overstayed his welcome with the greatest gentleness and utmost dispatch; his charm 'in six different languages'—all these were utterly unlike the traditional film tycoon's image.

Korda was ready to analyse himself, to offer at least some clues to the character that still puzzled, fascinated and amused the British.

"Is there a film I would like to do, a piece of work I would like to complete, were I to die tomorrow?" he asked himself in January 1936. "No. Faced with death, making a picture —so little a thing. Oh well, I should regret not seeing the Wells picture, 'Things to Come', in which we are so engrossed. But if there is a picture I want to make, then I make it. I'm doing the work I want to do—subject to the frustrations that everyone has in life—finance, other people's points of view, and so on."

He felt that there was not enough time in any active individual life to do anything—he, like others, was always in the process of snatching a little education, a little knowledge. He thought he knew nothing about the really interesting things.

"I have never seen anything—*really* seen it," he confessed. "I want 35 to 40 years of ripe age—let's say 60 to 95, healthy, vigorous, looking younger than I shall be—comfortably off —not rich. I want to do the things I intended to do when I was fifteen—to travel, to find out things that were so exasperating as youthful studies—the real value of mathematics, for instance, and of economy, the classics and languages. One of my greatest desires is to learn golf. I once tried to hit the ball for half-an-hour and couldn't. I play nothing. I get so sluggish. I must really learn this golf!"

He never did, of course. In his later years, he thought, he would probably retire to a nursing home or a monastery, where he could spend several weeks each year talking to nobody at all.

He had noticed that almost every crisis in his life was accompanied by illness. Not that the crises brought on the illness—somehow the illness was sent to allow him to collect his thoughts and look at himself.

By the end of 1936 Korda could look back proudly on the four years that had passed since 'Henry VIII'. His colleagues, even his rivals, regarded him with affection and respect; he had built a new prestige for British films all over the world. He addressed his appeal to the intellect—and brought it off. He had gathered a brilliant company of actors, writers and directors around him. The future looked bright indeed.

In November 1936 he became a British subject. It was during the shooting of 'Rembrandt' that the news came through. Work stopped and soon the champagne arrived for all—at three o'clock in the afternoon. A regular party! Everybody on the set shared in it, including the lowliest technicians. Korda looked like a schoolboy who had just received a prize.

Later, in the bar at Denham, Adrian Brunel, the veteran director, asked him why he had given up his Hungarian nationality. Alex grinned and said: "So that I can tell those other bloody foreigners where to get off!"

★   ★   ★   ★

Near the end of the year he summed up his creed:

"If the British film industry is to expand and grow, we must not just copy American ideas, but strike out on our own . . . I have observed audiences. I have seen them grow weary of hokum. The eternal triangle of Tom, Dick and Mary doesn't interest them any more. It is true that if Tom, Dick and Mary are famous stars, a certain proportion of the public will go automatically to see any film in which they appear. But the film won't make a hit—it will leave the audience dissatisfied . . . It is most essential that inspiration be allowed to take its own course in every department of film creation. When I choose directors, I seek the cleverest ones I can find, give them stories which suit them, and then allow them a free hand to make the kind of creative entertainment the public likes."

With a fine studio, with generous financial backing, with an entry into the world market, it seemed that nothing could stop Alexander Korda. But trouble was brewing, not only for him but for the whole British film industry, and 1937 brought a hurricane which only his courage and tenacity could weather.

CHAPTER VIII

CRISIS

ACCORDING to the experts, the history of the film industry is an unbroken roller-coaster sequence of boom-bust-boom-bust with crises and occupational disease. Such crises have the disconcerting habit of flaring up without warning. In November, 1936, *The Times* could still write: 'There are indications that the British film industry is approaching the time of its greatest opportunity. Its prestige abroad is rising and it has at least a footing in foreign markets, where its products are examined with interest and even with expectation . . .' This was a classic example of what *The New Yorker* calls 'the clouded crystal-ball'. Less than a month later a London weekly reported that during the previous month insiders had started to talk about a 'reckoning up' between Korda and the Prudential, his backers.

Not that Korda was alone in his troubles—if troubles they were. Nineteen-thirty-six had been a boom year. No less than 640 film companies had been registered in eleven years in England. By 1937 not more than twenty remained active.

Twickenham Studios failed with liabilities in the region of £500,000. Gaumont-British increased its overdraft by nearly the same amount in a year—due, as Mr. Mark Ostrer put it, to 'the failure to get into the American market'. The fact was that the cost of American distribution far exceeded the revenue. Pinewood Studios, owned partly by Mr. J. Arthur Rank and controlled by Richard Norton, had a tough battle to keep the stages occupied. In 1936 Denham itself had gone 'dark' for a short

time; but by the beginning of 1937 Korda had prepared a new
and ambitious programme.

The financial status of London Films during this period was
difficult and tangled. From April 28, 1935, to May 2, 1936, there
was a loss of £330,842. In the previous year (1934/35) the loss
had been £26,967. Expenses of £113,017 were incurred while
they awaited the completion of Denham Studios. At this time
the assets were valued at £2,229,973 for completed productions;
costs applicable to future films were set at £751,845; property
and equipment were valued at £564,149; other items in the
accounts included £19,250 compensation paid for cancellation
of contracts; £94,885 Debenture Discount account; £41,408
debtors; and £5,403 cash.

In the eight months of May 2, 1936, to January 2, 1937, however, London Films made a profit of £35,839. This was the first
uninterrupted period of operation of Denham; as the final cost of
the studio had been around £300,000, the 'loss' was in reality a
paper loss, for the studios represented a far greater asset than this
sum.

Still, the talk of crisis persisted, and it was only too real. Some
explained it by the fact that most of the film companies had
spent all their working capital on a big crop of ambitious pictures
and could not make any more until these had recovered their
cost. Korda immediately came forward to deny this.

"All this talk about only making cheap pictures for the British
market is rubbish," he said. "We can't ask British people to go
to the cinema for patriotic motives. This country has a right to
the best film industry in the world and will get it only by competing in the world market."

He pointed out that companies formed without the proper
personnel, technical or commercial, had either lost their money
or would lose it in the future. But this was no reason to decry the
efforts of those who were trying to build up a film industry in
England, and to damn their effort in advance. Was it fair to
generalize and describe all and sundry in pictures as wastrels and

fools who paid fabulous salaries simply because they liked doing so? He denounced the get-rich-quick promoters: "If an investor chooses to entrust his money to his tailor for the building of a ship, he deserves all he gets. In the last two years, lured by the fabulous earnings of film companies, investors have put money into film ventures without the least hope of success . . ."

If London Films was short of money, this was certainly not because its productions hadn't done well. 'Scarlet Pimpernel' and 'Henry VIII' had taken more than a million pounds between them. 'Sanders of the River' and 'The Ghost Goes West' grossed £450,000; 'Rembrandt' had earned £400,000 and 'Catherine the Great' £350,000. Even the H. G. Wells venture, 'Things to Come', had taken £350,000 at the box office, though because of the very high production costs there was a loss on this particular film.

So Korda spoke with authority when he said:

"It is not enough that the product should be made. The real job and the real difficulty start when it has to be sold. The same conditions apply to the cheap picture made solely —as it can be made—for the British market and the ambitious and more costly picture for the international market. England may be a nation of shopkeepers but the day of the small shopkeeper is over. Today the successful salesman must have the stability of a multiple chain store behind him. Selling and distributing pictures is an art that England still has to learn."

In all this there were curious echoes of the articles he had written about Hungarian films twenty years earlier. His thinking was still the same, only the framework had changed. A film that was made for £20,000 for the home market, he explained, is not necessarily profitable because it is cheap—it is only so if it can be sold for more than £20,000. A film made for the world market had to be sold throughout the world, not only in England and the U.S.A. There must not be a single country in the world where it was left unshown and unsold. "That is why I and my financial backers in London Films," he pointed out, "decided that I should become a partner in United Artists which has one hundred and twenty branches all over the world." Except in Russia, every film made by his company in the last four years had as wide a booking as the films of any of the biggest American studios. He admitted that they had to spend a lot of money and fight strong competition. After all, this was only the beginning; they had to build their studios, train their stars and technicians, establish their credit in different markets. They were well aware that in the first years, if they meant to realize their ambitions for a successful industry, they would have to be prepared for some loss —which was really an investment in the future.

"Today we have the best studios in Europe, the best staff for making pictures in Europe," he declared proudly, "and an organization which can gauge to a penny the cost of our productions and sell them all over the world. In producing a large number of pictures one must always be prepared for a certain variation in quality. Some will not be as successful, artistically or commercially, as the others. But our position is not the same as that of a man who risks his last penny on a single picture. One flop does not mean a bankruptcy. The risk has to be spread over the whole of the product. I can honestly say that London Films have made individual mistakes but we have never yet made a group of four pictures that did not bring in more and sometimes considerably more than their cost."

Beverley Baxter, writing in January 1937, in the *Daily Telegraph*, forecast that neither 'Things to Come' nor the 'superb' Rembrandt picture would get back their cost. But in his view these were financial failures out of which victory would eventually come. Korda's aim was to surpass Hollywood. "If his efforts to date show a loss of £350,000, does that in any way represent the value of Mr. Korda's services to Britain and the British film industry?" Baxter demanded.

Korda himself reacted sharply to the crisis-talk.

"They call it a crisis," he said in an interview, late in January 1937, "I would not say it was a crisis. It is rather a little 'scrap' from which we are going to learn a great deal. I have spent much money and time laying the foundations of a great new national industry. That work is not going to be wasted. There has been panic, yes. But I am not afraid of it. What has troubled me most is that as head of a great company employing thousands of people I have had to see many of them lose their jobs. I have learned several lessons. I have been forced to fix my mind on the finance of these films to the exclusion of all considerations. There have been times when it was all figures, when I felt more like an accountant than a film producer. My policy will still be to go all out for the big successes and I shall get them. It is true I shall be bearing this question of cost always in mind. That will be a new Korda. I hope the old Alexander Korda will not be killed in the process."

There was little fear of that—but there was no doubt about it that his financial backers were awakening to the fact: a film studio was a rather special piece of bricks-and-mortar. It had to be kept alive to produce profits—while with a block of flats it was sufficient to keep it in good repair, a studio needed new films and new capital investment to keep it going. And it was so very difficult to forecast whether a picture would be a financial success or not. No one, since the beginning of show business, has ever figured out actuarial figures for that.

So it was getting more and more difficult for Korda to obtain new financial backing from Prudential. There was no question of the money being cut off—London Films went on producing up

to the outbreak of the war—but the persuasive powers of Alex
had to work overtime.

One day Lothar Mendes was with him when he had to face
some of his financial backers who were in an angry mood. Korda
stood in front of the fireplace while the three City gentlemen
glared at him.

"You have every right to be upset," he started. "It was all my
fault. I was extravagant, I thought that to make money one had
to spend it. I'll take full blame for what happened . . ."

He went on in this strain and gradually the three men became
uneasy, restless. As Alex accused himself of more and more
heinous omissions and mistakes, they began to protest, to inter-
rupt and argue. Within half an hour they were begging him not
to take it to heart and castigate himself; if he had made any mistakes, they had been made in a good cause. Another half-hour
went by and they were literally pleading with him to accept
more money, to finish the production which had been suspended
because of lack of funds. The rôles were completely reversed
and while Mendes watched in fascinated admiration, Korda got
exactly what he wanted. The 'performance' was completely
sincere, the famous charm worked without visible effort. And
in the end the bankers had every reason to be satisfied.

In 1937 he had to change his policy. In February it was
announced that London Films would produce, under the unit
scheme, 'good entertaining pictures of comparatively little
expense, taking the cue from Hollywood'. These, of course,
would not be quota quickies and the 'super films' would still be
sandwiched in between them.

Korda was keenly aware of Hollywood's competition—old in
experience and rich in money, buying whatever talent there was
available in the world. "Could anyone expect," Korda said in
May 1937, "that in three years the British film industry should
have matched this experience? How could it? Nevertheless
we have achieved results to be proud of—four new studios
equal to any in the world, several promising directors, good

technicians and a score of players who are daily increasing in popularity."

Those who knew the facts certainly absolved him of blame for the crisis. But as a trade paper pointed out:

"It is ironical that Alexander Korda who did so much to bring world prestige to British films was also indirectly responsible for the crash. Korda spent more money than British films had ever seen before, gambling on big returns from America, as well as from this country. In the case of pictures like 'The Private Life of Henry VIII', 'The Scarlet Pimpernel' and 'The Ghost Goes West' his policy seemed justified. But his imitators spent equal sums on filming indifferent stories that had no hope of crashing the American market and as little hope of recouping their costs from the cinemas of Great Britain."

This was the true summing up of the matter. Korda produced big pictures. These were largely successful. Others tried to imitate him and, with notable exceptions, failed—because they lacked the know-how. When the crash came, Korda was accused of setting a bad example. What he did in reality, was to teach British film-makers to be ambitious; to think of themselves in American eyes. He even went one better than the Americans—in 'Things to Come' he tried to make a British film handle a story which was really important. It did not matter that the experiment did not quite come off—the great thing was that it was tried. One of the reasons it did not succeed was the British audiences' refusal to believe in the reality of totalitarian danger. When, in the film, fifty bombers crossed the East Coast, the audiences began to laugh at the 'absurdity' of what a scanty three years later became grim, tangible truth. The great tragedy was, as John Grierson pointed out, that the ambitious British picture turned into a racket. Many gamblers started 'to do the big thing' without the production ability and the supporting personnel.

They failed and destroyed the credit of the industry. A vast sum of money had been lost and *big* British production was in a bad way. The gamblers kept on making excuses—but they failed because their films were not worth the money they cost. As Joseph M. Schenck, president of 20th Century-Fox said in September 1937: "I do not know any British producer except Mr. Korda with whom I would trust my company's money."

Memories in the film industry are notoriously short; but Korda must have chuckled when he read these words in an interview—remembering how, not quite seven years before, the same company had sacked him for 'incompetence and disobedience'.

*   *   *   *

The general belief, even among those familiar with the history of British films, seems to be that Prudential, Korda's backers, suddenly decided to call it quits—and that, in consequence, Korda lost his studios, his company, all he had built up with such tremendous effort and energy.

According to Montague Marks and other close associates of Korda, this wasn't true at all. Actually, London Films and its associated companies made twenty pictures between the end of 1936 and the outbreak of the war. Most of these were financed by Prudential. Within the same period Denham Laboratories, the finest in Europe, were completed. There was no dramatic severance between Korda and Prudential but a gradual and amicable withdrawal. That in the end the great insurance company parted from Korda and Korda lost his cherished Denham Studios is, of course, established fact. There were several contributory causes—not only the film crisis which was clearly not Korda's fault, though he might have set a 'bad example' for his far less capable imitators, but a number of other mishaps and difficulties.

Denham was a Moloch—it had to be fed. Idle, its stages were

costing a lot of money in interest and maintenance. To keep them busy, London Films wasn't sufficient. Almost from the beginning Korda made a useful revenue for his company, leasing his stages to independent producers. (A practice that has become more or less general both in Hollywood and Britain.) Most of these worked under the United Artists releasing banner.

One of these producers was Max Schach, who has been described as a 'perky griffin behind an enormous desk'. He started at Denham but moved out in the winter of 1936, going to Shepperton Sound City studios—because they were cheaper. Not that Mr. Schach lasted long after that; by December 1937 he had to resign as chairman and managing director of his Capitol Film Group.

A little harder was the loss of Erich Pommer who came, a penniless refugee from Hitler's Germany, and joined Korda as the most important producer in the group. He was not only leaving his friend and colleague, but taking one of the greatest assets of London Films with him—Charles Laughton.

There is no doubt that 'Henry VIII' and 'Rembrandt' had established Charles Laughton as a top international star. But subjects and rôles were not easy to find to suit his vast and unconventional talents. Laughton, perhaps with some reason, resented that Korda became more and more involved with financial and administrative problems; he thought very highly of Alex as a director and artist, and felt that by becoming a great executive, he was betraying his art, his mission. It was, of course, the actor's, the artist's point of view. Korda may have shared it in his secret heart but there was very little he could do about it.

At last he thought he had found a worthy subject for his brilliant star. He bought the film-rights of Robert Graves's fine novel, 'I Claudius', and went to Majorca to discuss the screenplay with the poet-novelist. He assembled a brilliant cast—Merle Oberon as Messalina, Flora Robson as Olivia, Emlyn Williams as Caligula—with John Clements, Robert Newton, Everley

Gregg and Basil Gill in important supporting parts. He brought Joseph von Sternberg, Marlene Dietrich's favourite director, from Hollywood to do the picture.

Sternberg arrived, summoned all the technical staff to a production meeting and then had the doors locked so that no one could get in or out. He went through the script line by line, explaining every scene and passage, demanding opinions, conducting long arguments with each technician involved. The meeting started in the morning and was still going on in the late afternoon. Finally the staff, hungry and exhausted, were rescued by Korda, who carried off von Sternberg.

Though he had asked for him, Charles Laughton did not get on very well with Sternberg. Laughton was not an easy actor to direct—"he needs a midwife, not a director", as Alex had once ruefully said. Whenever he wanted to get into the right mood for Claudius, he used to play a record of Edward VIII's abdication speech, over and over again.

Work on 'I Claudius' began at Denham in the second week of February, 1937. In March it was suspended. Merle Oberon had been in a car crash and couldn't work; the relations of Laughton and the director were becoming more and more strained. In the end Vincent Korda's superb sets, the fine cast, the excellent script all had to be scrapped. Laughton's contract with London Films was about to expire and he did not intend to renew it. 'I Claudius' was to have cost £150,000; Korda claimed £80,000 insurance when it was abandoned. Perhaps Merle Oberon's mishap would not have been decisive; but Laughton's contract ended on April 21st. (The parting with Korda must have been a rather painful experience for him. More than twenty years later he still refused to speak about it, saying only that it was "best forgotten".) He formed his own company, Mayflower Films, with Erich Pommer and never worked directly with Korda again.

Another, though less costly, frustration was caused by a pet idea of Korda which he had nursed for a long time. He was making 'Things to Come' at Isleworth when he first decided to make a series of films dealing with the development of shipping, land transport and aviation throughout the ages.

Only the first of these was ever attempted. It was called 'The Conquest of the Air'. John Monk Saunders, the author of 'Wings', 'Dawn Patrol' and other flying films, was brought over from Hollywood to write the script; Zoltan Korda and Alexander Esway were assigned as directors. The picture had a fine cast—Laurence Olivier as Lunardi, the balloonist, Cameron Hall as Blanchard, Charles Le Faux as Blériot, with Margaretta Scott, Michael Rennie and Alan Wheatley also in the cast. Zoltan Korda shot the episodes of Blériot, Lilienthal, the Wright Brothers and several others; Esway did Leonardo da Vinci, the episode of Nero and the 'flying barber'—but after forty-five minutes of it were completed, the film was postponed. Later, Donald Taylor and Alexander Shaw revived it and finished shooting by October, 1937. But it had gone through so many hands—Charles Friend did the final editing—that it never came to life and had only a brief run in London.

Almost equally disappointing were the two co-productions with M. Granovsky involving the pictures 'Rebel Son' and 'Moscow Nights'. These were made in French and then English versions were prepared by Adrian Brunel and Anthony Asquith respectively. In 'Rebel Son' Patricia Roc got her first break and Bernard Miles made his screen début. 'Moscow Nights' starred Harry Baur, who came over to repeat his French rôle in English, supported by Penelope Dudley-Ward, Laurence Olivier, Athene Seyler and Robert Cochran. Baur didn't have a word of English, so he had to learn the part phonetically, syllable by syllable. It sounded all right in the projection room—but when it was finished, hardly anybody could understand a word Baur was saying. Yet even so, with Asquith's direction and a most amusing performance by Athene Seyler as a middle-aged, maternal spy, the film didn't do too badly.

*   *   *   *

Failures and frustrations—but they were more than balanced by a whole series of successful and challenging pictures.

In 1936 Anthony Asquith had been put to work on a screen-play about Queen Elizabeth. He collaborated with Dr. Harrison, the eminent historian. But this project was shelved and in the end Korda bought A. E. W. Mason's best-selling novel, 'Fire Over England'.

The picture was remarkable for several things. For Flora Robson, who had made her Korda début in 'Catherine', it brought a special triumph. She had considerable doubts about her being cast as the Virgin Queen; she thought there was no physical resemblance, that she did not have the strength or authority for the difficult rôle. Yet in the magnificent scene at Tilbury, in the great speech that hurled defiance at Philip, she proved what a fine actress she was—and justified Korda's choice. Leslie Banks gave an unusually subtle performance as Leicester; Raymond Massey was excellent as the tormented Spanish king. James Mason had a minor rôle in the picture; there were fine supporting performances by Morton Selten, Lawrence Hanray, Henry Oscar, Francis de Woolf and Robert Newton. But the real stars of the film were two young people who have since become the first lady and gentleman of British pictures—Vivien Leigh and Laurence Olivier.

Monty Marks told me the story of Miss Leigh's 'discovery', a story which, in turn, I told her more than twenty years after the event and which amused her considerably. One night Korda, Joseph M. Schenck, Murray Silverstone and Marks were dining at the Savoy Grill; talking, as usual, shop. About nine o'clock Korda suddenly remembered that he had two tickets to a first night in his pocket—one of the film critics had asked him to go and see the play because of a new leading lady. The two Americans decided to go along, even though it was getting rather late. They reached the theatre in the middle of the last act. A strikingly beautiful young girl was on the stage—and all four late-comers were instantly struck by her looks and her talent.

The play was 'The Masque of Virtue' and the girl Vivien Leigh. After the play ended, with many curtain-calls, the two Americans and Korda held a hasty conference. The Americans agreed that Alex should have 'first go'—if he could sign her up, they would retire from the competition. If he couldn't—well, then, let the best man win.

Korda went round to Miss Leigh's dressing-room. Within a few minutes she had agreed to join London Films. Next day her husband called on Monty Marks and the details of her contract were fixed. She was to start on a modest scale—£750 a year—but it was a five-year agreement and the salary, if the options were taken up, was to rise by annual increases to £5,000. And it allowed Miss Leigh to continue her stage-work.

It took two years before Korda found a rôle suited to her talents—though he went on record long before that as saying that she would become a world-famous star.

"It was during the making of *Fire Over England*," Lady Olivier told me, "that Larry and I met—and fell in love. Alex was like a father to us—we went to him with every little problem we had. We usually left convinced that he had solved it—or that we'd got our way, even when we hadn't. Well, one day we went to him and said: 'Alex, we must tell you our great secret—we're in love and we're going to get married.' He smiled and said: 'Don't be silly—everybody knows that. I've known it for weeks and weeks.' "

'Fire Over England' was one of Korda's most successful pictures; it did equally well in Britain and America. *Life* nominated it as 'movie of the week'; it won the Gold Medal of the impressively-named International Committee for Artistic and Literary Diffusion by the Cinema. And it launched Vivien Leigh on the triumphant career that led to 'Gone With the Wind' and so many world-wide successes.

'Knight Without Armour' was perhaps Korda's most expensive production—though not entirely intentionally. When the first budget was prepared for the screen version of James Hilton's

novel, it came to about £300,000. Prudential, according to
Monty Marks, protested that this was far too much. "I agree,"
Alex said, "the budget is all wrong. I guarantee that I can slash it
to £180,000." He did, too; only when the picture was finished,
elaborate retakes were needed and it ended up by costing in the
neighbourhood of £350,000.

To star in this story of the Russian revolution, Korda brought
Marlene Dietrich from Hollywood for her first British picture.
The blonde star of the 'Blue Angel' was guaranteed £50,000
and a number of other 'perquisites' which in the end increased
her 'take-home pay' to almost £80,000.

Marlene was partnered by Robert Donat, whom Korda considered one of his happiest and most valuable discoveries. It was
a hard blow when the beginning of the film also marked Donat's
first serious attack of asthma. Much upset, Alex suggested to
Marlene that the story should be changed and she should star
alone. She refused and for four weeks they 'shot around' Donat
until he was well enough to continue work. When he appeared
on the set, Marlene greeted him as 'Our Knight Without
Asthma!' A special apparatus was installed in Donat's dressing
room to enable him to breathe medicated air while he slept, and
he had to be handled with great tact until he overcame the
depressing effects of his illness. It was the first shadow that fell
upon the life of this brilliant actor who died almost literally
under the arc-lights of the studio—his last picture, 'The Inn of The
Sixth Happiness' was finished only a few days before his death
in 1958.

The cast included Irene Vanbrugh, Herbert Lomas, Lawrence
Hanray and—in the part of a drunken Red soldier—Miles
Malleson. The designer was the highly talented Lazare Meerson,
who died the following year of meningitis. But the greatest
chance the picture provided was for John Clements.

He had already done a few small parts for Korda when he was
called to do a test for the part of Poushkoff, a young Russian
commissar. He waited around all day until Jacques Feyder, the

director, was ready for him. In the meantime he studied the part, which was only a couple of pages—but a wonderful opportunity for any actor. He worked hard until the evening when Feyder came round and listened with an impassive face while an assistant director cued Clements. He put everything he had into his performance for his audience of one. At the end Feyder simply walked away. Clements thought he was a flop—but the assistant director told him that if he had failed, Feyder would have given him a piece of his mind. So he got the part—and won considerable praise for it.

The production went on for a long time. There was an unpleasant accident when a railway truck collapsed, throwing the extras down an embankment, injuring several people. A whole forest had been constructed on the set, complete with birds and bullfrogs, and Feyder, a stickler for detail (as his famous 'Kermesse Heroique' proved) had antique shops ransacked for contemporary furniture and fittings.

'Knight Without Armour' was also the beginning of Miklos Rozsa's association with Korda. Rozsa, a Hungarian, is today one of Hollywood's best-known composers whose work has won many awards; he is also a serious musician whose symphonic and chamber music is played all over the world. It was Jacques Feyder who suggested him for the music of 'Knight' and Korda agreed at once, giving Rozsa a long-term contract.

They became good friends and Rozsa came to know Alex intimately.

"Alexander Korda," the composer wrote to me, "had he been born under different circumstances, would have become beyond doubt a Prime Minister, the President of General Motors or of a Republic. He was born to lead—and a born diplomat who could handle people with dazzling skill. He used his perfect manners, natural charm and superior intelligence to train them as an animal-trainer shapes wild beasts. The technical side of film-making interested him far less than the preparatory stages of a production; the acquisition of funds, the building and organization of studios, the choice of subjects, the combination of political ideas (and through them, various governments), high-level negotiations, combinations with distributors, insurance companies, the foundation of production firms—in other words the whole 'big business' with all its variations and dangers. It would be an exaggeration to say he wasn't interested in success; but I somehow felt that he was always in his true element whenever there was trouble; like the captain of a ship who can only show his mettle when there's a storm. The tougher the situation, the more interested he became to get his threatened enterprise out of a hole or obtain a new private or government loan. Whenever it was simply a matter of persuading people, he knew in advance that his case was won. In the first months of the Second World War Lord Haw-Haw called him the Disraeli of British films; and certainly, there was some similarity between the great statesman, the Empire-builder, and the brilliant juggler who created British film production out of nothing. Both of them possessed a smooth and convincing manner, wit, literary erudition, a deep general intelligence and tremendous persuasive power together with inborn shrewdness. He was loyal to his friends and associates, clinging to them through thick and thin. If he grew fond of someone, his affection lasted a life-time and he defended him against any attack. He ignored the cold and cruel Hollywood yardstick according to which anybody was exactly as good as his last picture. For him a person's value was measured by his worth as a human being . . ."

'Knight Without Armour', presented in the summer of 1937 in the United States and in September in the British cinemas, received high critical praise. Paul Holt pointed out what a truly international effort it was—Korda, Lajos Biro, the scriptwriter and Miklos Rozsa were Hungarians; Marlene Dietrich, German; Robert Donat, James Hilton and Arthur Wimperis (who again worked on the dialogue), British; the technical adviser Zinovieff, Russian; the director, Jacques Feyder, French. There was some trouble with the bath-tub scenes in which Marlene showed a little more of her 'fabulous chassis' than usual—these were actually all cut out in the American version. But this time the box office did not respond to the critics; the picture was only moderately successful and did not earn back its production cost until a considerable time had elapsed.

'The Squeaker' and 'Paradise for Two' were more modest pictures. The first, a well-knit thriller, starred Edmund Lowe, Ann Todd and Sebastian Shaw; the second was a musical with Jack Hulbert, Patricia Ellis and Arthur Riscoe. Both were 'bread-and-butter' films made under Korda's new policy for more modest budgets.

Shortly after the completion of Denham, Victor Savile had a disagreement with Gaumont-British, where he had made a series of successful pictures. His friend Alex was happy to welcome him to his company. Savile formed his own production unit with Joseph Somlo and began work at Denham in 1937. He made four films which were all substantial successes: 'Dark Journey', 'Storm in a Teacup', 'Action for Slander' and—the most important of them—'South Riding.' Korda gave him a pretty free hand; by now Alex was beginning to get cured of the 'itching fingers', the often irresistible impulse to interfere with his directors; or perhaps he trusted Savile's great experience. Even so, when he saw 'Storm in a Tea-Cup', he said: 'Victor, you must spend another £10,000 to make the picture look less good." Probably he felt the settings of this small-town comedy were a little too sophisticated; and though he was 'more British than Churchill', as one of his associates put it, he had a few blind spots, and English humour sometimes puzzled him.

'The Dark Journey' starred Conrad Veidt and Vivien Leigh; 'Storm in a Tea-Cup' had Rex Harrison, again with Miss Leigh as his partner, with Cecil Parker, Sara Allgood and Mervyn Johns. 'Storm' was especially successful in New York—within a few weeks Korda had three of his films showing at the most important cinemas of Broadway. 'Action for Slander' brought Korda's old friend, Clive Brook, to Denham, where he was partnered by Ann Todd, Margaretta Scott and Ronald Squire. It was a polished film which drew praise even from the highly critical Graham Greene.

'South Riding' was beyond doubt Victor Savile's most important picture for Alex. Many people felt doubtful whether Winifred Holtby's fine novel could be transferred to the screen without much being lost—but the result justified Savile's and Korda's faith. It probed deeply into character and disdained the usual facile division into hero and villain, black and white. It was acted by a whole galaxy of brilliant players. It gave Ann Todd one of the finest parts of her career. Edna Best, Ralph Richardson and John Clements gave equally brilliant performances, and in her moving rôle of Midge, Glynis Johns showed what a fine actress she was bound to become. Korda was only the presiding spirit over it all; it was Savile's film but the Denham team of actors, technicians, writers, created by Korda, made it possible.

       ★   ★   ★   ★

The quest for the 'Elephant Boy' began in January 1935, when Robert Flaherty, the eminent documentary director announced that he was looking for an Indian boy who had personality and character in his face—"probably a lad who has worked with elephants and understands them". After a long search his ideal youngster was found by Osmond Borrodaile, the cameraman, in the elephant stables of the Maharajah of Mysore.

The picture took well over a year to shoot and at one time three directors and three cameramen were working on it. Its original budget was £30,000, but when the cost reached £90,000 Alex became somewhat alarmed and sent his brother Zoltan to

G

India. At first Zoltan refused to be associated with the project, but finally agreed to the responsibility. The many months had produced only 2,500 feet of film and another 7,000 were needed. In the end the picture was finished at Denham; even there considerable difficulties arose. The actors had to spend nights and nights in Denham Woods, complete with elephants and distracted assistant directors. Poor Sabu, in a loin-cloth, almost froze in the October cold and had to warm himself between takes at a roaring fire. Alan Jeayes, the veteran actor who appeared in more Korda pictures than almost anybody else (because Alex 'liked his mug') recalled how Korda used to come down in the early hours, complete with walking stick, to encourage his brother. But even the Korda charm could not extract the wayward elephant that got stuck in the river. Robert Flaherty was a great help to all at 4 a.m., with a bottle of whisky in his pocket—and Alex smiled as usual. Finally the elephant was persuaded to move and at 8 a.m. everybody retired to a well-earned rest.

Sabu, the penniless, illiterate youngster, born in the Karapur jungle, became a star in 'Elephant Boy' which won the Venice Prize for the best-directed film and the Cup of the Nations. The eleven-year-old new star was supported by Walter Hudd, Alan Jeayes, W. B. Holloway and Wilfred Hyde White—but the real stars of the film were the elephants themselves. 'Elephant Boy' led to a whole series of films made under the Korda banner which used India for a background.

An ambitious and star-studded picture, 'The Divorce of Lady X', was an expanded remake of the early London Films production, 'Counsel's Opinion'. It starred Merle Oberon, Laurence Olivier and Ralph Richardson with Binnie Barnes, Gertrude Musgrove and Hugh McDermott in the cast. In the tiny part of an office boy Lewis Gilbert, today one of the leading young British film directors, made his début. The picture was later attacked in a book called *The Film Answers Back* (by E. W. and M. M. Robson) for its 'major psychological mistakes' and generally low moral attitude. This was like breaking a butterfly on a wheel—for 'Lady X' wanted to entertain and nothing else; in this it succeeded admirably. To expect from *all* films a realistic attitude, a reproduction of actual life, is absurd. Films, like opera or painting, have their conventions. For one thing, they must be selective; no film can show every detail of its subject or it would be unbearably tedious. I doubt whether Korda took very much notice of high-brow attacks and censures.

He knew very well that he couldn't please everybody all the time. When he produced 'Henry VIII', 'The Scarlet Pimpernel', and 'Sanders of the River', he could do no wrong. Then followed 'Things to Come', 'The Man Who Could Work Miracles' and 'Rembrandt'—and everyone said he was getting too high-brow. So he made 'Knight Without Armour', 'The Squeaker' and 'Action for Slander'—all with a strong popular appeal—and the critics said that they expected better things of a man like Korda. It was significant that in 1937 his most popular picture was not the star-studded 'Knight Without Armour', but the small yet exquisite jungle story, 'Elephant Boy'.

Korda always maintained that there could not be a 'trend' in films; he refused to play follow-my-leader as so many lesser producers have done since the beginning of films. (Someone has success with a picture about racial relations—and there is a whole flock of films about coloured people!) He wanted variety in subjects, in their treatment. In 1936 he was criticized for ignoring the distressed areas, the topical problems of England, and for turning his back on 'indictment and indignation' as portrayed on the screen. Perhaps it was in answer to some of this criticism that Korda (with Erich Pommer producing) made 'Farewell Again', originally called 'Troopship'. The story originated in a true incident of 1936. A troopship put in at Southampton for a few hours with hundreds of British soldiers on their way home after five years' service in India. On the way to the harbour the ship was recalled to the East; after six brief hours she put back to sea with its many scores of disappointed servicemen. It was Wolfgang Wilhelm, the German refugee screen-writer, who saw the possibilities of this incident and wrote an original story based on it.

The film was directed by the Irish-American Tim Whelan; the script was the joint work of Clemence Dane, Patrick Kirwan and Wolfgang Wilhelm. It had a huge cast, headed by Leslie Banks and Flora Robson; but almost every outstanding British character actor seemed to draw a part in it. The film was hailed as a 'small miracle' by one critic; another called it 'one of the best pictures that England has ever made'. The other reviews were equally complimentary and Dilys Powell declared that this picture proved a complete answer to the alarmists who were afraid that the British film industry was dying. Korda had shown that he and his associates could tackle an intensely British subject and do it without a single false note. In a way, this was his 'naturalization film'.

Equally successful was 'The Drum'—though the *Left Review* denounced it as a 'further prostitution of Robert Flaherty's discovery, Sabu . . . The Korda brothers have skilfully timed the completion of a sop to the decayed romanticism of the Empire's outposts.' It is rather doubtful whether Alex or Zoltan Korda had anything of the sort in mind.

Besides Sabu and Roger Livesey, whose performance was singled out for special praise, 'The Drum' marked the début of a new star, Valerie Hobson.

She was eighteen and had just come back from Hollywood when she met Alex at a studio party. He asked her whether she would make a test for him and of course, she agreed. When she got to the studio, she found, somewhat to her surprise, that it was as a singing and dancing star she was to be tested. She performed some Ginger Rogerish numbers for the camera and waited for the verdict.

Finally she was told that the test was most satisfactory—but that Alex had decided she should become a dramatic actress . . . And so he put her in 'The Drum'.

Miss Hobson, who became one of the most versatile British

film-stars, was apparently a most level-headed and self-possessed young lady before she came of age. "Alex and I had a lot of arguments," she told me. "Somehow I puzzled him. He used to tell me: 'You've no business to *know* so much at eighteen!' For him I was someone quite different from American, even English girls. He couldn't quite understand that I had my own ideas about my work and future . . . In a way I was fond of him— but I didn't *like* him very much . . ."

Still, Miss Hobson went on making films for Korda or his organization for quite a while—and later, as Korda aged and mellowed, found that she had far more understanding and sympathy for him.

In addition to Sabu, Roger Livesey and Valerie Hobson, 'The Drum' starred Raymond Massey in one of his sinister Indian rôles with Francis L. Sullivan, Leo Genn (as a blind beggar), Ralph Truman, Esmond Knight, Amid Taftazani (a genuine Egyptian actor), Edward Underdown and Bernard Miles in the large cast. Truman had the somewhat frustrating experience of spending weeks and weeks in the studio, only to find that in the end his contribution to the picture had been reduced to a single —and appreciative—*belch* after a sumptuous meal.

The film grossed £170,000 in the United States and it won the City of Venice Cup at the International Film Festival in September 1938. India liked it much less; in several cities it was banned. In Bombay there were even riots, and finally the local government asked the British Board of Censors that, in future, reports should be submitted before the release of any British film in which Indian life was prominently depicted. 'The Drum' was the first Korda picture which showed how colour *should* be used; its restrained but effective employment contributed a good deal to the film's success.

The other Korda pictures of this period—with the notable exception of 'Four Feathers'—were less successful. For 'The First and the Last' (later re-titled 'Twenty-One Days') Alex brought the veteran stage and film director Basil Dean into his organization. He gave him an excellent cast—Leslie Banks, Laurence Olivier and Vivien Leigh headed it. But the production ran into difficulties.

One day Dean was working on a big set, shooting a scene with Olivier and Vivien Leigh. His schedule called for remaining on the same set for at least a week. In the middle of the morning Korda sent for him. There was a long, desultory conversation about the weather, politics and other general topics. Finally Dean began to fidget and explained that he was in the middle of shooting.

"Well, Basil," Korda said, "I'm afraid I have bad news for you. That set must be struck tomorrow—we need the stage . . ."

"B—but . . ." Dean was taken aback, "we were going to stay on it for another week or more . . ."

"Never mind . . . go and do something else. You have exteriors to shoot, haven't you? Just rearrange your schedule . . ."

Dean did as he was told though it cost a lot of money. He didn't know, of course, that Olivier and Miss Leigh had gone to Korda and told him—they very much wanted to go to Elsinore, to play 'Hamlet'. And Korda had said that they could go. When they returned, the set was rebuilt and production continued. The finished film did not please Korda but later it was taken over and released by Columbia.

'Over the Moon', scripted by Robert Sherwood, starred Merle Oberon and Rex Harrison with Zena Dare, Ursula Jeans, Herbert Lomas and a large supporting cast. When, years later, I talked to Rex Harrison about this and other pictures he had made at Denham, he wasn't very complimentary about Korda as a director—though he had been one of Alex's personal friends. True, Harrison had only been directed by him for a week; but he thought Korda's methods did not suit his own talents. Alex was too dominant a personality, Harrison said, he gave no latitude to an artist's interpretation. This, Harrison added, might be his personal view and others might feel differently. Indeed, Mr. Harrison had a dissenting opinion in his own family. I talked to him in the presence of his wife, Kay Kendall, and she protested instantly. "Alex directed me once—for three hours," she said. "It was heaven! I never felt so much in tune, so happy with any other director!" I must confess that in the end I left the famous couple to fight *this* one out among themselves.

Repeats and sequels are seldom as successful as originals. This was the fate of 'The Return of the Pimpernel', produced by Arnold Pressburger, in which Barry K. Barnes replaced Leslie Howard as Baroness Orczy's formidable hero. Sophie Stewart played Lady Blakeney and James Mason had a minor part as Talien. Perhaps it was made too soon after the original; in any case, it did not repeat the first 'Pimpernel's' success.

*   *   *   *

In May 1938 Irving Asher, the American producer, resigned his position as production chief of Warner Brothers' Teddington Studios and joined Korda as associate producer at Denham. The two men, utterly different in character, became efficient teammates. Asher, who had a very pronounced Mid-Western drawl, liked to tease Alex about *his* English. Once he picked up a phone in Korda's office and demanded, dead-pan: "Does this phone talk with an accent?"

In August 1938, Columbia Pictures made arrangements to produce a series of British films at Denham, and Asher was appointed head of production for Columbia, though he remained associate producer for London Films. 'Q Planes', 'The Spy in Black', 'Prison Without Bars', 'The Challenge' and several others were made under this arrangement. These were not, strictly speaking, London Films productions but they were produced, directed and acted by Korda's executives and contract artists. And Alex, of course, couldn't entirely keep his fingers out of them.

Brock Williams, the well-known screen-writer, went to Denham with Irving Asher. For weeks nothing happened—then one day Korda sent for him.

"I hear you're an expert on India," he said. "I'd like you to write a story for Sabu."

Williams had to admit, regretfully, that he had never been near the place. Alex seemed to be a little surprised but didn't insist. Again a few weeks passed and there was another summons.

"I've just seen a newspaper story," he told Williams. "About a plane that went up—and never came down. I think it would make a good film."

"What happened?" asked Williams.

"How should I know?" replied Korda, a little testily. "It's for you to work out the rest of the story . . ."

Brock Williams had his doubts—but he went away and started to write. Once again he returned to Korda and asked him what cast would be available for the picture? "Oh, I don't know," Alex said, "what about Valerie Hobson, Olivier and Ralph Richardson?" Williams was delighted—he had never expected such a galaxy of stars. Korda told him to take his time—which again was a new and delightful experience for Williams, who was used to doing screen-plays in a month or less, harassed by small-budget producers.

In 'Q Planes' he created the figure of Major Hammond, the rather lackadaisical Secret Service man whom Ralph Richardson brought to life as a delightful scatterbrain. Korda liked 'Hammond' and told Williams that he could 'have him'—use the figure for other films, books or plays. It was only months later that Williams discovered—Alex had forgotten about this promise and had 'given' the same character to some other writer. By then he had written 50,000 words of a novel—still drawing his salary. Then war broke out; the salary stopped and Williams went home —without finishing the novel.

Another director who joined Korda in 1938 was Desmond Brian Hurst. He was working at Associated British when Alex sent for him and offered him more money than he had ever been paid. Hurst was staggered, went back to his employers, telling them that he'd be glad to stay—if they gave him half of what Korda had offered. But they wouldn't—so he went to Alex.

His contract was for three pictures, but only one ('Prison Without Bars', one of the many versions of 'Mädchen in Uniform') was actually made. This starred Corinne Luchaire, who later became rather notorious as a collaborationist in Vichy France; Barry K. Barnes, Edna Best, Martita Hunt, Mary Morris and Glynis Johns also had important parts in the picture.

The producers were worried about costs and Hurst was told to hurry with the shooting. There was a production conference in Korda's office and he agreed that speed was necessary. When the discussion ended, he called back Hurst and said, with a smile: "Brian, you do not hurry—you make a good picture—take extra two weeks . . ."

The film ran into trouble and Hurst, an outspoken man, had a fight with Asher. Losing his temper, he told the producer in no uncertain terms what he thought of him. Asher went to Korda to complain about 'insubordination'. Alex sent for Hurst and began to talk about politics, the latest play—everything except the matter in hand. Then he rang for his secretary and asked for a large sheet of paper and a pair of scissors. While Hurst watched him, puzzled, he started to fold the paper, made various cuts and then held up the result—a swastika.

"This is a trick the Duke of Kent taught me," he said. "You like it?" Then he added, as an afterthought: "Now, Brian, be a good boy—do not tell your producer to go and drown himself. It's better to apologize; because, you see, he won't drown himself, anyhow."

Hurst, who had put it a little more strongly, laughed and promised to be a good boy. Later he was put to work preparing a picture on Lawrence of Arabia. (He was well qualified for it; he spoke Arabic and had known Lawrence personally.) One day as he was deep in work, surrounded by books, letters, newspaper cuttings, Korda wandered into his office. "Brian," he asked, "have you any nice idea for a thriller? We need one for Clive Brook."

The director looked up. "I must have notice of that question," he said and went back to his research. Alex retired meekly; nothing was ever heard of the Clive Brook picture. On the other hand, nothing ever came of 'Lawrence of Arabia', which Korda announced for 'imminent production' half a dozen times.

Colonel Lawrence also haunted John Clements, who starred in the highly successful 'Four Feathers'. He had played minor parts in earlier pictures—but this was his first great chance. The reason for his rather belated emergence as a full-fledged star was a long-drawn-out argument about his contract.

Following his success in 'Knight Without Armour' Clements was offered a long-term exclusive engagement. But he was far more interested in the theatre and refused to tie himself down. The lawyers came back with much improved terms. He still refused. Finally Korda sent for him.

"I hear we've offered you a contract, my boy," he said, "and that you've refused it. How much did they offer you?" he went on, without waiting for an answer. "Don't tell me—double it!"

This was so typically the big tycoon that Clements had to laugh. Then he explained that it wasn't the money; he just wanted to go on acting on the stage. Korda showed considerable understanding and finally a contract was worked out that demanded only twenty weeks of each year of his time. "The money was big —so big I just couldn't afford to refuse it," Clements told me.

Three times he was notified that he would be playing Lawrence of Arabia. Twice this was followed by the announcement that Leslie Howard or Robert Donat would play the part. It all became something of a joke. He was cast in the ill-fated 'I Claudius' as Valens, Messalina's lover. He had his costumes made, there were a few rehearsals—but his part was never shot. Then came 'Four Feathers'. Clements travelled out to Cairo—only to find a telegram from Zoltan Korda at his hotel saying that there was no hurry. So he had a pleasant time exploring Luxor and the

Pyramids. He had to store up energy; the eight weeks in the Sudanese desert were gruelling enough.

One night he was in his tent, washing off the grime of his disguise as the blind beggar who slips into Khartoum. The tent flap opened and Zoltan Korda came in. Without a word, he took a cable from his pocket and handed it to Clements. It was from Alex and it instructed them both to stay on in Egypt in readiness to begin 'Lawrence of Arabia'. Clements looked at Zoltan; neither of them said a word. Clements handed back the telegram and continued his ablutions. Neither of them heard anything again about the project—at least, not for months. Then, when Clements returned to London, Alex discussed what he had in mind for him. There were three possible rôles—one of them 'Lawrence of Arabia'.

"Now, look, Alex, you don't really mean it, do you?" protested Clements.

Korda sighed. "No, I don't," he said. "I can't make the picture—not as long as the Turks are our friends. Now, if someone would just start a little war to bring them to the other side . . ."

'Four Feathers' was based on A. E. W. Mason's novel; R. C. Sherriff wrote the screen-play and John Clements was co-starred with Ralph Richardson, C. Aubrey Smith and the charming June Duprez. The settings were designed by Vincent Korda, it was photographed by Georges Perinal; Charles David was associate producer. The editor was Henry Cornelius, who became one of our best-known directors until his untimely death in 1958.

The film was extremely well received; Guy Morgan ranked it as one of the four best pictures ever made. J. Brooks Wilkinson, Secretary of the British Board of Film Censors, told Korda: "The British nation should be grateful to you for producing such a film at such a time, Mr. Korda." A left-wing paper thought differently: "The reason for Alexander Korda's continuation of production of films which seek to justify Imperialist policies, becomes very clear when it is realized that his principal backer is the Prudential Assurance Company . . . It is a justification for the policy of appeasement and a place in the sun for aggressive dictators . . ."

If the writer had known how much Alex hated the dictators— all of them—perhaps he would have been less denunciatory. Or again, perhaps not.

*   *   *   *

The crisis deepened. The film trade continued its rather pointless arguments whether the world wanted to see pictures based on British prestige and traditions—or 'international spectacles', no matter where they were made. Korda had very decided opinions on this problem:

> "Our difficulty is that you cannot convey a proper sense of the British spirit unless you go down to the roots," he said in an interview in May, 1938. "Roots strike deep into history and may be very local things. In America, where the roots are near the surface, they are not easily interested in what lies deep down in other countries—and unless we can interest America there may be no great market for our films. The most definite phases of life in this country, for screen purposes, are not local but national. We can occasionally produce a film like Michael Powell's 'The Edge of the World', which is a first-rate epic of local life, but I think that we are compelled, as far as world markets are concerned, to stick to stories based on broad issues of national life. However, I'm not going to dogmatize about it; all that I can say, based on screen experience, is that stories that dig deep into national roots start with a handicap."

In June 1937, on his return from one of his numerous American visits, he announced a film called 'Tempest Within', starring

Merle Oberon, 'Four Feathers', 'Mutiny in the Mountains' (this
became later 'The Drum'), 'Bicycle Made for Two' (which was
never made) and 'Playboy' with Jack Hulbert, Patricia Ellis and
Rex Harrison—which ended up as 'Over the Moon'. A year
later, coming back from New York in May, he spoke of 'Prison
Without Bars', 'Four Feathers', a third film, with Lynn Fontanne
and Alfred Lunt, 'Calcutta', an original story by A. E. W. Mason,
to star Sabu and to be directed by Michael Powell; and the peren-
nial 'Lawrence of Arabia'. He pointed proudly to his three
pictures running simultaneously on Broadway, with 'The Divorce
of Lady X' and 'Paradise for Two' doing especially well. He
also said that in the future he would be primarily interested
"in actors and not stars. Few stars are worth their salaries. The
only thing that matters about a star is whether he or she is a
good actor or actress." On this point he must have changed his
mind rather rapidly, for in the previous September he had said: "To
have a star, the right star, is safety—insurance. You pay for that.
No star in the world is worth what he or she gets for the work
done in the film. But like any other well-advertised merchandise,
the star is worth extra money because of the goodwill he or she
carries with filmgoers . . ." Or maybe the two views are not
opposed to each other, merely different expressions of the same
basic idea. Certainly, Korda seldom made a film without the
sort of 'insurance' he talked about.

Korda was waging a crusade, acting as a missionary, preaching
his faith in British films. In January 1938 a leading article in the
Daily Sketch acknowledged these efforts. It was headed 'THANK
YOU, MR. KORDA!' and continued:

"Thank you for—

1. Refusing to be pessimistic about the future of British
films.

2. For saying that there is too much talk about 'bad'
British films.

3. For emphasizing that there is no feeling among American audiences against British films merely because they are British.

4. For boldly announcing a brave £1,800,000 scheme for film production in Britain—and

5. For telling the world that the real enemies of British films are the British producers who send bad British films to America."

Although, as the *Manchester Guardian* pointed out, Korda had never permitted setbacks to upset him, the struggle was hard and the fight was taking its toll. Korda hadn't had a real holiday in seven years. Once he went away for a rest with a friend—and then discussed film scripts the whole time. Now his hair was turning grey and he was beginning to show the strain.

He told his associates that he wanted to lie unmolested in the sun and think about nothing at all—particularly not about pictures. Between October 1936 and 1937 his company had finished or nearly finished seventeen films; the artistic, financial and administrative tasks were beginning to weigh heavily upon him. Yet by the spring of 1938 he was buoyant and full of fight again.

Many of his friends told me that he always spoke about being 'terribly tired', 'completely exhausted'. Some of this was no doubt a pose—but gradually the pose was becoming reality.

One day he sent for Victor Savile. "Victor," he said, "I'm tired. I can't carry on. I want you to take over the studio. You'll be the boss. Of course, I'll give you all the help I can—but I want to retire."

Savile said nothing; he thought it was a joke. But Korda summoned all the studio heads, the various department chiefs, and introduced Savile to them as the new chief. They all received the announcement quietly, neither protesting nor expressing particular enthusiasm.

Next day Savile came to the studio and went to his usual office. He never heard of Korda's retirement again; nor had he expected to.

Though Korda often spoke of his desire for a peaceful and serene old age, he really hated the idea.

During the making of 'Hobson's Choice', he met Laughton again, for the first time in several years.

"We're both growing old, Charles," he said.

"Yes—and I'm glad," the actor replied. "I don't want to go through *that* again. These are the good years, Alex."

"What's good about them?" Korda said, almost savagely, and walked away.

* * * *

The crisis did not rise to any violent climax; yet Korda came to another parting of the ways. The liabilities of London Films had reached about £1,000,000. The Prudential was both chief shareholder and chief creditor. Korda carried on his gallant battle and managed again and again to extract new support from his backers. But in the end he was beaten. He had to give up the great Denham studios he had built himself—which, in three brief years, had created a tradition of great names and films. To the Prudential it seemed that the studios were the only tangible assets of London Films worth taking. A highly complicated deal was arranged between J. Arthur Rank, Richard Norton, C. M. Woolf, Korda and the insurance company, and a new company, D. & P. Studios Ltd., was created which took both Pinewood and Denham into its possession.

Montague Marks, who had left Korda some time before (and joined Douglas Fairbanks sr.) told me that there had been a simple 'fading-out' of the Prudential interest, mostly because of the international situation and the ever-increasing threat of war. For Korda it must have been a great blow to lose his empire. When he returned from Hollywood in February 1939, the

Denham-Pinewood merger had already been completed. Talking to the press, Korda said nothing about his disappointment; he spoke about the films he planned—'The Thief of Baghdad', 'Jungle Book'—both with Sabu; he also hinted that he might do some films in Hollywood.

Yet the loss of Denham rankled deeply. He felt it was his greatest failure. "Every time I travel along the Oxford road," he told a journalist later, "I look for the sign that says: 'To Denham Studios'. The sign is no longer there—for Denham is dead. Sold. That is my greatest defeat, indeed . . ."

With the studios he had to give up the majority of the shares of London Films; but he kept the laboratories and, after some years, was to buy back all the films which he had made with the Prudential backing.

I asked Monty Marks what was the real upshot of this episode in Korda's career? How much had the great insurance company lost?

"I wanted to find out myself," Mr. Marks replied, "so I asked somebody who ought to know—someone fairly high up in the company. And he told me they hadn't lost a farthing."

This sounded a little unlikely to me; when, later, I discussed the matter with a well-known film executive, he cried out in pained protest: "No! don't rob me of my faith! I've nursed all these years the happy belief that Korda had taken big finance for a ride—that for once a producer got away with making pictures as he wanted to make them, with somebody else footing the bill . . . I *want* to go on believing that the Pru lost three or four million pounds . . ."

I was sorry to disappoint him; but as far as careful and thorough investigation can make out, the informant of Mr. Marks was right. The total investment of the Prudential was around £1,100,000. For this they kept Denham Studios, which during the war were let at a comfortably high rent and later sold. They had the preference shares in London Films and any income the pictures still yielded. And it was through Korda and Marks that they made another, far more lucrative investment in British Technicolor. So, as it happened with most of Korda's financial backers, they had no reason to complain in the long run. The loser was Korda who, for the third or fourth time in his life, had to start afresh.

CHAPTER IX

KORDA GOES TO WAR

WHILE the financial backing of the Prudential had petered out and he had to work at Denham as a tenant instead of a landlord, Korda had no intention of giving up film-making. In February 1939 he announced that he would be making 'The Thief of Baghdad' and a Merle Oberon film at his former studio, and that his plans included making two pictures a year in Hollywood. Shooting on 'The Thief' began in the late spring.

About the same time he was busy denying that he was married to Merle Oberon—but he didn't 'exclude the possibility'. The marriage took place on June 3rd at Antibes Town Hall; the witnesses were Henri Guenod, President of the Antibes Travel & Development Association, and Maître Suzanne Blum, a French woman-barrister.

When, almost twenty years later, I asked Miss Oberon to put down her memories of Alex, she wrote from Hollywood:

"I am no writer—I shall not attempt to do so. However, I am sure you must know that my opinion of Alex was and is and always will be that he was one of the finest human beings I've ever known . . ."

★　　★　　★　　★

In 'The Thief of Baghdad' Korda made another star—John Justin.

Justin was the last man to be tested for the lead. He didn't believe for a moment he'd get it. He was in a play and had only done small bits in pictures. So he hammed the test—flexing his muscles, showing off his torso as if he were trying to become Tarzan Number Eleven. Greatly to his surprise, he was chosen for the rôle of Ahmad.

As soon as the contract was signed, the various departments went to work on Justin. They decided that things had to be done to his nose, his eyebrows, his hair—to all of which he submitted meekly. But then the question of his name came up. He liked his own and didn't want it to be changed (as the publicity department wished) to something like Michael Steel or John Ironside. (They were looking for something that would give the impression of strength.) For weeks the argument raged and Justin was getting angrier and angrier about it. Finally he told John Ware, the assistant chief of publicity, that he wouldn't stand for it—either they left his name alone or he would quit.

"Just be patient," Ware replied. "We'll work out something."

Finally there was another production conference and at the end of it Ware came out, grinning broadly. "It's all right, John, you can keep your name," he told Justin.

"But how did you manage it?"

Ware burst out laughing. "Well, your name came up again— as it has, regularly, for the last six weeks—and everybody had his own ideas. Then Alex walked in and asked what we were discussing. We told him. 'Yes, yes,' he said, 'we must give the boy a name.' So I spoke up: 'What about Justin, Mr. Korda? John Justin?' Alex rolled it around his tongue. 'Justin? Yes, that is good. John Justin. Yes, that is even better. You're a bright boy, Ware.' "

But there were other difficulties. Korda had brought over Ludwig Berger, the veteran German director, to do the picture. Unfortunately he didn't like the way Berger worked and there were many arguments and quarrels.

One day Alex was berating Berger and Berger was on the point of exploding. So was Justin. He leapt to his feet and decided to give them a piece of his mind. At that moment somebody yelled: "Lunch break!" Justin's fury disappeared—which was perhaps lucky for him.

Nicholas Rozsa, whose music for 'Four Feathers' had been acclaimed by the critics, also worked on 'The Thief of Baghdad'.

Alex sent for him and said: "My boy, our next picture is a most important musical job and I want you to do it." Rozsa thanked him for his confidence and waited for the contract. It was the spring of 1939 and there was a great deal of confusion around the studio. Korda had founded his own company; war was threatening and one director after the other was sacked as they were found unsuitable by the new financial backers. The script consisted of a few loose pages—yet the film had to be started at a certain date. Somebody different would have been plunged into despair by all this; but the greater the trouble, Rozsa recalled, the brighter the smile on Alex's face and the longer the cigars between his teeth.

Ludwig Berger had directed a successful French musical and when Alex signed him up for 'The Thief', he stipulated that the songs in the picture should be composed by the same Viennese maestro who had worked with him on his last film. He agreed reluctantly that Rozsa should contribute the orchestral background music—once the picture was finished.

Korda sent for Rozsa and explained that the film had to go on the floor and so he was forced to accede to Berger's demands. "Just leave everything to me, my boy," he added. And Rozsa did.

The ageing Viennese composer lived in Vichy; the songs he wrote for 'The Thief of Baghdad' arrived by mail. They were waltzes, arias and ensembles in the style of early Viennese operettas. All this for an Oriental fable—in 1939.

Muir Mathieson, the musical director of the studio, was frantic. With his broad Scottish accent he explained to everybody that the music would ruin the film. Of course, his unvarnished opinions soon reached the ears of Alex and Berger. One day Mathieson and Rozsa were summoned to Alex's office.

"What's the matter?" they asked his secretary.

"I don't know, but he's awful mad," she replied.

The next moment the door opened and they entered the room. Alex sat behind his huge desk, looking like Jupiter the Thunderer; Berger stood in a corner with a triumphant grin, looking like Alberich of the *Ring*. There was deep silence. Finally Alex spoke.

"Boys," he said tonelessly, "I want you to understand that Mr. Berger is in charge of *all* artistic operations regarding the 'Thief of Baghdad'. He alone will decide what music will go into the picture and you will have to follow his wishes, whether you like it or not. That's all."

Rozsa and Mathieson stood there like shamed schoolboys. Mr. Berger left with a smile of triumph. Mathieson gritted his teeth and Rozsa was about to follow him through the door when he felt a tug at his sleeve. It was Alex.

"Come back," he said. "What's that music like?"

"Awful. Third-rate Viennese *schmaltz*."

"All right," said Alex with a smile. "Go home and do every number afresh but don't tell anybody. I've got to start this film —otherwise we can't pay any wages next week. I can't make it without Berger. That's why I must accept everything he wants —for the time being. When you've done your work, come back."

In two weeks Rozsa composed the new songs and hurried to Alex. "It's done," he panted. "Good," said Alex. "I'm giving you an office with a piano—next door to Berger's. You must play your pieces over and over again, all day—so he can hear them."

For almost a week Rozsa played his songs from morning to evening. Finally Berger fell for the bait. "What are you playing?" he asked.

"Oh, I'm just improvising on a few ideas I had for the picture,' the composer replied.

"Would you play it for me again?"

Rozsa did; Berger listened in silence, then left without a word. An hour later Alex phoned the composer that he had made an appointment next day for him to see Sir Robert Vansittart, who was to write the lyrics. Berger had capitulated and it was *he* who suggested to Alex that Rozsa should compose the songs.

That was how Rozsa's long collaboration with the future Lord Vansittart began. A little later the Paris *Figaro* published an article declaring that France was happy to hear that the chief diplomatic adviser of the Foreign Office had the leisure to write lyrics. Obviously that meant no imminent danger of war. The date was August 1939 . . .

"Vansittart and Alex were close friends," Nicholas Rozsa told me, "but after this experience I was sure that Korda was giving Sir Robert lessons in diplomacy and not the other way round!"

Berger couldn't finish the picture and Korda was unable to pay the full sum agreed. "I promise to pay the rest as soon as the film has earned its cost," he told the director. Somewhat reluctantly, Berger agreed.

The war separated them. Berger had a difficult and dangerous time in German-occupied Europe. It wasn't until 1948 that he visited England again and called on Korda.

"Just wait a moment," Alex told him, and disappeared. Berger waited, a little puzzled. In ten minutes Korda returned. "I've checked our books," he said. " 'Thief of Baghdad' has made a fair profit. Here's what I owe you—and a little over."

And he handed the dazed Berger a cheque for £2,000.

*   *   *   *

Korda had no illusions about the dictators. Late in August 1939 his old friend Andor Zsoldos visited him in London. Alex was having trouble with his eyes and he was in a bad temper. The world seemed to be full of fear. Suddenly he said:

"Do you remember Ferrer's execution—almost thirty years ago? When I climbed on that table outside the Café Abbazia . . . to protest . . . to rouse the world? What could I do today? War is coming—maybe tomorrow, maybe next week . . ."

"Oh no, it won't!" Zsoldos protested violently. "It can't, Alex!"

Korda smiled and shrugged. "It can, Andor," he said. "You're still the President of the Self-Improvement Circle—but I'm no longer the secretary of the Literary Section!"

Because of his friends in high places and because of the unofficial and unorthodox intelligence work London Films was doing, Alex had known very well that war was unavoidable—ever since Munich. He knew that Europe, his beloved continent, was doomed and that the beauty and gaiety of his youth and middle age would disappear with it. He had so many friends for whom he was anxious; who he knew might be engulfed in the darkness and horror.

On that September day when Neville Chamberlain announced that Great Britain was at war with Germany, some of Korda's closest friends and associates were in his office. His wife, his brothers, Sir David Cunynghame—who had worked with him ever since the early Paramount days in Paris—and Miles Malleson, the distinguished actor and writer.

Merle Oberon broke down and cried. Korda comforted her but his voice carried little conviction. Everybody was moved and a little afraid—not of defeat and disaster but of the unknown.

Korda was half-way through his picture—rather in the position of a man who has put one foot through a trouser-leg when the ceiling collapses on him. Most of the studios were immediately requisitioned; only a few escaped this fate by the end of the war. Of those in operation at the outbreak of hostilities only two remained open out of a total of sixteen.

Miles Malleson had been collaborating with Lajos Biro on the script of 'The Thief of Baghdad', writing the part of the Sultan for himself. Their partnership was a happy one but they made very slow progress because of the repeated changes of directors. In the middle of the work Malleson had to go to the States for six weeks to appear in a play. When he left, they had reached page 85 of the script. When he returned, he found that they were still on page 86!

But at last the screenplay was finished. Malleson had a rather uncomfortable time during an early air-raid alarm. In the film he was riding a horse—high up in the air. Of course, this was done on a trick-horse, suspended on guy ropes. When the siren went, all the technicians, conditioned by weeks of air-raid drill, departed—leaving him high and dry. He felt most vulnerable and conspicuous, hanging in mid-air for quite a while before someone remembered him and saved him from his perilous perch.

*   *   *   *

Korda's first thought was how he could best serve his adopted country. He had been anxious to make a British propaganda film ever since the days of Munich; but his own organization opposed it—fearing that any political stand taken by a film company would hurt the chances of its costly and important feature pictures.

Even now he could find no financial backing for his plans. But within four days of the outbreak of the war he had raised money on his life insurance policy and went into production with 'The Lion Has Wings'. The story was by Ian Dalrymple, who came to Korda when Denham was built. There were three directors: Michael Powell, Brian Desmond Hurst and Adrian Brunel. There was no question of the usual leisurely Korda methods; the actual shooting was completed in twelve days and the picture finished in five weeks. Its cost was about £30,000.

It began with a picture of Britain at peace, a sequence of fields ready for the harvest, of new factories and the leisurely pursuit of sport—an idyllic picture which ignored the existence of slums and distressed areas.

Then came a contrasting image of Nazi Germany, parades, banners, Hitler's frantic speeches, mass hysteria and the frenzy of war. There were pictures of the very early days of the conflict,

seen especially from the angle of the R.A.F., with the climax of
the famous and successful Kiel Canal Raid. The R.A.F. and the
Air Ministry collaborated whole-heartedly—even to the extent
of lending one of the only two Spitfires then in existence!

Never before or since could a British documentary boast of
such an all-star cast. Ralph Richardson and Merle Oberon headed
a brilliant group of players, including June Duprez, Raymond
Huntley, Brian Worth, Robert Douglas, Anthony Bushell,
Derrick de Marney, Miles Malleson, Ronald Shiner, Bernard
Miles, Flora Robson and Milton Rosmer.

'The Lion Has Wings' was dubbed into French and shown in
France, Belgium and Switzerland. It was sub-titled for exhibition
in Spain, Portugal, Holland and the Scandinavian countries. It
was extremely well received; within a month of its completion
it was playing in two hundred British cinemas and afterwards
received extensive bookings in New Zealand, Australia, Japan,
Canada and South America.

The Germans were furious about it. They managed to get hold
of a print in a Lisbon laboratory, copying it secretly, and it was
flown to Berlin. Soon there came threats over the German radio
to 'bomb Denham out of existence'.

Steven Pallos was sent with a copy to Rome during the brief
few months when Italy hadn't yet entered the war. He had the
important mission of arranging some private showings—
especially for the top-rank Fascist officials. Through a personal
friend he was introduced to Ciano, who saw the film and arranged
for Mussolini to view it. Later there was a showing at the British
Embassy in Rome to which the cream of Italian society was
invited.

One night Pallos was sitting in the Excelsior bar with some
Italian friends when Udet, the German air ace, deputy of Milch,
who commanded the Luftwaffe, walked in. He was in full dress
uniform with a double row of decorations; Mackensen, the
German Ambassador to Rome, was giving a dinner party in one
of the private dining-rooms.

Udet, one of the greatest stunt-flyers of all times, had worked for Korda when 'Conquest of the Air' was being made and Pallos knew him well. They looked at each other for a moment; it was an awkward situation, citizens of two countries at war meeting on neutral ground. Then Udet walked over to Pallos and greeted him most effusively. Pallos, a little embarrassed, could do nothing but return his greetings. Udet asked about mutual friends.

"Why is the German radio broadcasting all those threats?" Pallos asked after a while. "Why do you want to bomb Denham?"

"Because you have made that terrible film—about the Lion and its Wings," Udet replied. "The Führer is very angry. He's so angry, he's stopped showing that other picture of yours which he liked so much . . ."

Pallos knew which film the flyer was referring to. No picture made by London Films was ever exhibited in Nazi Germany. But a copy of 'Fire Over England' had been 'captured' in Prague when the Germans marched in. And apparently Adolf Hitler fell in love with it. Several prominent Englishmen who had visited him brought back news of the Führer running 'Fire Over England' again and again and praising it lavishly.

"Well, you've made a film about your Polish campaign," Pallos said. "We had to do something, too . . ."

"I suppose so," Udet agreed surprisingly. "But he's still very angry . . ."

This was perhaps the most glowing testimonial given to 'The Lion Has Wings' which, made hastily, was no masterpiece but served its purpose admirably. Every artist, from Ralph Richardson and Flora Robson downwards to the smallest bit player was paid the same fee—£5. But when the picture started to make money, every actor was compensated fully and received a warm letter of thanks from Alex.

*   *   *   *

The phoney war dragged on and Korda began to realize that it would be extremely difficult for him to continue film-making in Britain. In January 1940 he flew to the States to publicize 'The Lion Has Wings', which he did with great success. Already in February 1939 he had said that he planned to make pictures in Hollywood. The parable of the sausage-factories and sausage-shops was still valid. The pictures of London Films had great moral triumphs in the United States and made money; but not enough money. The answer was to produce pictures in America —if not an entire programme, at least some of them. Korda still had his distribution contract with United Artists and during that brief visit in January his decision must have been taken. There was a personal reason: after finishing her part in 'The Lion' Merle Oberon had flown to Hollywood to take up her contract with Warners. Zoltan Korda went later but before Alex, to finish 'The Thief of Baghdad'.

Today, almost twenty years after the events, the bitterness and hostility around the exodus to America seem to have died down, the arguments are almost forgotten. Yet, as Sir Michael Balcon told me, in those days there was plenty of both. 'Gone With the Wind Up' was about the kindest thing said about the stars, directors and producers who preferred the safety of California to the besieged island-fortress. Some had actually left months before the German attack on Poland. Others pulled up stakes when Hitler's armies overran Europe. Sir Michael and many others felt especially bitter about a few prominent refugees from Nazi tyranny who had been befriended in Britain, given the chance to start new careers—and then hastily decamped when the bombs began to fall. Having lived through the war in London, I can well understand this attitude; but I can also see the point of view of people like Conrad Veidt and Elisabeth Bergner, who realized that if a successful invasion took place, *they* would hardly find a place on the few ships evacuating V.I.P.s to Canada. It was a question of nerves and of faith.

Michael Balcon called the British film personalities who had gone to America 'deserters' and his attack, published in the *Sunday Dispatch*, pulled no punches.

Was Alexander Korda a 'deserter'? Did he run away?

I don't think so. Neither does Sir Michael today, though he told me that he had felt very bitter at that time about Alex going to Hollywood.

The two producers once had a long argument. Sir Michael could not budge his friend and opponent from his attitude; so, in final exasperation, he said:

"But, Alex, we had a gentlemen's agreement!"

"Ah, but Mickey, you need two gentlemen for that!" replied Korda.

When Sir Michael recalled the story, he added, a little pensively: "I wonder which of us he meant . . ."

I asked about twenty people who were closely connected with Korda in those fateful months of 1939–40. Unanimously they said that it was unthinkable—that Korda had never run away from anything in his life.

I spoke to several of his intimates who were with him during the terrible days of the fall of France, the beginning of the long night that descended upon Europe. He was deeply distressed, especially because there were so many friends of his behind the barbed wire of Hitler's vast concentration camp. He worried about their fate and indeed, a good many perished. Perhaps he had moods of depression; he certainly realized that the struggle would be long and would cost millions of lives.

But it wasn't his personal safety that concerned him—though he was fairly high up on the Nazi Black List (and very proud to be on it). If it ever had, he wouldn't have made so many war-time crossings of the Atlantic, all of them hazardous, most of them very uncomfortable.

In 1941 there was another attack on him—Frank Owen had written an article about the 'Hollywood Exiles' in the *Evening Standard*. Adrian Brunel sent the cutting to Korda, and Alex replied in April, 1941:

"I was very interested in the article," he wrote. "I can really say very little about it. I left England really because there was absolutely nothing for me to do, however hard I tried. I hope that when I return, which I expect will be very shortly—either in June or July—that things will be a bit better in this direction."

This was perhaps the simplest, most straightforward reason he could give—there was 'absolutely nothing for me to do'. Nor was his departure exactly precipitate. He was still in England in June 1940—and, of course, he did not spend the whole time of the war away. By 1943 he was back in London permanently as production chief of British M-G-M.–London Films Ltd., and he made many trips to England in between.

But did Korda go—or was he sent? There are many of his friends who assured me of the second alternative. London Films and its chief had done a certain amount of economic intelligence work before the war. I spoke to some Hungarians who had asked him to be a go-between when Hungarian liberal elements wanted British support in their fight against the Arrow Cross, the Hungarian brand of Nazis. Alex had a huge circle of friends and acquaintances, a widespread web of contacts. Perhaps if Lord Bracken hadn't died after his long illness, I could offer a more detailed answer to the question. He was one of Alex's closest friends—according to some people *the* closest. They were kindred souls, both witty, cynical, worldly-wise, tremendous workers, with strong loyalties. They both had a deep and enduring admiration for Britain's wartime leader. And here perhaps one could find the best proof of Korda's impeccable war record. Sir Winston wasn't a man who would condone or reward cowardice. Yet Alex received his knighthood in the middle of the war, after he had gone to the States and before he returned to London to settle. According to the legend, he was informed of this honour in Churchill's bedroom after one of his quick and dangerous trips to England.

I can offer you only two clues. One is Korda's close friendship with the late Bill Donovan, the wartime head of America's O.S.S. The other is on record—on the Congressional Record. The Senate Foreign Relations Committee held hearings in 1941 to look into the problem of foreign agents in the United States. There was a law that obliged all such agents to register—whether they were Nazi, Fascist or British. Senators Nye and Vandenberg, both strongly isolationists, accused Alexander Korda Productions of being an espionage and propaganda centre for Britain.

One of their strongest arguments was a piece of celluloid— the Korda picture called 'Lady Hamilton' (or, characteristically re-titled in America, 'That Hamilton Woman'). The Senate Committee—or some of its members—wanted to establish that Korda and Pallos had broken the law and should be expelled from the United States.

The scene on which they based their charges was set in the board-room of the Admiralty. Laurence Olivier as Nelson delivered an impassioned speech against dictators, declaring that one should never make peace with them. He spoke about Napoleon, of course, but the implication and the parallel were clear enough. What Senators Nye and Vandenberg wanted to know was whether Korda and his associates could provide any proof for the historical accuracy of this scene.

Of course they couldn't. It was something that Korda, Walter Reisch and R. C. Sherriff, the scriptwriters of 'Lady Hamilton', had invented and deliberately inserted in the picture.

Korda and Pallos were summoned to appear in front of the Committee; though Alex was in the middle of a film, the Senators insisted that he should drop everything and come to Washington. The date of the hearing was set for December 12, 1941.

On the 7th, as we know, something happened that made such investigations rather silly and pointless. The Japanese planes dived over Pearl Harbour and America was at war.

★   ★   ★   ★

In September 1939 John Justin had joined the Air Force
Reserve; but though he pressed for his call-up, they did not
seem to want him. In the meantime, 'The Thief of Baghdad' was
still moving slowly towards completion. In spite of air raid
alarms, Georges Perinal still insisted on his famous clouds being
right—so that it sometimes took days to line up a single shot.

Finally Justin plucked up enough courage to go and see Alex.

"I'm sorry, sir," he blurted out, "but I can't finish the picture."

Korda looked at him, more puzzled than angry.

"Why not?"

"I'm in the Air Force," Justin said, a little untruthfully, for he
was still far from being 'in'.

Alex reached for the phone. He buzzed his secretary.

"Would you get me . . . what's-his-name? The gentleman in
charge of the Air Force."

"Do you mean Sir Kingsley Wood?" Miss Fisher asked.

"You ought to know whom I mean—but get him."

While Justin waited, awe-struck, Korda was put through to the
Minister. They chatted amiably, obviously old acquaintances.
Then Alex said: "By the way, we have a young man here . . .
Justin, John Justin. He's in the Air Force, he says—but we need
him to finish a picture. Do you mind, Sir Kingsley?"

The answer was obviously in the negative. Korda reassured the
Minister: "Yes, of course, we'll let you have him back when we
no longer need him."

Justin, feeling about 'half-an-inch tall', was dismissed with a
fatherly warning—not to do it again. He moved to Hollywood
with the rest of the cast which included Conrad Veidt, June
Duprez, Sabu, Mary Morris and Rex Ingram—though, of course,
the bit players finished their parts in England.

Still the production dragged on and on; Justin became more
and more restive. Every day at 11 a.m. sharp he and Alex went
through a little ritual. Justin appeared in Korda's office and asked:
"When can I go back to England?" Every day Korda said: "In a
little while." Sometimes he added: "Don't be impatient, John.

This is going to take a long time—you'll get plenty of chances to break your neck . . ."

Justin had both personal and patriotic reasons for his home-sickness—there was a girl in London he was in love with—and he chafed under the long delay. But finally one day Alex returned the long-hoped for answer to the regular question:

"Here's your passport and your ticket, John. Good luck!"

*   *   *   *

'The Thief of Baghdad' had its London première on December 19, during the darkest period of the war. The picture was enthusiastically reviewed on both sides of the Atlantic and made a very comfortable profit.

Two days later, 83 Avenue Road, Korda's London home, was shattered by a near-miss. Peter Korda who, rejected by the army, had joined the London Ambulance Service and remained in England throughout the war, was covered in dust and debris but escaped injury.

The next year and a half Korda spent shuttling to and fro between Hollywood and London. During this time he made three pictures—'Lady Hamilton', 'Lydia' and 'The Jungle Book', all of them for United Artists release, two of them substantial box office successes. He made them for his new company, Alexander Korda Inc. When his British financial support ended, he had taken 'Four Feathers' to America and raised a bank loan on this collateral. The New York and California banks which advanced funds had no cause to regret their investment. Money wasn't exactly plentiful but he established himself at Las Palmas Avenue, Hollywood, and his cigars, his hospitality, were just as lavish as before.

"We made 'Lady Hamilton' in six weeks," Vivien Leigh told me. "It proved that if need be, Alex could work in a hurry—though he hated it—and still turn out a fine job.

David Lean finds his angle before shooting a sequence in the 'Sound Barrier'

Sir Carol Reed and Korda look at the former's Cannes Festival Grand Prix Award for 'The Third Man'

'Everybody's Woman' (Vienna, 1924)

Left, Mary Morris and Conrad Veidt in 'The Thief of Baghdad', and *right*, the Oliviers in 'Lady Hamilton'

Yet there was some skimping and ingenious saving on the production. When, as the ageing Emma, I had to wear a rubber mask, we could only afford to cover the upper half of my face so that I was always photographed at a certain angle. Yet the wonderful Alex found the money to bring my mother and daughter to Canada—something I have never forgotten . . ."

Even before the Congressional investigation, 'Lady Hamilton' ran into trouble. Alex was almost half-way through the picture when he remembered that he had forgotten to check the script with the American censors. He asked R. C. Sherriff (whom he had taken to the States with him) to go and see Joseph Breen, head of the Hays Office.

Sherriff took the screenplay along; Breen read it and told him: "You can't possibly make this picture."

"Why not?" asked the author. "Is there any particular scene you dislike?"

"The whole story," replied Breen. "Here's a man living in sin with another man's wife, his own wife is still alive—and neither of them shows the slightest remorse or even consciousness of doing wrong! Impossible!"

Sherriff went back to Korda with the sad news. "But I can't stop!" Korda cried. "We've already shot the Battle of Trafalgar! You must think of something . . ."

Sherriff and his co-author, Walter Reisch, did some more research and a good deal of thinking. They discovered that Nelson's father had been a parson. So they wrote the now famous scene in which old Nelson, in his wheelchair, berated his son for his love-life; and Nelson replied that he knew he was doing wrong—but couldn't help himself.

This single scene saved the picture—the censor was completely satisfied. And it turned out to be one of the most effective sequences in the picture.

There were enough crises and difficulties even without the

H

censorship or Congressional investigations. One day Melchior Lengyel went to see Alex to discuss with him his story 'To be or not to be', which was later filmed with Jack Benny.

Suddenly Korda's business manager burst in, pale and dishevelled. He reported that the bank had phoned—unless a deposit of $100,000 was made, the property of the company would be seized and sold.

"How much money have we in our account?" asked Korda.

"A few hundred dollars," replied the manager.

"And when do they want the $100,000?"

"By noon."

"What's the time now?" Alex continued.

"Half past nine . . ."

Korda smiled. "What are you worrying about? We've plenty of time . . ." And he continued to discuss the script with Lengyel. By noon he had the money at the bank.

C. S. Forester, the creator of the great Horatio Hornblower, had a delightful wartime memory which must date from Korda's more prosperous days in Hollywood. With a large party he was enjoying himself at Korda's house—which was always open to all his friends. There were complaints about the swimming pool —the water was too tepid. Korda must have heard about it, for an hour later a huge lorry drove up—loaded with ice. Dozens of blocks were tipped into the swimming pool and the water became most invigorating. "I thought that was a truly magnificent gesture," Forester said, "not at all vulgar or ostentatious—yet still worthy of a film-mogul . . ."

'Lady Hamilton', without being blatant, served as wonderful propaganda for Britain's war effort. The parallel was obvious— in the Napoleonic Wars Britain also stood alone for long periods and had her 'finest hour'. Nelson's and Lady Hamilton's love story, however idealized, provided a brilliant vehicle for Laurence Olivier and Vivien Leigh. No wonder that Winston Churchill was reported to have seen it eight times and cried over it on every occasion! No wonder, too, that some of the film-makers in

Britain felt a little jealous of the man who, they thought, was making films in a safe place while they braved bombs and war-time discomforts in Britain.

After the war there was a meeting in London at which the demand was voiced that those who had 'deserted' England in her need should not be allowed to make films in Britain.

Alex, who wouldn't have come under the ban for he had returned late in 1942 to London, got up and said:

"I was in the first world war—but on the other side. What are you going to do about me?"

The speaker advocating the ban insisted that it should be carried out.

"Excuse me," Korda said, "how many wars d'you have to be in to make a picture in Britain?"

Then somebody made an ironic remark about 'homing pigeons'. Del Giudice, whose English wasn't always up to idiomatic expressions, interposed: "What is all this talk about racing pigeons?" he demanded plaintively. "I do not understand . . ."

The meeting dissolved in laughter; the subject was never mentioned again.

*　　*　　*　　*

'Lydia', the second picture of Korda's wartime Hollywood period, starred Merle Oberon and Joseph Cotten, with Duvivier directing; it was only moderately successful. This was followed by the 'all-Korda film', based on Kipling's great *Jungle Book*. The screen-play was by Laurence Stallings; Zoltan Korda directed and Vincent designed the whole production.

Apart from Sabu, the picture starred Joseph Calleia, John Qualen, Frank Puglia, Rosemary de Camp, and Faith Brook. The music was again by Miklos Rozsa. It cost about £250,000 and made a handsome profit. There was no possibility of locations in India so about ten acres in California's Sherwood Forest were used for the jungle, with a good many wild animals, elephants, bears, leopards, panthers, wolves, jackals, pythons, crocodiles and a cobra among them. All in all, 'Jungle Book' was one of Korda's most successful and harmonious achievements.

Not that all his Hollywood experiences were so pleasant or harmonious. Early in 1941 he made an agreement with his first wife about alimony, stipulating that if his income dropped under $6,000 a month, she would only receive one quarter of it. But in August Maria was suing him in Los Angeles, asking for their 1930 divorce to be annulled on the ground that they had co-habited after the final decree in 1931. Korda denied this and pointed out that his ex-wife had in 1935 publicly announced her engagement to a Count Teleki; this she would have hardly done if she had still considered herself married to *him*. The verdict of the court went against Maria Corda.

By February 1942, Korda was making his fourteenth Atlantic crossing since the outbreak of the war.

It was winter and the weather was rough. The Liberator bomber had taken off from Newfoundland and most of the flight was to be made at night. The North Atlantic storms were lashing the ocean and there was much turbulence in the air above the waves.

Quite a few important passengers were huddled in the cramped space of the bomb-bay, half-sitting, half-crouching in the uncomfortably restricted area. For Alex the journey was becoming increasingly uncomfortable. His bulky parachute didn't make a very soft seat.

Finally he shook the shoulder of the high-ranking R.A.F. officer sitting next to him and yelled into his ear:

"What are our chances if we come down in the sea?"

"Very slight," was the answer.

"How long would I stay alive in the water?"

"In this weather—maybe half an hour."

"That's just what I wanted to know," Alex said. "Then I needn't wear this dam' thing any longer."

He undid the uncomfortable harness and flung the parachute to the end of the bomb-bay.

To Korda, the confirmed globe-trotter, these wartime journeys were no particular hardship, however much he liked his comfort. On this particular occasion he reached his London office within fourteen hours of leaving New York. Quietly he sat down at his desk and called the faithful Miss Holloway.

"But you're in America!" she gasped.

"I'm not, my dear," Alex replied. "I'm in my office, and I'd like some coffee."

The uncomfortable trip in the bomb-bay had a very important reason. Korda was to be knighted—the first film producer to be so honoured and certainly the first naturalized Hungarian to achieve such distinction since Sir Aurel Stein, the explorer. On this occasion he stayed in England well over two months. A few days after his return to America, 'To be or not to be', the Melchior Lengyel-Jack Benny film was shown in London. Korda had helped Walter Wanger to set it up by obtaining $100,000 for him. In June there was the first private pre-view of 'Jungle Book' in England.

The trip he made across the Atlantic in February caused quite a stir. Captain Shaw, M.P., asked in the House of Commons why a former alien was allowed to fly in an R.A.F. bomber? The question drew a mild ministerial answer; Korda himself, when interviewed about it, said that it had been no joy-ride and that he would have gladly yielded his place to any member of Parliament.

He made another lengthy visit to Britain in the same year, paving the way for his permanent return. Vincent Korda came back at the end of 1942.

The arrangement which Korda made with M-G-M. was to revive London Films and combine it with the British branch of Metro. Mr. Ben Goetz was to represent the American interests; Korda was appointed Chairman, Managing Director and Production Supervisor. In May 1942 he had already announced an ambitious production programme: 'War and Peace', which he intended to shoot either in Canada or around Smolensk, with Merle Oberon as Natasha and a screen-play by Orson Welles and Lajos Biro; another picture dealing with Britain in the year after Dunkirk; and a third about the past, present and future of London for which he hoped to get H. G. Wells to write the scenario.

The news that Korda intended to resume work in England led to more attacks on him both in the press and in Parliament. He found it somewhat distasteful that he had to justify himself. In an interview he gave after his return to Hollywood, he pointed out that he had made about fifteen Atlantic crossings since the outbreak of the war and that on his last visit he had spent two and a half months in England, while on the previous occasion he was in London for three months. He emphasized that he had gone to Hollywood with the approval and support of the British Government. After a while the hostile criticism died down—especially after the great success of 'Lady Hamilton'.

Many people gave me wartime glimpses of Alex—some of them chance encounters, others meetings of great importance. John Justin who, after returning from Hollywood in 1940, had become a fighter pilot, received a summons from Alex during one of his short periods of leave. He went to Claridge's, where Korda had established himself after his Avenue Road home had become uninhabitable, wondering what Alex wanted. He was offered drinks and they talked, rather desultorily. It seemed that Korda expected Justin to say something; but the young R.A.F. officer couldn't think of anything. Finally, after about an hour, Korda became restless and Justin stood up to say goodbye. Then Alex blurted out, rather shamefacedly:

"Look—I know what it is, to be in the Air Force. If you need money at any time, John—just let me know . . . I'll arrange it."

Justin was deeply moved—not only by the offer of help but by the manner in which it was made . . . as if Korda were apologizing for being kind to him. As it happened, he didn't need the money—but he knew he could have had a thousand pounds and Korda would have never asked for its return. "Ever since I made 'The Thief of Baghdad'," Justin added when he told me the story, "I felt that there was almost a father-and-son relationship between us which endured even when we didn't meet for years . . ."

Donald Taylor found him in a different mood during the war when he visited Alex in his penthouse apartment at Claridge's. He seemed to be terribly lonely and depressed; almost pathetically grateful for company. He told Taylor that he had been for a week in England and no one had got in touch with him; it looked as if no one wanted him in the country he loved. Taylor told him that all this was nonsense, and near the end of their talk Alex cheered up.

Taylor was one of many who spoke to me about Korda's quickly changing moods which ranged from buoyant optimism to deep depression, bordering on misanthropy. And as his moods changed, so did his setting. There was the young executive producer of the Denham days who liked modernistic furniture, whose office walls were decorated with a few choice French paintings. There was the setting at Belgrave Square, headquarters of his British M-G-M.-London Films period, where flunkies gave the place an almost eighteenth-century atmosphere, with wood panelling and heavy brownish canvases to emphasize it. And finally at 146 Piccadilly, a mixture of the two, the framework of the august film magnate.

Basil Dean made a wartime crossing with Korda on the *Queen Mary*. The great liner had been converted into a troopship and quarters were cramped, food austere. Alex spent most of the eleven days—for the ship had to make a wide detour in convoy—playing gin rummy. Once a day, however, he appeared in the big drawing room to listen to the news broadcast which Dean did through the public address system. These were the days of the North African landings, and as Korda's mood brightened with the victories, his card-playing became worse and worse. But he was quite cheerful about his losses—considering them as a small contribution to the war effort. In New York the two men stayed together at the St. Regis and did some strenuous play-going.

Carol Reed also met him on one of his journeys; Alex was stranded at Prestwick, waiting for a take-off that was repeatedly delayed. This long, enforced idleness certainly benefited the director—for Alex discussed with him in great detail Reed's projected picture, 'Odd Man Out'.

When the film was made, Alex told Reed: "I've put far more work into that picture than in many of my own—and for my rivals, too!"

It was during this meeting that the two men began to discuss tentatively their future co-operation which proved such an exciting and successful partnership.

Korda played an active part in the film-side of political warfare. His close friend, John Ford, was one of the heads of the American Armed Forces film organization; Alex himself took part in many of the long and complex conferences which the Film Division of the British Ministry of Information organized. His presence always electrified the atmosphere. He was a pioneer in the interchange of films between Britain and Russia—he gave all the pictures he controlled to be exhibited in the U.S.S.R., though the Russians, of course, did their own picking and choosing. The preparations for making 'War and Peace' were going on at the same time, which may have had something to do with Korda's desire to co-operate with the Russians. Not that he wouldn't rebel occasionally against everything this entailed.

One day there was a showing of Russian films at the Tatler Cinema, followed by a supper party at the Hungaria, where vodka flowed less quietly than the Don, but just as abundantly. Korda was the guest of honour—and also the life and soul of the party. But after an hour, Alex bent close to Catherine de la Roche, who used to work at London Films' story department and was now in charge of Russo-British film exchanges. He asked in a whisper:

"Can I go now? This is hell!"

Miss de la Roche asked him to stay for a little longer—and very heroically, he did.

*   *   *   *

In March 1943 the London Films–M-G-M. merger was completed and Korda announced that he would return to London within a fortnight to start organizing his 'ten-million-dollar production programme'. His artists included Vivien Leigh and Ralph Richardson; the new arrangement, he said, would not affect his partnership in United Artists, of which he still owned 25 per cent.

The home of the new company was a large mansion in Belgrave Square. Here Alex was enthroned in a huge, softly-carpeted office. A Hungarian chef looked after the meals which, for wartime London, were an exquisite surprise. But Alex was the first to volunteer as fire-watcher and there was quite an argument when Ben Goetz pointed out that Korda would be the most expensive fireguard in all Britain and that it would be slightly cheaper to hire somebody for the job.

He settled down to assemble a roster of stars, writers and directors. Robert Donat was, of course, happy to return to the man who made him a star. His partner in the first (and only) film Alex made in wartime Britain was an unknown, Deborah Kerr. She had been Gabriel Pascal's discovery and later The Archers (Michael Powell and Emeric Pressburger) gave her the lead in 'The Life and Death of Colonel Blimp'. Now Alex took her under his wings.

It took a long time to prepare the script for 'Perfect Strangers'. (In the States it was re-named 'Holiday from Marriage', which wasn't a very happy choice.) Korda had almost thirty writers under contract and it seemed that all of us had a hand in it at one time or another. Finally it was Clemence Dane who co-ordinated the disjointed efforts and received the sole credit.

It was a story very much in the Korda tradition—a little satirical comedy and tragedy handled with a master's easy-going, yet never leisurely or diffuse touch. A marriage going on the rocks, stifled by dull routine—and then, the electrifying effect of war. Husband and wife—beautifully played by Donat and Miss Kerr—were separated not by the horror or danger, but by the exigencies of military service. War divided them and they discovered that they were 'perfect strangers'—but war brought them together again in the end. The picture was shot on location in West Scotland and the interiors at Denham, where Korda was a welcome tenant; though it must have always caused him a nostalgic pang to drive through those gates.

Donat and Miss Kerr were most ably aided by Glynis Johns, in the part of a pert and worldly-wise Wren. Ann Todd played a widow for whom war was sheer tragedy.

"I wanted to do it in a very low key," Miss Todd told me, "as unmitigated tragedy. But Alex said: 'No, do it differently, darling—very gay, very light at the beginning—then deliver the punch, drive home the point with double force . . .' He was right, of course. He was the magician who always drew the best out of any actor . . . And he was a friend, too; I went to him with all my problems, artistic or personal—and he always seemed to have time and always helped whenever he could . . ."

Soon after he started this long-deferred film, Korda cut himself off from Hollywood by selling his shares in United Artists. He had come back to England to stay—because he believed in the future of British films.

The large-scale Korda–M-G-M. programme needed a home—and so Alex and his associates bought Elstree studios from Prudential. These magnificent studios had been originally built for Simon Soskin but had passed through many hands, including Mr. Rank's. They were never actually used for film-production

and were now taken over by the Ministry of Works for storage.
Korda made strenuous attempts to get them de-requisitioned,
claiming that they served no essential purpose—but he failed.
So he now had a wonderful roster of stars, writers and directors
—but nowhere for them to work. A very frustrating position.

★　　★　　★　　★

It was in April 1944 that Korda paid $1,000,000 into the
Treasury; a minor but welcome dollar-windfall for Britain,
starved for hard currency. His connection with the remaining
partners wasn't entirely broken for he was to make films later in
association with Sam Goldwyn and David Selznick.

Upon his return, Korda found a new and important factor in
British films—Mr. J. Arthur Rank. Mr. Rank, who was to
become the second peer in the film business after Lord Archibald,
was the complete antithesis of Korda. They both understood
each other's limitations. Alan Wood, in his brilliant Rank
biography, quotes him as saying: "I've always told Alex that he
should stick to making films. He's brilliant at anything to do
with them—he can produce or direct or write the script or do
anything else he likes. But he should never have got tied up with
this business of running companies . . ." While Korda was
reported to have said: "I only wish I knew as much about
finance as Arthur. But when it comes to films . . ."

In any case, Korda was to plunge into finance again. He was
once more frustrated, not being his own master; however deep
the respect and admiration Ben Goetz had for him, there was
still the 'head-office' and Mr. Louis B. Mayer in Hollywood—
and behind them the 'front-office' in New York whom he had
to consult and whose decisions he couldn't override. With no
studio and very large overheads, it was a very costly business to
run British M-G-M.–London Films. The Americans, not without
cause, protested that to give scores of people long-term contracts
when there was little prospect of using them, was a waste of

money. Alex, of course, planned for the future; he knew that when the war ended, the world-markets would be opened again to British films and that very large pickings were going to be had. He was also a little tired of dancing attendance on Mr. Mayer, whose background and character were so utterly different from his. "To hell with roast goose," he said once in a moment of exasperation, meaning the lavish dinners which Mayer used to give in his palatial home and which bored him to tears. So, having made 'Perfect Strangers'—which wasn't released until 1945—he decided to make himself independent again and revive London Films as an independent company.

For this, as always, he needed money. He had sold his United Artists shares and this gave him a certain capital. His wartime Hollywood films, with the exception of 'Lydia', were highly successful financially; so was 'The Thief of Baghdad' and 'Four Feathers' which were not included in the pictures Prudential took in the final settlement. He sold Denham Laboratories for a good price to the Rank Organization. And then he made a deal which was to be the most lucrative of his life.

Prudential had decided to sell the twenty-odd Korda films which it owned. They always had a very high regard for Korda and thought it would be only fair to give him first refusal.

They asked Steven Pallos to act as go-between. At first Alex was dubious—in 1943 re-issues of old films were not exactly promising—but then he quickly realized the possibilities. The total sum he paid—£42,500—was certainly a bargain basement price. And Korda made the most of his opportunity. As Alan Wood puts it:

"(He) was a brilliant overseas salesman, always ready to get into a plane, and never minding how much money he spent on international telephone calls. His pre-war films, released again through the world, were still remarkably popular; and with the proceeds Korda was able to launch a programme of production, at first on a small scale. The success of the re-issues was a complete vindication of his policy of quality production, a proof that money invested in Korda for high-class films might always get a return in the very long run, and a tribute to the way the prestige of his name was still remembered in Europe."

It was certainly remembered in Germany, where Korda founded Deutsche London Films with his old friends Joseph Aussenberg and Karl Klär handling his pictures. They earned more than a million German marks, not to mention the money made by his current productions.

London Films was in business again. Alex bought 144 Piccadilly, next door to the house King George VI and Queen Elizabeth occupied when they were Duke and Duchess of York. Soon he acquired Nos. 145 and 146, installed a chef and a private cinema. The war was over. Between V.E.- and V.J.-Day Korda's second marriage had also ended. In June 1945, Merle Oberon obtained a divorce in Juarez, Mexico. The ground was 'incompatibility'. She had announced six months earlier that "our efforts for the past two years to work out separate lives and careers have failed; but our parting is most amicable." Now Alex was a bachelor again and his loneliness, his absorption in his work became even more marked. Again, he was faced with the task of building a new life and a new empire.

CHAPTER X

BRITISH LION AND THE OLD LION

"ALEX always asked my advice," Joseph Somlo told me, a little ruefully. "But he never took it."

This was exactly the case when Korda decided to acquire an interest in the British Lion Film Corporation and in Shepperton and Isleworth studios. British Lion was a distributing organization with declining fortunes; the two studios badly needed modernizing. Somlo, consulted by Alex, told him it was unwise to sink his own money into such a speculative venture. "You're a very dear and honest friend of mine," Alex replied. "But I'm still going ahead."

He was moving fast. He resigned the chairmanship of M-G-M.–London Films in October 1946. He paid £250,000 for a controlling share in British Lion, where his associate was Sir Arthur Jarratt, formerly with J. Arthur Rank at Gaumont-British. Shepperton was rebuilt and re-equipped and Vincent Korda was made production designer. Once again Korda had what he wanted: studios and an organization to sell his films.

The 'new era' at British Lion was announced in the trade papers early in January 1947. At his Piccadilly headquarters Alex had all his old associates: Sir David Cunynghame; his casting secretary Miss Holloway and many others. Mr. Harold Boxall, who was to play such an important part in the later period of London Films, had also joined him. Boxall had forsaken law for films after the First World War and was production manager of that notable British silent film 'Woman to Woman'. Later he became studio manager of Gaumont British and in 1937, during Michael Balcon's brief association with M-G-M., went with him to the American company. It was Harold Boxall who brought Ted Black, one of the most dynamic men in British films, to Gainsborough. Boxall met Korda when the M-G-M.–London Films merger was in operation and followed him to 146 Piccadilly, to remain at his side until his death and afterwards serving as one of his executors.

Production under the London Films–British Lion set-up began on a modest scale with a few 'finger-exercises'—yet by the end of the year it was in full swing. In the meantime Alex was finding many things changed in post-war Britain which weren't exactly to his liking. The A.C.T., the trade union of film technicians, had achieved great unity and power under the guidance of its capable and tough general secretary, George Elvin. Working hours and conditions were much improved; and the union became a closed shop. Korda always liked to start his working day late and finish it late—and this was getting to be more and more difficult and costly. "My players," Alex complained once, "can't start making love at nine o'clock in the morning—at least, not very convincingly." And in November 1947 he wrote plaintively in a letter to *The Times*:

> "Some of the 'crisis' talk comes from some of the trade union leaders in the film industry. They should, perhaps, remember that, to ensure a continuance of this output of quality pictures, reasonable working conditions in the film industry must also be maintained. Before the war film studios worked 66 hours a week. Now a five-day week of 44 hours has been established. It is obvious that so long as this is in strict operation films can be made neither as quickly nor as cheaply as before."

This statement brought him an accusation of being 'anti-labour'. Yet Korda had always been extremely friendly to unions, a partisan and supporter of craft organizations. He had broad understanding for the views and problems of others—

whether they were writers, carpenters or musicians. Donald Taylor recalled how one day a meeting was arranged between the 'big men' of film production and the producers of documentaries and short films. Mr. Rank was there, exactly on time, but the representatives of the 'small fry' didn't feel that he was particularly interested in their problems. Then Alex arrived, late as usual, flinging hat, coat and walking stick at a flunkey, apologizing for his lateness, greeting most of those present by their first names. He sat down and said: "Wasn't it Madame Sévigné who once wrote to her daughter: '*Forgive me, I haven't time to write briefly today*'? Believe me, I know how much harder it is to make a good short than a big feature. What can we do to help you?"

Immediately the atmosphere changed, the mood became friendly and by the end of the meeting something useful had been worked out. This might be a very unfair illustration of the different temperaments and characters of Lord Rank and Sir Alexander. That they were as different as salt and sugar, no one could deny. Alan Wood made a point in his Rank-biography of emphasizing these differences:

"The career of Korda was to bear much the same relationship to Rank's as Disraeli's had to Gladstone's; and, like rival political leaders, they were never in power at the same time. When one was up, the other was down. Nor could anyone ask for a better dramatic contrast than between the two men, for Korda has always been everything that Rank was not. Korda was a Cavalier where Rank was a Puritan; Korda was a Bohemian where Rank was a Methodist; Korda had an artistic conscience where Rank had a Sunday School conscience. Korda was divorced and Rank was happily married; Korda had the gift of tongues and every social charm; Korda had perfect taste in food and drink; Korda was steeped in cultural and intellectual interests; Korda—though this is often forgotten since he became a financier—was a film director in the first rank before he put on too much glamour . . ."

The differences are important to establish; for in Korda's last ten years much of his career, many of his activities were unavoidably tied up with the personality and principles of Lord Rank. Once there was even an attempt to have the two giants join forces. Nothing came of it and nothing could; that was amply evident after the first few minutes of the meeting. Their approach to film production was too different, and however much respect they had for each other, their collaboration couldn't have lasted.

Yet in 1947 and the subsequent years Rank and Korda were facing problems that made them, on certain issues, comrades-in-arms, fighting to save British film production which once again had entered a critical period.

* * * *

Basically, I think, there has always been a deep cleavage of opinion (and perhaps of interest) between the two branches of the British film world, production and exhibition. Cinema-owners have always fought for the showing of American pictures and, with some notable exceptions, were often less eager to exhibit the home-made product. For one thing, American pictures had been tested for box-office reactions before they came to Britain; and though tastes varied on both sides of the Atlantic, a spectacular U.S. success was rarely a failure in London. Therefore a protectionist policy was unavoidable unless British film production was to die.

I have spoken of the 1928 Quota Act which started with a 5 per cent Exhibitor's Quota and a 7½ per cent Renter's Quota. In 1938 the Second Quota Act raised the obligatory screen-time for British films to 12½ per cent and the Renter's to 15 per cent; it also specified the minimum production cost, thereby killing at least the worst type of the cheap and nasty 'quota quickies' made solely to fulfil the letter of the law.

In 1948 the Third Quota Act was due. The battle started in 1947 as to its provisions and both Korda and Rank were involved in the struggle.

The film technicians campaigned for an abolition of the Renter's Quota on the ground that the studios had plenty of work without it. Korda was accused of 'having extreme protectionist views' and was violently attacked by the Cinema Exhibitors Association. He was criticized even within the British Film Producers Association, which objected to a 'private memorandum' he had submitted to Sir Stafford Cripps, then Chancellor of the Exchequer. Korda replied in a strongly worded statement:

"These recommendations which have been criticized so strongly were not mine as an individual. Whatever I have written or recommended has been in my capacity either as a member of the B.F.P.A. or the Films Council. I wish that when people quote me they would do so correctly, with full knowledge of the facts. Of course I am against Renter's Quota. But I am not against American companies making pictures in this country. What I am against is government action forcing them to do so."

The argument continued for several months. But by mid-May 1947, it was evident that Korda's plan for the quota—involving a 'grading' of pictures according to budget and quality—would be adopted. This was a considerable achievement. He repeated again and again that quality was still the only important consideration and that the 'trustification' of the film industry, the big combines and powerful interests would invariably neglect this all-important fact.

Korda realized that the fine films turned out in Britain were inspired by the large-sized subjects they dealt with, subjects that no longer were acceptable to the war-weary audiences. Not to mention the fact that the 'thin line of British stars' needed an infusion of new blood.

The British-Lion–Korda 'empire' was a small one compared to Rank's at the beginning. But doggedly, persistently Korda set to work to enlarge his domain. In April the famous film-making team of The Archers, Powell and Pressburger, left the Rank Group and joined Alex. The 'raiding' of the Rank stables was to go on until more than half of Rank's best directors, writers and artists had passed from 38 South Street, the Rank headquarters, down the short stretch of Park Lane and Hamilton Place to 146 Piccadilly. In July 1947 an agreement was signed between London Films and 20th Century–Fox about the distribution of Korda's films throughout the American continent. Korda explained that this contract had a guaranteed minimum value of $14m. for the British Lion group and might reach twice as much. It must have been a wryly satisfying thought for Alex that Sol Wurtzel was involved in this agreement—the man, who seventeen years before, had dismissed him summarily . . .

★   ★   ★   ★

Quality not quantity was Korda's constant refrain, the point he tried to drive home again and again. Perhaps he remembered his unhappy experiences at Denham where the stages had to be kept busy, no matter how. He took up Mr. R. J. Minney's statement in a letter to *The Times*—a statement in which Mr. Minney, a distinguished writer and producer, had quoted Alex as saying that the British film industry was capable of making 150 pictures a year.

He pointed out that no enormous number of films was needed for survival or even prosperity—what was wanted were pictures of the highest possible quality. For this the most important requirement was the number of creative people available—a number that was steadily growing in Britain.

Then Korda took up the cudgels against his special *bête noire*, the British system of distributing and showing films.

"The greatest waste in handling films today in Great Britain," he wrote, "results from the policy of some of the large circuits in only playing films for one week, however much the public may want to see them. We saw several examples of this last year when one of the largest circuits took first-rate British films out of their theatres after one week in order to put in what often proved a much inferior article. This is a practice that does not exist any more in any country in the world. All the world over, if a film is appreciated by the public, it is kept in the programme just so long as the public is willing to support it. The Music Hall in New York, for example, which is the world's largest cinema, used 40 films in 1935 to fill its programmes. Last year it used only seven. The Astor Cinema, also in New York, showed between 40 or 50 films in 1935. Last year it only showed four. Surely if British films are good and if the public is willing to support them in the cinemas for more than a week, it cannot be against the interest of any individual cinema and can be very much in the national interest to keep them in the programme for as long as there is a sufficiently large public willing to pay to see them? This would give good and popular British pictures longer playing time and a larger income, and would eliminate the necessity of showing a number of mediocre films . . ."

This was plain common sense; which is perhaps why Korda's suggestions still haven't been fully adopted. He forecast the policy of 'road-showing' for important films; hiring or setting apart a 'show-case' for a costly and successful production as it has been done all over the world by the late Mike Todd, by Mr. Samuel Goldwyn or for such spectaculars as 'The Ten Commandments'. It wasn't until early in 1959 that Mr. John Davis, Lord Rank's deputy, indicated a change in the mechanical rota-system of 'general releases'—and then only because film production and cinema attendances had both fallen disastrously. Korda knew that where production and exhibition were linked, as in the case of the Gaumont-Odeon or ABC circuits, this system of 'one-week-only' for all pictures actually hurt the companies' own interests.

*   *   *   *

'Korda in Clover' ran the headline of a weekly's article in April 1947. And Korda was, indeed, in clover at the beginning of his British Lion Days. London Films was a private company, all but 2 per cent of the shares being owned by Alex and his family. In 1946-47 it made a profit of £283,000. In July British Lion Studios paid a dividend of 15 per cent—the first since 1936. Their net profit was a respectable £61,154.

In the end the Quota was fixed at 45 per cent, an increase of 25 per cent in the screen-time for British films. This would have been a triumph for Korda and his allies—except for the fact that in the meantime that great Anglo-American film war had taken place. A war in which, as in so many, both sides turned out to be losers—though Britain came out rather worse than America.

The British Labour Government was becoming anxious about the amount of dollars American films took out of the country. In the two-way traffic the balance was heavily in favour of the U.S.A. Mr. Rank made a long and exhausting trip to the States, trying to arrange wider distribution for his films; Korda had made an arrangement with 20th Century-Fox. American companies produced a few pictures in Britain; but even so there was little prospect of the account in dollars being balanced.

Dr. Hugh Dalton was Chancellor of the Exchequer and Sir Stafford Cripps was at the Board of Trade—the two ministries concerned with dollars and films. At first it seemed that the Americans would agree voluntarily to 'freeze' part of their dollar earnings in Britain. But on August 7, 1947, an *ad valorem* duty of 75 per cent was suddenly introduced on all new American films entering the country.

The Americans reacted instantly and drastically. They refused to pay the tax; and the only way of not paying it was to ban the exhibition of all new American pictures in Britain. The embargo or boycott was enforced completely and immediately.

Mr. Rank, who had made an important deal with the big cinema circuits in America, complained with some bitterness: "All my work was thrown away. My two months in America went for nowt—right down the drain . . ." Korda must have felt exactly the same.

The British Government, though shocked by the prompt and drastic counter-measures, couldn't retreat from the difficult position into which it had jockeyed itself. So the Government told British film producers that this was their great chance—the wonderful opportunity to fill the screens with British pictures. Rank responded at once by announcing a programme of 47 films —at a total cost of well over £9m. This, as Korda forecast, proved a disastrous move. Too many pictures, not enough creative talent—that was the story not only of the Rank Organization but of London Films and British Lion. It wasn't enough to make the pictures; you had to get the people into the cinemas to see them. Three months after the embargo British producers were already being blamed for 'not rising to the challenge'; though in the same breath they were accused of meeting it with wasteful extravagance! Once again Korda wrote to *The Times*:

> "It is rather bewildering to read in the newspapers the various speeches and announcements about a great crisis in the British film-producing industry. What the reason for these statements may be I do not know, but I am afraid that the British public, who so generously support the products of British film studios, must, like myself, feel rather astonished and wonder how it is possible that, in spite of their support, there should be a crisis in British film studios. Con-

sequently, they will draw their own conclusions as to the
efficiency of our film-makers . . ."

He denied the existence of a crisis and pointed out that more
pictures were being made than ever. In America only 24 first
feature films were in production; in Britain 20—which certainly
did not compare unfavourably. In a single month five important
British films were to be presented in the West End.

"I think it should also be mentioned," Korda continued,
"that all the British studios put together hardly possess as
many stages as *one* of the big studios in Hollywood, and the
number of people employed is something like 15 per cent of
the number . . . in Hollywood . . . Faced with these facts, I
don't think that any accusation against the efficiency of
British film producers is justified, or that loose statements
about the critical position in which the British film studios
find themselves have any foundation whatever. Quite the
contrary. If the quality of our pictures goes on standing up
to the demand of the public, British films have never had a
better opportunity for success."

When Sir Stafford Cripps replaced Dr. Dalton as Chancellor
of the Exchequer and Mr. Harold Wilson took over the Board of
Trade, they soon realized that the 'confiscatory tax' hadn't
stopped the dollar-drain at all. American films still earned large
amounts in Britain—but they were re-issues or new films already
in the country before the introduction of the tax. So the Government had to swallow its pride and negotiations began—during
which, characteristically, British film producers and distributors
weren't consulted at all. Finally an agreement was reached under
which the annual film remittances to America were fixed at
$17m.; but the remaining sum was left to the American com-
panies to use for various, vaguely-defined purposes. In addition
to the seventeen millions, the Americans could draw dollars to

the extent of the dollar earnings of British films. This was intended to encourage American distributors to show British films—but it was more than balanced by the considerable ill-will and bias that had been created in the States by the rash Government action.

Korda was closely affected by this feeling; he had two big and costly films—'An Ideal Husband' and 'Anna Karenina'—ready for release in 1947. They both suffered from the Anglo-American film war, though Spyros Skouras, head of 20th Century-Fox did take them for US showing.

*   *   *   *

British Lion handled product other than that of London Films; but its most important source of films was obviously Korda. Alex refused to become 'Chief Production Executive' and, indeed, especially in later years, there were many films with which he had very little to do and which were still distributed by British Lion; he was content with the title of 'production adviser'—the implication being that he only gave his advice when he was asked for it.

In the meantime he was constantly seeking new ways of getting his films in front of the public. In May 1948, he made an arrangement with David Selznick under which they would handle each other's pictures—or at least some of them. Carol Reed told me how Korda rang him from New York and asked him to fly over at once for a conference. He found Alex and Selznick in an office high above Fifth Avenue. The subject to be discussed was a screen-version of 'Tess of the D'Urbervilles' which Selznick wanted to make with his wife, Jennifer Jones, in the title-part. Korda was rather lukewarm about the project but there was agreement about another picture. Selznick was dictating while Alex looked down from the dizzy height at the scurrying cars and discussed the various makes with Reed. Now and then Selznick would ask: "O.K., Alex?" And Korda would say, non-

chalantly: "Yes, yes, anything you want, David . . ." The upshot
of this somewhat absent-minded attitude—though Korda could
be sharp enough when important things were involved—was a
law-suit and considerable unpleasantness between the two partners; not that it lasted—as seldom did a quarrel in which Korda
was involved end in final estrangement.

A few days after the Korda–Selznick arrangement was announced—a trade paper called it 'a product of the film tax'—
another deal became public. British Lion and Associated British
Picture Corporation had signed a contract under which Korda
acquired a long lease of British National Studios, one of several
built in and around Boreham Wood. This was to increase the
production capacity of the Korda–British Lion group by six or
seven big features a year. A similar arrangement as the Korda–
Selznick one brought Korda and Samuel Goldwyn into partnership—though this, too, ended in litigation.

When, in June 1948, the new Exhibitors' Quota was announced, Korda welcomed it as a new safeguard for British films.

The picture was not as rosy as Korda's optimism suggested.
By October 1948, the Rank Organization had acquired an
overdraft of more than £13½m. Too many films—not enough
film-goers; too much product—no world market. This was
the explanation of such financial decline; but there was also
the Entertainment Tax which took £40m. a year out of the
film industry. Out of a total of £109m. of box-office receipts in
1948 British producers were left with about £7,500,000—just
about *seven per cent of the gross*! It was calculated that in eleven
years they had provided the Exchequer with £327m. in tax!

The Labour Government decided to do something to help the
producers—among whom Korda was perhaps in greatest need
of working capital. The National Film Finance Corporation was
set up by Mr. Harold Wilson and provided with funds of
£5m. The money was to be used to finance production—but
not to be given directly to the producers. To their 'amazement
and horror', as Alan Wood put it, the N.F.F.C. loans were to be

made only through distributors—the creative side of the industry was to be subordinated to the administrative side.

Mr. Rank declared that he did not want any of the N.F.F.C. money. Korda had no such scruples—or perhaps he did not have the National Provincial Bank behind him with its generous over-draft facilities. By the end of September 1948, NATKE, the trade union of the Theatrical and Cinema Employees was launching an attack on the Korda-group, with the charge that it was gradually becoming a government-subsidized organization.

The negotiations dragged on for some weeks. Korda could not have the money directly; but British Lion could. The sum of £2m. was mentioned—a considerable chunk of the N.F.F.C. capital. In October Korda stated that he would explore the possibilities of South Africa for co-production and distribution; he admitted that though the Anglo-American film dispute was officially settled, in actual fact the stalemate continued; he had not yet been able to secure releases for his new batch of pictures —which meant that these would have difficulty in earning their production costs, let alone make a profit without the American market.

On November 11 it was announced that British Lion had received a £1m. loan from the N.F.F.C. The interest rate was fixed at 4 per cent. The loan was made on the basis of a statement from the distributing company that it planned to handle eighteen British-made features next year; it was to provide additional working capital for Korda and his associated producers.

Ten years later, Mr. Nicholas Davenport, who had been one of the original directors of the N.F.F.C. and, at an earlier stage, a director on Alex's invitation of M-G-M.-London Films during their marriage, wrote a two-part article in *The Spectator* and told the story of the loan with the objectivity the distance of time had made possible:

"On the initiative of Mr. Harold Wilson, then President of the Board of Trade, it (the Labour Government) passed the Cinematograph Film Production (Special Loans) Act which set up a National Film Finance Corporation to make loans to film producers provided they were unable to obtain finance 'on reasonable terms from an appropriate source' (this silly restriction was not removed until the Act of 1957). Now, Sir Wilfred Eady at the Treasury had already decided that the greater part of the rescue money should be lent to the British Lion Film Corporation (then controlled by Sir Alexander Korda) which was financing all the leading independent producers and was already in financial difficulties. I happened to be an original member of the board of the N.F.F.C. and I remember that we were called to the Treasury for our first meeting and asked to approve a letter to British Lion (already drafted) offering an immediate loan of around £2m., which was subsequently increased to £3m."

This was the background of the loan; British Lion was in a bad way and had to be saved. Whether it was a good or bad thing for the Government to enter, however indirectly, into film production, has been debated for the last ten years and I don't think that adding to the mass of argument would be any use. In 1949 the Board of Trade insisted that production and distribution should be strictly separated wherever state aid was invoked. As a consequence Sir David Cunynghame and Harold Boxall resigned from the board of British Lion to make this separation 'quite legal'. When, a few weeks later, Korda was asked why the British film industry had to depend on Government aid while the Americans could manage without it, he replied: "The British film industry is not identical with the American industry. We want to live . . ." He added, candidly: "I have to admit that I know nothing of what the public wants . . . But the courage of producers is the support of this great industry."

There were many attacks, inside and outside Parliament, on

the N.F.F.C. loan to British Lion, especially when the loan was increased from £2m. to £3m. Harold Wilson gave a straightforward explanation: "Outside the Rank Organization the greater number of independent producers were associated, directly or indirectly, with the British Lion Corporation and that seemed to us the quickest and surest way of preventing the complete breakdown of production . . ."

Being associated with British Lion meant in effect being associated with Alexander Korda. Though the money British Lion received was used to make a good many pictures with which Alex had little to do, in the public and official mind he was the responsible man, the figurehead and guiding spirit. This may sound flattering but in the long run it turned out to be extremely damaging.

Korda was at great pains to point out his new position. In October 1948 he stated that his pictures would no longer carry the 'Sir Alexander Korda presents' credit-line; he was no longer a 'producer' in the strict sense of the word, but an administrator. In a reminiscent mood he recalled that in thirty years he had been responsible for 109 pictures in six different countries. The London Films–British Lion group of producers already included Carol Reed, Anatole de Grunewald, Michael Powell and Emeric Pressburger. He emphasized that because of the loss, temporary or permanent, of the U.S. markets, production costs would have to be scaled down. The 4 per cent interest on the £2m. government loan would alone represent £80,000 a year; but they hoped to repay it within three years. Bank charges would add another 3½–5 per cent to the overheads. In spite of these heavy burdens and his changed status, Korda plunged with enthusiasm into a large-scale programme of new productions.

*　　*　　*　　*

The Government loan was made to British Lion in November 1948; by April 1949, Mr. Harold C. Drayton, the city financier who had become chairman of the company, warned his board that a loss of £700,000 was to be expected. In April the trade papers reported that British Lion wished to increase its borrowing powers to £6½m.—of which the N.F.C.C. money would be only about half. *All except two* of the films were showing a loss. This was a necessarily short-term view and we have seen how Korda, *in the long run*, usually managed to make a profit on all but his most expensive and least successful pictures. Nor was he, of course, responsible for *all* films distributed by British Lion. By the end of 1949 London Films owed, according to Mr. Drayton, the sum of £1,350,374 to British Lion.

Yet this was the year in which Korda visited South Africa and established valuable contacts there; it was also the year of the founding of Deutsche London Films. A credit of 400,000 DM was obtained from a German bank, which was soon repaid from the considerable earnings of the old and more recent Korda films. Hamburg became the site of the company as it was in the British Zone. Between 1949 and 1955 Korda was to pay five visits to Germany and see his films earn a net profit of more than a million marks for him. Later Deutsche London Films entered into production and within three years became one of the leading German distributors. This was useful to Korda not only for the revenue it brought, but also because he could finance some of his Continental productions through it.

The most successful Korda picture in Germany was 'The Third Man', which was reissued several times; 'The Thief of Baghdad', 'Jungle Book', 'The Four Feathers', 'State Secret', 'Catherine the Great', 'Lady Hamilton' and 'Tales of Hoffmann' did equally well —while 'Hobson's Choice' and 'Richard III' had long runs in the so-called art houses.

Another important step was taken in June 1949, when the Canadian distribution of London Films was taken over by Eagle-Lion Films of Canada. This meant that, at least in the great Dominion, Korda's pictures were handled by his rival, the Rank Organization. The same year London Films acquired a substantial holding in Laurence Olivier Productions Ltd., forecasting the co-operation of the 'two premier knights of film business'.

In November 1949 the annual meeting of London Film Productions was held. The expenditure had been about £1,500,000; it was stated that about £500,000 represented non-recoverable story properties. The old Korda films were valued at £2m. Korda forecast that in Germany alone 15 million marks would be earned by them. In less than five years his old and new pictures had earned £1,760,000 in Europe—though a large part of this sum was unfortunately still frozen.

Korda pointed out, with justified pride, that this had been "contrary to everything predicted by experts in film finance". It proved that films had an infinitely longer life than generally expected. 'Four Feathers' alone had been reissued four times and while 'Rembrandt' and 'The Shape of Things to Come' had been financial failures originally, even their production costs were gradually being recovered.

*   *   *   *

Some of Korda's associates told me that he was to a considerable extent responsible for the Eady Plan. This was named after Sir Wilfred Eady, the Treasury official whose son David started his career at London Films as a cutter, becoming later a director and producer. Its purpose was to create a fund to help producers; this was achieved by putting an extra penny on the price of seats and the producer's share was in proportion to the box office receipts. It was meant as a makeshift measure but it has survived almost ten years and became more important as time went on. Obviously it only benefited the producer who managed to get his pictures into the cinemas; and as it could not be calculated in advance, it did not aid production as much as it should have done. The producer was still left with little more than 13 per cent of the box office receipts but at least his losses could be reduced by the

Eady Fund. There were also special provisions for short films and for children's pictures.

In June 1950 Korda repaid the London Films debt to British Lion by transferring certain rights and assets he possessed. In December an agreement was signed between London Films and the Lopert Film Distribution Company. This brought Robert W. Dowling, the American financier, into British films. Dowling had already helped Alex by putting up money for some American stars who came over to appear in Korda's pictures. He was President of the New York City Investment Co. and head of about three dozen other financial companies; Ilya Lopert, of Lithuanian origin, began to distribute Continental films in the U.S. in 1947 and later entered production. These two men were destined to play important parts in the final phase of Korda's career.

The British Lion board was reconstituted. It included Harold C. Drayton, Sir Arthur Jarratt, Wilfred Moeller. Korda's title was 'chairman of the executive committee'.

In the same year John Woolf, son of C. M. Woolf, who had been connected with London Films in its early years, set up an independent release organization inside British Lion; not much later he was to become a good deal more closely associated with Alex. An important gain for the Korda organization came in August 1950, when David Lean also left the Rank group and crossed over to the rival establishment.

The year's trading hadn't been very bright for British Lion and London Films. Both showed substantial losses; that of Korda's company amounted to £127,000, though the next financial year promised to be better. And in spite of the difficulties and the gathering storm, the flow of films continued in 1951; and Alex continued his efforts to sell them. By May 1951 he was able to announce an improvement in the finances of the company when the accounts of London Films up to August 31, 1950 were made public. The parent company's accounts—for Alex had set up quite a few subsidiaries—showed a profit of £6,225—modest enough but still an improvement. He was constantly extending his distribution field, signing in July an agreement with an Argentine company for the showing of twenty pictures. British Lion itself opened a reissue department which handled, among others, 'An Ideal Husband' and 'Anna Karenina' with some success. Harold Drayton, the chairman, showed a little more optimism when he declared that his company expected at least half a million pounds extra revenue within the next three years from the Eady Plan, whose operation had been extended. Production costs had been reduced by an average of 45 per cent— which proved that both Korda and British Lion knew how to reduce expense in line with a new 'rationalization' policy. This policy continued all through the next year; though production values were maintained, the next group of films was shot in a much shorter period and were much less spectacular than the earlier Korda pictures.

Maybe it was too late—maybe it wasn't enough. The financial storm-clouds were gathering. In March 1952 negotiations started for the repayment of the loan to British Lion, which had been due in October 1951. Mr. J. H. Lawrie, the managing director of the N.F.F.C., said early in May that though about £1m. of this loan might never be recovered, there was "a great difference between a debt being bad and one that is still owed". Mr. Lawrie was something of an optimist as it proved in the end; the Labour Government's method had only shown, as Alan Wood put it, that one could make a number of first-rate films at an overall loss. This both Rank and Korda had discovered to their grief.

Korda was looking for other sources of capital. He offered to N.B.C., the American TV network company, an arrangement under which he would make 26 feature films in Britain for American TV, at a cost of £65,000 each to the Americans. This plan did not materialize; but late in May he signed a contract with the City Investment Company of New York which involved the sum of half-a-million dollars. This was not a partnership but a pure investment, giving the Americans

The 'Perfect Strangers': Deborah Kerr and Robert Donat

Korda directing C. Aubrey Smith and Michael Wilding in 'An Ideal Husband'

Orson Welles in a typical 'Third Man' scene

Robert Morley and Maurice Evans have a difference of opinion in 'Gilbert and Sullivan'

The crookback king eyes Jane Shore: Olivier and Pamela Browne, 'Richard III'

a percentage share in the gross world receipts of three forth-coming Korda pictures.

In July, British Lion applied to the Board of Trade for support to build additional stages at Shepperton; these were actually finished in March 1953. In September the distribution company was able to pay two years' arrears of dividends on its preference shares, bringing payment up to date. Harold Drayton was still pinning his hopes on the Eady Fund, though in 1951/52 British Lion had received £120,000 less from the Fund than he had forecast. In December the Treasury made a statement that still expressed confidence in British Lion and Korda.

★　　★　　★　　★

I have told the story of the five years, 1947 to 1952, from the financial point of view first—because in these years Korda, perhaps against his will, was far more concerned with legislation and international film diplomacy, with balance sheets and loans than with making films. Some of his friends told me that he became more interested in high finance than in pictures. The truth is, I think, that he enjoyed both—but that he could just as little give up making films as he could give up breathing.

But in the final analysis the films he made are far more important than the financial losses or gains. I have gone through the long list of pictures made during this period with one of his close associates. About one third of them were failures—but the remaining two-thirds either broke even or produced very sub-stantial profits. Yet the structure of film finance is so involved and, in a certain sense, so crazy that these profits could not offset the very substantial losses on such costly mistakes as 'Bonnie Prince Charlie', 'The Elusive Pimpernel' and a few others. The British film industry was in poor health and no makeshift measures or Government action could cure it. But film-making all over the world was in the same unhealthy condition, reflecting the general economic instability in almost every country. This

I

is not meant to provide Korda with an alibi. No doubt he made serious mistakes, some of which could have been avoided. The greatest mistake, a close friend of his told me, was to go on making films. In 1947 he could have retired and watched his old films earning a comfortable fortune. But he was unable to do it. He was still trying to be a father not only to his own family, his immediate employees, his friends—but to the whole British film industry. And in the end it proved too much for him.

*   *   *   *

Almost the first two people who joined Korda when he 'opened up shop' at 146 Piccadilly were Ted Black and Leslie Arliss, who together had produced for Gaumont-British 'The Wicked Lady', 'Love Story', 'The Man in Grey'—all highly successful pictures. Ted Black, whose early death (he literally worked and smoked himself to death) was a heavy blow to British film production, wanted to do a film about Bonnie Prince Charlie; Leslie Arliss, the writer-director was put to work on the script. But difficulties arose and finally Arliss did 'A Man About the House', based on a successful stage play, instead.

Here, too, there were difficulties about the screen-play. Black liked it; Arliss didn't. Korda was unable to see them until a few days before production was due to start; Arliss, with some difficulty, persuaded him to read the script over lunch-time. Those who, like myself, have actually watched Alex read a script know what an awe-inspiring and amazing sight this was. Using only one eye, standing or sitting with the light behind him, he would go down a foolscap page in a few seconds. It seemed impossible that he should take in anything he read at such speed—yet he remembered every scene, every pertinent line of dialogue.

When they returned after lunch, Korda told Arliss: "You are right. We postpone production by a week—and you'll rewrite the script in three days." Arliss protested but Korda wouldn't

give him more time. In the end he went on the floor a week after
the original starting date and kept dashing off from directing to
rewrite frantically.

'Man About the House' starred a dark, good-looking newcomer, the Irish boy Kieron Moore, who had a rather chequered
career under Korda's wings. Margaret Johnston, Dulcie Gray,
the veteran Felix Aylmer and Lilian Braithwaite were co-starred.

When the film was finished, Korda looked at it. Arliss, sitting
next to him in the darkened theatre, saw him yawning, squirm-
ing, changing his position, and thought that the film must be
awful. But at the end Alex said: "You have made quite a nice
little picture . . ." Then he proceeded to tell the director what
scenes he should re-shoot and how. "You can have another week
for re-takes," he said. "No more, no less. That should be enough
to make the film really good."

Leslie Arliss told me: "He was the only genius I ever met. I
was truly awestruck as I watched him at work."

Though Arliss signed a four-year contract with Korda (passing
up an important Hollywood assignment) he only did one more
picture for him—the screen-version of Paul Vincent Carroll's
play 'Saints and Sinners', for which the dramatist and Arliss
wrote the script. This warm-hearted story of an Irish village
which believes in Doomsday coming upon it almost at once,
was not very warmly received in England but earned most
enthusiastic praises in America, where it ran for several months
in several 'art-houses'. The leading players were Kieron Moore,
Marie O'Neill and Michael Dolan. Christine Norden, one of
Korda's discoveries, struck a somewhat incongruous note as the
'girl from the city' among the well-characterized Irish types.

*   *   *   *

About the same time as Leslie Arliss, Guy Morgan also moved
into the Piccadilly headquarters. Morgan, a former film-critic of
the *Daily Express*, had fought with distinction in the war and had

12

tasted the rigours of a German P.O.W. camp. He was hired by Korda, rather casually, at a party.

Alex waved his magic wand and had a 'writers' room' equipped where Morgan sat for a few weeks, doing nothing. He was given a script secretary, a charming and efficient girl. Then workmen arrived and started to put up bookshelves all around the room. Obviously, writers had to have the right setting. A day or two later the same workmen turned up with huge crates which they opened, and proceeded to fill the shelves with volume upon volume. When they were gone, Morgan and his secretary inspected the books. There wasn't a single English volume among them—most of them were in Hungarian, a language which the screenwriter had unfortunately neglected to learn.

Morgan acquired a very high reputation with Alex—for the simple reason, he told me, that his abilities were never put to a real test. Korda would buzz him on the phone and he would go downstairs to his office.

"I want to make 'A Woman of No Importance'," he would say. "Do you know it, Guy?"

Morgan said he did. "Very well, take the book, read it and tell me how I can make it."

The screen-writer would go off, read the play, prepare his notes and wait for the summons. The next time Alex would present him with another book or play and ask him to do the same thing. Again he would get ready as if for a severe examination—but it never came. Before long Morgan would have had five or six similar summonses and be prepared to give his 'considered judgment' on five or six 'properties'. But he never got the chance. Then one day Korda called him down and introduced him to one of his producers.

"You can rely on Guy's judgment," he said. "He's always right, you know. I trust his opinions."

This time Morgan did tell the producer what he thought of his story and script—which wasn't very much—and, acting on his opinion, Korda rejected the proposition. The film was made for another company—and was a huge success. "But as he never put me to the test himself," Guy Morgan said, "my entirely undeserved reputation for a sound and shrewd judgment remained."

There was nothing more difficult than to get Alex to read a complete script or story. But if you did force him, the result was terrifying. "I don't need to read them," he told Morgan, "to know whether they are good or bad. A few pages will tell me —and I have never been surprised yet by any writer . . ."

It was always safer, then, to tell him a story; because this way there was give and take, his reactions could be taken into consideration promptly, his opinions respected. Of course, there were many writers who couldn't stand this—and there were occasions when Korda's judgment faltered, too.

Morgan's first task was to write the script of 'Night Beat', with T. J. Morrison—a picture Korda wanted to use to 'warm up' the studios he had bought. It was produced by Harold Huth, starring Anne Crawford, Maxwell Reed, Ronald Howard (the great Leslie's son) and Christine Norden, who was supposed to have been discovered in a cinema queue. It was a forerunner of 'The Blue Lamp' and many other British films that attempted to show the police 'from the inside'. As it happened, it was press-shown in a week in which there were no other films, so that the critics could concentrate all their attention (and some of them, their venom) on the modest offering. "Strangely enough," Morgan told me, "it was the only picture in that year among the Korda productions that showed a substantial profit!"

One of Korda's big films which was adversely affected by the Anglo-American film war was 'Anna Karenina' and Guy Morgan was also associated with it. The script had been written originally in the South of France by Jean Anouilh, the eminent French playwright, and Julien Duvivier, the equally eminent director who had worked with Alex before. When it arrived, it created some consternation at London Films headquarters. Anouilh, in a most original approach, had transposed the story to France and the early years of our century. This wasn't at all what Korda wanted and he brought in Guy Morgan to work on the screen-play with Duvivier.

"It was a great and startling experience for me," Morgan recalled. "I was young and deeply impressed by the genius of these two men. I found Duvivier wonderful to work with. He would act out each scene from the director's point of view and then leave the writing to me."

But then, almost every night, there was a story conference in Korda's Claridge suite. It followed exactly the same pattern every time. It began with a wonderful dinner, exquisite wines, brandy and cigars. Then Korda changed completely; he was no longer the charming host but the ice-cold, ruthless executive producer. He tore into the script, using colourful expletives and did not spare anybody's feelings. Duvivier would get angrier and angrier; until, in a towering rage, he would gather up his papers, announce that he would abandon the picture and return to Paris.

Alex and the director would shout at each other from opposite sides of the room while Morgan would sit on the sofa, his head swivelling from one to another. Sometimes Korda's doctor would arrive, take him into the bathroom to give him an injection—but the argument continued through the open door. Every night Alex would let Duvivier get as far as the threshold—and there would stop him dead in his tracks with a subtly calculated final insult. The director would turn back, react, argue and forget about his decision to leave. In the end something constructive would be achieved—but next night the same scene would be repeated with slight variations. What happened to the picture was tragic enough—it turned out to be too long, had to be cut drastically (in America about twenty minutes were scissored out of it) and this, with some miscasting, turned into a comparative failure something that should have been a triumphant success.

Even so, 'Anna Karenina' was a considerable achievement. Duvivier conceived the tragedy of the main characters against the crowded, bustling, vivid setting of a Russia that died in 1914 and had been dying since 1905. The railway stations, the opera, the parties, the balls of upper-class society created a pattern that was extremely attractive. Perhaps they were bound to distract the audience's attention from the main characters. Where its weakness lay was in the acting—though here some notable exceptions must be made. Vivien Leigh, who has perhaps the finest diction among British stars, presented a pictorially perfect Anna—but emotionally deficient. Too cool, too self-possessed, she made it impossible to believe her jealousy and despair, her maternal grief at losing her son. She remained aloof as if viewing her part from the outside. Only in the last scenes did she come to convincing life. Kieron Moore—and he was Korda's choice— was stiff, gauche, unconvincing as Vronsky. The real star of the film was Sir Ralph Richardson, whose tortured Karenin acquired a far greater significance than his lines.

Perhaps there was another factor that worked against the success of 'Anna Karenina'. Many filmgoers remembered Garbo in the rôle—and who could hope to equal her? Perhaps if the film had been in colour, instead of black-and-white, this handicap would have been balanced.

Korda's own swan-song as a director—apart from a few occasions when he took over 'unofficially'—was 'An Ideal Husband'. He had intended to bring over Paulette Goddard to play in a Carmen picture—Lajos Biro and myself were working on a script—but decided to do the Oscar Wilde play instead which Biro transposed to the screen in a witty, charming scenario. Michael Wilding, Hugh Williams and Diana Wynward co-starred with Miss Goddard, and Alex directed it with all his cunning, his feeling for period and character. It was photo-graphed by his old comrade, Georges Perinal. The film was sophisticated and light-hearted; yet it failed to become a box office success—perhaps because the Edwardian period was not yet in fashion, perhaps because of the lingering consequences of the Anglo-American dispute.

*   *   *   *

Anthony Kimmins joined Korda almost immediately after the war. They had met frequently before; Korda had often enlisted Kimmins's help while the latter was Chief P.R.O. at the Admiralty.

"He liked me and he liked my wife," Commander Kimmins told me. "During the war whenever I had shore leave, we dined at least once together at Robert Sherwood's country house which was near my cottage. For me these dinners were at first terribly embarrassing. Half-way through them Bob Sherwood would uncoil his giant's body at the head of the table, get up and make a most eloquent speech of welcome to us all. Then Alex would get to his feet and make an equally eloquent and witty speech. When he had finished they both looked at me and I realized I was expected to 'say a few words'—which I hated. I swore the first time it would never happen again—but I was always caught. It was a kind of game those two played, a sort of intellectual cricket— and I wasn't in their class."

When war ended, Anthony Kimmins was in the Pacific. Korda sent him a cable which reached him in San Francisco: "Want you as director-producer. When can you start?" Kimmins had been working for Ealing Films but succeeded in arranging for his release and he joined Korda happily.

The first picture he did was 'Mine Own Executioner', based on Nigel Balchin's penetrating and original novel. Korda brought over Burgess Meredith, one of Hollywood's most intelligent actors, to play the lead with Kieron Moore and Dulcie Gray as his partners. It won considerable acclaim and is still shown occasionally at film festivals.

Far less happy an experience for Kimmins was his next picture. With Ted Black's death, 'Bonnie Prince Charlie' became Korda's direct concern. He had borrowed David Niven from Goldwyn, he had made a good many other commitments and the film had to be made. Kimmins was more or less 'drafted' into the job. He had just finished 'Mine Own Executioner' and was about to fly off to Cannes to show it at the Festival. Then came a summons from Alex. He told Kimmins that he needed his help; he knew it wasn't fair but other directors had tried and failed, a great deal of money had been spent—he was to take over 'Bonnie Prince Charlie'.

Kimmins protested that he knew next to nothing of history and even less about Scotland; but Alex insisted. Kimmins drove home and told his wife about his dilemma.

"You know very well," Mrs. Kimmins said, "that Alex will bring you round—he always does, with everybody— so why don't you save time and energy and give in right away?"

Kimmins did and found it a very hard task. A host of writers had worked on the script but it was still only half-written and he had to do a fair amount of it himself with the aid of the historical expert who was called in. He found that Niven was thoroughly unhappy—indeed, years later the star wrote to me that it was an experience he preferred to forget—and that some of the casting was, to put it mildly, erratic.

Ronald Adam, who played in many Korda films, had done a long stint on 'Bonnie Prince Charlie' and then went to Rome on another film with Charles Goldner. To Charles's astonishment, he learned that he (Goldner) had been booked for additional scenes being written for the picture—and the part was that of a Highland captain. Now Charles was a Central European and very perturbed because of his accent. Adam tried to comfort him by pointing out that even if he were a Scotsman, speaking broad Scots, the rest of the world would hardly understand him; but he remained very worried.

They returned to England and to work. Korda, looking at the rushes of Goldner's first days in his Scots part, said to Bill O'Brien, the casting director: "Why do you have this man?"

O'Brien explained that Goldner was a fine actor and that

Anthony Kimmins had wanted him. Korda said: "But why a foreigner playing a Scots part?" O'Brien, placatingly, said: "Well, Sir Alex, he's a Hungarian." Whereupon Korda exploded: "Then why the hell don't I understand a word he says?"

The picture was first shown in October 1948 and the critics condemned it almost unanimously—at least the English did, for the Scots loved it. Two years in the making, it had cost half a million pounds; it was beautifully photographed and about an hour too long. David Niven was obviously unhappy with the part of the ill-starred prince; the best he could produce was a certain petulance and boyish charm but no tragic depth. The script was also rather inept. Only Margaret Leighton as the lovely and moving Flora Macdonald and Jack Hawkins as Lord George Murray gave fully satisfactory performances; the brave show of tartans and kilts was lost in the confusion of local colour and aimless posturing. The final verdict of the press was 'too much soda with Scotch'.

Korda's reaction to all this was rather surprising. He tried to do one thing he had never done before—argue with the critics. He started a large-scale and costly poster and newspaper campaign— there was a huge billboard in Piccadilly Circus—in which he declared that the critics were wrong and he and his associates were right. A trade paper called it 'a grand publicity gesture which, it is hoped, will not go unrewarded'. There was even a rumour (until better counsels prevailed) that the BFPA considered abolishing press shows of films. Unfortunately, the critics were proved right in the long run. 'Bonnie Prince Charlie' was one of Korda's rare mistakes, "and if I make one, it's a beauty," he confessed. But in the very long run, as Anthony Kimmins told me, the picture recouped most of its cost and it is still being revived in Scotland every year.

The next two pictures Kimmins did for Korda were far more modest but also more successful: the first 'Mr. Denning Drives North', scripted by Alex Coppel from his own novel starred Sam Wanamaker, Herbert Lom, John Mills and Phyllis Calvert; the second, 'Who Goes There?', a gentle frolic about a grace-and-favour house and a sentry who gets into trouble. For this picture Valerie Hobson returned to London Films after a long interval; Nigel Patrick, Peggy Cummins, A. E. Matthews, George Cole (as the unfortunate guardsman) and Anthony Bushell supported her. The picture did very well; but the most successful picture Kimmins did under the Korda wing was 'The Captain's Paradise', which he both directed and produced. The script was by Alec Coppel and Nicholas Phipps; the story of the literally amphibious ferry captain, shuttling between the decorous Victorian atmosphere of Gibraltar and the delights of Tangier, provided Alec Guinness with one of his most delightful parts. Yvonne de Carlo was the Tangier siren who hankers after domesticity; Celia Johnson, the staid matron on the Rock who blossoms out into something quite different in the end. The film had a very warm reception in the cinemas and was one of the pictures that established Guinness as a truly international star. It brought off something that is rare enough in the cinema: intelligent satire, flouting of conventions, high comedy without the bad taste of excessive slapstick.

*   *   *   *

Carol Reed had made 'Odd Man Out' for the Rank Organization but he wasn't happy under the growing influence of John Davis, who had become Mr. Rank's most important executive by the end of the war. Those wartime discussions with Alex bore fruit at last; in 1947 Reed signed a contract for five pictures with London Films; a contract that was soon extended. Of all the producer-directors working with Korda, Reed was the most successful and his relationship with Alex the most harmonious.

His first Korda film was 'The Fallen Idol'. The original story called 'The Basement Room' was discovered by Alex in a volume of Graham Greene's short stories. He introduced the novelist to Carol Reed; and then, knowing that he had two highly competent artists at work, he left them pretty well alone.

The short story was developed into a striking screen-play and 'The Fallen Idol' provided one of the most sensitive and original pictures in Carol Reed's career. Above all, he showed how beautifully he could handle children—for Bobby Henrey, the small, unself-conscious boy, was the most important character in the film, who lived his rôle instead of acting it. (At least Reed made it appear so.) Michele Morgan, Sir Ralph Richardson and Sonia Dresdel gave equally brilliant performances. Altogether Reed's start under the Korda banner was certainly a most auspicious one.

I have already spoken of my own very modest and all-but-invisible share in the beginnings of what was one of the most successful post-war London Films productions—'The Third Man'. Korda must have discarded at a very early stage the project of making a comedy with the background of shattered Vienna. According to Carol Reed the idea was suggested to Korda by *The Times* correspondent in Austria, who gave him a graphic description of the once-proud Habsburg capital, now divided between the four occupying powers, on the very edge of the Iron Curtain and (as in 1920, when Alex arrived there first) a happy hunting ground of profiteers, spies and black marketeers. It was Korda who suggested that the happy collaboration of Reed and Graham Greene which began with 'The Fallen Idol' should continue.

Graham Greene told Korda and Reed that he'd always wanted to do a story about a man who meets an old friend in the Strand —someone whom he'd believed to be dead. That was the germ of the idea and Greene agreed to go to Vienna. After five weeks he came back with the story of 'The Third Man'.

David Selznick was financially associated in the production; he provided the necessary dollars to pay Joseph Cotten and Orson Welles, who co-starred in the film with the beautiful Italian actress, Valli; Britain's contributions to the cast were Trevor Howard,

Bernard Lee and Wilfred Hyde-White and on the Austrian side there were the well-known actors Paul Hoerbiger and Ernst Deustch.

Korda had a special affection for the 'boy genius', as Orson Welles had been dubbed early in his spectacular career; a nickname he had found difficult to live down. But at the same time Alex was very much aware of Mr. Welles's volatile temperament and his habit (part of his genius) of doing too many things at the same time. These views of Korda somewhat affected the making of 'The Third Man', as Sir Carol told me.

He was in Vienna, shooting the picture, when the telephone rang. It was Alex, calling him from Claridge's. There had been some difficulty with Welles about arranging the dates of his stay in Vienna; he could only give them a certain number of weeks within a definite time. Alex told Reed that Welles would mean considerable trouble—maybe it would be better to cast the part with somebody else. Reed wanted Orson Welles very much but found it difficult to argue with Korda.

At this moment the other telephone rang—it was Welles calling from Rome.

Reed hesitated for a moment—and then he did an 'awful thing'. He hung up on Alex as if they had been cut off. He talked to Welles and arranged everything amicably. Then he called back Korda in London, pretending that the connection had been broken. As soon as Alex heard Reed's voice—maybe half-an-hour had elapsed between the two calls—he shouted.

"Carol, my dear boy, come right up! I've been waiting for you!"

It took a little time until Reed was able to explain that he was in Vienna, nine hundred miles away and that he couldn't very well 'come up' to Korda's pent-house apartment in Claridge's.

In the end 'The Third Man' triumphantly justified both Korda's initial idea and Carol Reed's casting. A stroke of genius made the zither of Anton Karas world-famous; no one had before dared to use a single instrument for the entire musical accompaniment of a film. But Korda and Selznick went to law over the picture—and Korda lost. When he was asked why he had originally agreed to terms that were obviously to his disadvantage, he confessed candidly: "My dear fellow—I didn't know it would be such a wonderful success!"

The third Carol Reed picture was a difficult subject. 'The Outcast of the Islands' had been suggested to him by Sir Ralph Richardson. Korda had always been a great admirer of Joseph Conrad and he fell in readily with the suggestion. The result was a most distinguished and artistic picture but not a great box office success. It gave Trevor Howard perhaps his most original part; Ralph Richardson gave another of his striking character studies and Kerima, the Indian girl, was a sensuous and most attractive heroine—though not exactly heroic. The film used an exotic background to tell a universal human story of weakness and strength, of friendship and betrayal, cowardice and love. The script was by William Fairchild and the production was once again designed by Vincent Korda; much of it was shot in Malaya.

'The Man Between', Sir Carol's fourth picture in this period was, in some ways, a sequel or parallel to the famous 'Third Man' —only it was set in post-war Berlin instead of Vienna.

James Mason came back to star in it after having appeared in small parts in earlier Korda pictures. In 1946 Korda signed a two-picture contract with him (one of these was supposed to be 'The King's General', the screen-version of Daphne du Maurier's novel which still remains unfilmed) and advanced $50,000 to Mason who was settling in the U.S. But a dispute arose over the contract and Korda sued his star for return of the money. In the end the matter was settled without rancour—in Alex's favour. "As soon as we had patched up things legally," Mason told me, "I came to England to appear in 'The Man Between'."

How little rancour there was, must be evident from a postscript in the letter Mason wrote to me: "Alex, incidentally, was one of the forerunners after whom we named our boy Alexander

Morgan. It seemed to us that the two names embraced a fine collection of conquerors, millionaires and pirates."

In this Carol Reed film Mason played an amoral hero, a man uneasily poised between East and West, crime and love. Claire Bloom was the innocent abroad, caught in the grim realities of a defeated country. Hildegard Neff gave a most appealing performance as a German girl married to an Englishman, conscious of both worlds and their dangers. Carol Reed's direction was as deft and tense as it always had been; still it would be wrong to pretend that he repeated his previous success. Maybe Berlin did not offer the same opportunities as Vienna; maybe the story was less original and logical. The film did well but wasn't an outstanding hit.

*   *   *   *

Anatole de Grunwald produced 'The Winslow Boy' for London Films, with Anthony Asquith directing this screen-version of Terence Rattigan's play; later de Grunwald scripted 'Home at Seven', based on R. C. Sheriff's stage-hit and co-produced 'The Holly and the Ivy' with Hugh Perceval, doing the screen-play as well. These were comparatively modest films which, on the whole, made quite considerable profits.

Carol Reed was followed by Michael Powell and Emeric Pressburger in the exodus from the Rank Organization. Indirectly, Korda had been responsible for creating the fruitful partnership of the Archers who were responsible for making some of the most interesting and provocative pictures since 1939.

Powell was first assigned to direct 'The Spy in Black'. A well-known novelist had written a script which Powell disliked considerably. One day he and the novelist were waiting in Korda's anteroom. The novelist said, rather bitterly: "I hear Alex has got some Central European to rewrite my script. I bet he's mucked it up. A fellow named Pressburger . . ."

At this, a small, round-faced man, sitting in a corner, interposed: "Excuse me . . . my name is Emeric Pressburger . . ."

The novelist glared at him but before he could say anything, the door opened and they were all invited into Korda's office where Irving Asher, the associate producer of the picture, joined them.

"I believe Emeric has some ideas about the script," Alex said.

Pressburger produced his notes and explained the somewhat drastic changes he proposed in the story-line. The novelist snorted, Powell listened with growing interest—for here was somebody who obviously knew his craft. Asher said nothing. At the end, Korda rose: "Well, this seems to be all very sensible. Get on with it."

Emeric Pressburger found his compatriot a most sympathetic and understanding employer. The novelist disappeared—Powell and Pressburger went to work and the result was a tight, exciting picture.

After that they collaborated on several films until they formed The Archers, a partnership which was responsible for 'The 49th Parallel', 'The Life and Death of Colonel Blimp', 'A Canterbury Tale', 'A Matter of Life and Death', 'Black Narcissus' and several others. The Archers were an important part of the Independent Producers Group operating under the Rank banner. But with their picture 'The Red Shoes' they ran into trouble. The script had been originally commissioned by Korda while Pressburger was under contract to him. Later the two partners bought it back from Korda and, after a long search, found their ideal star in the enchanting Moira Shearer.

The picture proved very costly; both Mr. Rank and Mr. John Davis became very worried about it. Before it was quite finished, they had it screened with Pressburger present. At the end, the two high executives departed in a stony silence. Powell and Pressburger thereupon went to Korda.

"We believe in this picture," they said, "but the Rank Organization doesn't. Are you willing to take it over?"

"Yes," replied Alex without a moment's hesitation.

"It means £500,000 in cash," Powell warned him.

"I think that can be arranged," smiled Korda.

The two partners returned in triumph to South Street. But there they were told that no such sale was contemplated and they were given enough extra money to finish 'The Red Shoes', which became one of the fifty biggest money-earners of all film-history. But this experience convinced The Archers that they would be happier under the London Films banner.

Actually, though their relations with Korda were always friendly and harmonious, ill-luck seemed to dodge most of their pictures done for him. 'The Small Back Room', based on Nigel Balchin's novel, starring David Farrar, Kathleen Byron, Jack Hawkins and Leslie Banks, had a comparatively modest budget and was successful. The story of a 'boffin' contained one of the most exciting sequences ever shot in any film—the dismantling of an anti-personnel bomb to learn its deadly secret—and also some startling, though perhaps slightly exaggerated visual probing into the subconscious.

The next two pictures both ran into trouble. The first, 'Gone to Earth', was a co-production of Korda and Selznick. For the screenplay, based on the Mary Webb novel, Selznick provided the services of Jennifer Jones, his wife, who had risen to stardom after her great success in 'The Song of Bernadette'. Selznick was disappointed with the picture and litigation followed with unhappy results for all concerned.

It was during this dispute that Alex once leaned over the table, facing Selznick, and asked with deceptive gentleness: "You don't really think you can out-trade me, David, do you?" Selznick, taken aback by this direct challenge, reflected for a moment and replied softly: "No, Alex, I don't."

The second Archers' picture that came to grief was 'The Elusive Pimpernel', for which Sam Goldwyn sent over David Niven; Margaret Leighton, Cyril Cusack, Jack Hawkins and other highly competent players co-starred in it. It cost a great deal of money—£450,000 was the figure I heard quoted—and when Powell and Pressburger presented it to him Goldwyn refused to accept it for American distribution. Various re-takes added another 6 per cent to the cost but the result was still unsatisfactory and there was a second lawsuit. How it ended, must be told in Mr. Goldwyn's own words:

> "Alex and I became embroiled in a double lawsuit—he sued me and I sued him. Months later when my wife and I sailed for England, the lawsuits and hard feelings were still going strong. During our last evening on the ship I mentioned to my wife that as much as I always enjoyed visiting London, this time we would not have the pleasure of seeing Alex. That old friendship was over.
>
> My wife admitted that she had been thinking of Alex and added certain impolitenesses about friends who get into lawsuits.
>
> As we arrived in our room at Claridge's the telephone began to ring. Alex was on the wire asking us to dine with him that evening. First, I said, we'd be delighted, then took the precaution of saying, 'Alex, I hope you know I'm still suing you.' Alex replied: 'Of course, and so am I you, but not during dinner, Sam.'
>
> Alex was always a charming host and companion but perhaps this evening he proved doubly so. Anyway, I was very surprised when my wife broke in with, 'Sam, Alex—it's after two o'clock. Don't you think it's time you started patching up that lawsuit?'
>
> Alex's voice was soft. 'Frances, why didn't you mention it before now?'
>
> Yes, Mr. Tabori, we settled the suit."

They did indeed—to their mutual satisfaction and the complete restoration of their friendship. The Korda charm had worked again—or maybe it had been the famous common sense of Mrs. Frances Goldwyn.

The most spectacular and lavish contribution the Archers made to London Films was 'Tales of Hoffmann', one of the most expensive and ambitious films they ever made, though not the most successful.

It was, as usual, produced, directed and scripted by Michael Powell and Emeric Pressburger; the distinguished services of Sir Thomas Beecham were obtained to conduct the score and those of Frederic Ashton for the choreography.

The cast was headed by dancers with a sprinkling of actors, including Robert Helpmann, Pamela Browne and Moira Shearer; Frederic Ashton, Leonide Massine, Ludmilla Tcherina added their considerable talents while Margherita Grandi, Owen Brannigan and others supplied the voices. The picture was a feast for the eyes; but it was much too long and highbrow for the general public. Nor did it appeal to Alex himself. One of his stars told me how he saw the film at the 1951 Cannes Festival. As it went on, he became more and more fidgety; then he murmured his excuses and left. Half an hour later he returned, holding a quadruple whisky. He took one look at the screen and grunted: "My God, it's still going on!" and retired again.

Perhaps he had a blind spot for the art of ballet; just as in Michael Powell's view, he basically disliked original stories. He thought in 'big properties', preferring a world-famous classic, a hit play—something that was 'pre-sold' by its reputation, like 'The Scarlet Pimpernel'. Or if it had to be an original story, he liked it to be built around a famous historical character. Whether this attitude developed gradually (for in Austria and Germany, not to mention the first Hollywood period, he had often filmed original subjects) or was ingrained, would be difficult to decide. But he wasn't happy about 'The Tales of Hoffmann'. It was the last film the Archers made for him.

★ ★ ★ ★

Among the 'solo' producers under the Korda banner, there was Emlyn Williams, the distinguished actor and writer who wrote and directed 'The Last Days of Dolwyn', a moving and often funny Welsh picture, dealing with the fate of a village doomed by the building of a new dam. It was—and it was meant to be—a modest, 'off-beat' film but Williams was very nervous of tackling the whole thing himself—yet dreaded official (and officious) interference.

"Korda was the ideal impresario," Mr. Williams recalled. "He said, one day at 146 Piccadilly, smoking a cigar and looking out of the window at the trees of Mayfair: 'I leave it all to you, my dear Emmaleen, you know what you want, I will give you all the expert technicians I can' (he did) 'and please come to me in doubt and trouble' (I did) 'for I have been through the whole bloody mill.' It's impossible to catch on paper not only the unexpectedness but the elegance with which he would suddenly swear. 'It will be a nice film, though of course I know and you know there won't be a damned penny in it' (there wasn't) 'but it's worth doing, before the whole business gets in a worse state than it is already—oh, films are finished, I'm an old man. I'm finished. Kaputt. Good luck.' From anybody else this send-off would have been depressing and even exasperating, but from him it was somehow a challenge, to do the film as well as he thought it might be done; there was again an avuncular twinkle in his eye as he shook hands as if to say: 'Don't believe a word I say, my dear Emmaleen, I've been gambling with films all my life and it's wonderful, I love it.' "

'The Last Days of Dolwyn' had a reasonably warm welcome and the acting of Dame Edith Evans, of Hugh Griffith and Barbara Couper (not to mention the performance of Williams himself) earned considerable praise.

Another actor, Robert Donat, also tried the same experiment with 'Cure for Love', which he directed himself, collaborating on the script and appearing in the leading part. His co-stars were his wife, Renée Asherson, and Dora Bryan, whose pertness as a brassy barmaid attracted the first real notice this very clever and funny actress received. It was one of the low-budget films which Korda decided to do—to prove that they could be done well. All three of these were considerable box office successes (they cost £50,000 apiece), but this did not balance the losses suffered on the more costly and elaborate productions.

The Boulting twins, John and Roy, also did a 'single turn' for Alex. They came to him with the idea for the tense and original 'Seven Days to Noon' which was scripted by Frank Harvey and Roy Boulting and directed by John. They had one or two friendly arguments with Alex about story and script but stuck to their guns and finally had their way—for Korda always respected true craftsmen. This taut, gripping story of a scientist carrying destruction in his bag through an unsuspecting London, was played by Barry Jones, Olive Sloane, Andre Morell and Sheila Monahan and it had a world-wide success. Again, there was some argument over the distribution terms and the Boultings left London Films.

There were other producers who appeared briefly under the Korda banner. Gregory Ratoff made 'My Daughter Joy'; Karl Hartl, his old associate, was responsible for the English versions of two Continental pictures (neither of them, alas, very successful). One of the three 'small' pictures in which Alex took a special interest was 'Home at Seven', produced by Maurice Cowan and directed by Ralph Richardson. It was shot in 13½ days—almost revolutionary for London Films. Speed was achieved by fifteen days' rehearsal before the film went on the floor. Another Richardson picture was 'The Holly and the Ivy', a gentle, heart-warming story which was also completed in less than a month. Joseph Somlo returned to his old friend to produce 'The Man Who Loved Redheads', scripted by Terence Rattigan from his play 'Who's Sylvia?' Directed by Harold French, this brought John Justin back to Korda. He co-starred with Moira Shearer, who played the enchanting 'redheads', all the loves in Justin's life.

This was Miss Shearer's first direct engagement with Alex. He sent for her to discuss her contract. She was very young and shy and inexperienced. She sat in a big armchair in his huge office, overlooking the garden at 146 Piccadilly.

"He soon realized," Miss Shearer told me, "that I hadn't the faintest idea of business or law. So, while he paced the floor, smoking his cigar, he said: 'Now, this is what you ask me to give you . . .' and reeled off the terms and conditions, figures and dates. Then he sat down behind his desk and said: 'Well, Miss Shearer, what *do* you want?' I repeated what he told me to ask for; he argued a little—in this case, he was arguing with himself—and in the end we settled every detail. It was so characteristic of Alex—and it helped me, of course, tremendously!"

Moira Shearer and John Justin were partnered by Roland Culver, Gladys Cooper and Denholm Elliott. The film was witty and charming even if it somehow failed to catch the public's fancy.

★   ★   ★   ★

After Sir Carol Reed and The Archers, Frank Launder and Sidney Gilliat also joined Korda. This famous partnership had started in 1943 and is still going strong. They began at the B.I.P. studios in Elstree and joined forces as a producer-director-writer team, alternately directing and producing for each other though sometimes they separated for a particular project. They formed their own company in 1945 and became part of the Independent Producers group under the Rank Organization. But differences arose over one of their most successful pictures, 'The Blue Lagoon' —according to Alan Wood, Launder was offered less money than Gilliat because his two previous films had been less successful at the box office than his partner's—whereupon they departed. "We left," Launder said, "because the Organization was heading for more centralization and more control." Their path also led to 146 Piccadilly.

The films they turned out for Korda were almost without exception successful and Alex interfered very little with their work. The series began with 'State Secret', scripted and directed by Gilliat; it presented a new kind of thriller, witty and original. It was partly shot in the Dolomites and some of the stars, with no heads for cliffs and mountaineering, had a somewhat dizzy time. Douglas Fairbanks jr. came over from Hollywood to co-star with Glynis Johns and Jack Hawkins, who was especially brilliant in his rôle as an amoral totalitarian Police Chief. Then came 'The Happiest Days of Our Life', a very happy success indeed with Alastair Sim and Margaret Rutherford enjoying themselves hugely. This was followed by 'Lady Godiva Rides Again', a good-natured romp with jokes that *did* come off—though Korda, as Gilliat told me, wasn't at all enthusiastic about this project (perhaps the very Englishness of its humour puzzled him). The leading players were Dennis Price, John McCallum, Stanley Holloway and George Cole, with the distaff side represented by such delectable ladies as Bernadette O'Farrell, Kay Kendall and Diana Dors.

Launder and Gilliat stuck to comedy with 'Folly to Be Wise', their next production, and starred Alastair Sim again with Roland Culver and Elizabeth Allan; the screen-play was by John Dighton and Frank Launder. Then came their biggest and least successful picture for Korda—'Gilbert and Sullivan', which marked the 21st anniversary of London Films. Launder and Gilliat directed and produced, the script was written by Gilliat and Leslie Bailey. It was a vast, very difficult project—the material was so rich and not only two eventful lives but the entire range of the Gilbert and Sullivan operas had to be covered. It wasn't made easier by the fact, as Sydney Gilliat told me, that one of the American financial backers of the picture was a G & S fan—though his passionate interest was almost entirely restricted to 'The Mikado'.

Korda showed a close interest in 'Gilbert & Sullivan'. There were innumerable story conferences, long discussions as to this or that piece of music being included or left out. The film threatened to become a three-or four-hour epic.

Once, Gilliat recalled, they were discussing the merits of some aria or duet. The arguments became somewhat heated; suddenly Alex said:

"There's one piece of music we absolutely must have . . ."

"Which one?" Gilliat asked.

"Why—that famous hymn. You know—'Onward, Christian Scientists!'"

A moment later Alex noticed his slip of tongue (in these days his memory had sudden, brief black-outs). He grinned and the rather tense atmosphere changed into one of good humour.

"It was this keen sense of humour," Gilliat told me, "which made you forgive him what you considered the most outrageous fits of temper. And he had the greatest possible consideration for his associates."

The three film-makers travelled together to the Berlin Film Festival where 'Gilbert & Sullivan' was to be shown. An hour or two before the performance Alex rang the two director-producers at their hotel. He apologized most profusely for a slight that had been done to them—their names appeared *under* his on a poster. Gilliat and Launder, thinking that this was done on all publicity, became a little incensed; Alex promised that he would remedy the matter at once. Finally it turned out that the 'insult' was restricted to one, small, hand-lettered poster on a staircase in the Festival cinema.

After many retakes and arguments the picture was at last finished. It had an outstanding cast. Robert Morley was part-nered by Maurice Evans, who returned to England and London Films after twenty years. Eileen Herlie, Peter Finch, Martyn Green, Dinah Sheridan supported the stars and the singers included the foremost Gilbert and Sullivan 'specialists', headed by Webster Booth, Owen Brannigan, Marjorie Thomas and Elsie Morrison.

The film was beautifully photographed by Chris Challis in colour; the sets were opulent and the performances faultless. Yet 'Gilbert & Sullivan' wasn't the expected success; perhaps because too much had been attempted; perhaps because the time wasn't ripe for it. 'Biopix', as the American trade paper *Variety* calls the genre, are always tricky—and this was no exception.

Launder and Gilliat soon made up for this disappointment by their wildly hilarious picture, 'The Belles of St. Trinian's', based on Ronald Searle's uninhibited and fearsome schoolgirls. Alastair Sim again headed the cast in which Joyce Grenfell, George Cole, Hermione Baddeley, Irene Handl, Guy Middleton entered whole-heartedly into the fun. 'The Belles' provided one of the few cases when a sequel was just as successful (if not more so) as the original offering; three years later Gilliat & Launder repeated the mixture in 'Blue Murder at St. Trinian's' and won even greater triumphs.

★   ★   ★   ★

Ian Dalrymple also came back to the Korda fold, which he had left for the Rank Organization in 1946. His first production was 'The Wooden Horse', based on Eric Williams's best-selling prisoner-of-war story. The script was by Williams himself; the director was Jack Lee. The all-male cast included Leo Genn, David Tomlinson, Anthony Steel and Bryan Forbes.

Leo Genn had appeared in 'The Drum', where he had played a rather villainous Oriental type. (Before that he had three lawyer-parts in a row, having come to films from the Bar.)

'The Wooden Horse' wasn't quite right when Alex saw it. "This was one of the few occasions," Genn told me, echoing Leslie Arliss unwittingly, "when I saw genius at work. Alex saw the roughcut reel by reel—stopping after each part and telling us without the slightest hesitation what to do, where to re-shoot, cut or add . . . It was a real bravura performance which I never forgot. Everything Alex said was just right—in a few sentences he summed up where we had gone wrong and how it

could be remedied . . ." Later Dalrymple produced 'The Heart of
the Matter', the screen-version of Graham Greene's sombre and
gripping novel, directed by George More O'Ferrall. It cost about
£120,000 and was a satisfactory success. Maria Schell, the
German actress, came to Shepperton to star in it with Trevor
Howard, Denholm Elliott, Peter Finch and Elizabeth Allan;
Anthony Squire took a special unit on location for the exotic
settings the film demanded.

The last arrival in the Korda camp was the brilliant David
Lean; the two pictures he made for British Lion and Alex were
both extremely successful though widely different. 'The Sound
Barrier' was based on an original script by Terence Rattigan.
This taut, highly topical subject provided grateful material for the
assorted talents of Ralph Richardson, Ann Todd, Nigel Patrick
and John Justin. Joseph Tomelty, the brilliant Irish actor, was
given his first chance together with Denholm Elliott. Richardson's
portrayal of an aircraft manufacturer whose job forces him to
ignore all human considerations, was especially brilliant. Ann
Todd gave one of her sensitive and delicate performances; Nigel
Patrick and John Justin proved again what capable actors they
were. After the film's success, Korda offered young Elliott a long-
term contract.

"What was amusing," Mr. Elliott told me, "was that the
decision to give me a contract took place in mid-sentence. Alex
turned to an aide and said: 'By the way, before I forget, we had
better give this boy—what's his name? Elliott?—a contract; now
as I was saying about etc., etc. . . .' and completely changed the
subject. I'm glad he didn't change his mind!"

'The Sound Barrier' did equally well in England and America
and was one of the most solid successes of Korda's final period.
So was Lean's next picture, 'Hobson's Choice'. Taking a semi-
classic play, he fashioned it into a delightful comedy. For the
part of Hobson, the pig-headed Lancashire shopkeeper, Charles
Laughton came back to London Films for the first time since the
ill-fated 'I Claudius'. The cast was a most accomplished one with

John Mills, Brenda de Banzie, Daphne Anderson, Richard Wattis, Joseph Tomelty and Helen Haye giving performances that provided able backing to Laughton's usual brilliant character-study.

Zoltan Korda's first picture in a long time was a brave and striking experiment—the screen-version of 'Cry the Beloved Country', the moving Alan Paton novel; a searching and deeply tolerant examination of race relations in turbulent South Africa. It was a long time in the making; Paton wrote his own script and much time was spent in and around Johannesburg, where one of Zoltan Korda's minor problems was that his coloured and white actors could not stay at the same hotel or even eat publicly at the same table. In Canada Lee, Sidney Poitier, Edric Connor, Lionel Ngkane, Charles Mcrae and Albertine Temba, Zoltan assembled perhaps the most distinguished group of Negro actors; Joyce Carey, Charles Carson, Geoffrey Keen and Michael Goodliffe provided the white counterpart to them. The picture received enthusiastic and unanimous praise from the critics and deservedly so; because of its theme it unavoidably met 'sales resistance' in some parts of the world.

★   ★   ★   ★

The final break between Korda and British Lion—or rather, the withdrawal of the Government support—seemed to come suddenly, yet actually it had developed over many months. In 1952, the British Lion deficit had increased by more than £400,000. In October of the same year Korda had to lend £50,000 to his own company to finance the re-issues of earlier pictures and it was announced that he would go back into production on his own account. In November, during the debate on the Cinematograph Bill in the House of Commons, there was a sharp attack on him by Mr. William Shepherd, M.P.

"I have reached the conclusion," he said, "that it might be well and to the advantage of the British Lion Film

Corporation if they had a new executive producer and someone other than Sir Alexander Korda should take on that job.
Sir Alexander Korda was associated with the lush days of the
film industry, and he is not attuned to making films at a
cost of £120,000 a time. I understood from his recent public
pronouncements that he is very interested or more interested
in television, and I think it might be to the advantage of
both the Corporation and the country if someone else took
over his job. If not, I suggest that someone else should take
on the job of Mr. Drayton, who is a public-spirited man,
who took on the chairmanship of the Corporation at a time
when things were very difficult. He is doing a job as a
public service but how can he have effective control over so
difficult an organization as a film company if he has forty or
fifty directorships to look after at the same time? I do not
think that the job of containing Sir Alexander Korda can be
done as a part-time job, and therefore I suggest that if Sir
Alexander Korda remains as executive producer, a full-
time chairman should replace Mr. Drayton."

The N.F.F.C. had been created by the previous Labour Government and the loans to British Lion had also been made during
their term of office. Both Labour and Tory members now
defended the record of British Lion and Korda, among them
Mr. Harold Wilson, Sir Tom O'Brien, General Secretary of
NATKE, Mr. Thorneycroft (then in charge of the Board of
Trade) and Mr. H. Strauss, his Parliamentary Secretary. All
of them spoke of Korda in very warm terms. Mr. Shepherd's
personal attack on him resulted in a special meeting of the studio
staff at Shepperton; they passed a resolution in 'anger and
indignation' which stated: "We pledge wholehearted support and
continued loyalty in your endeavour to maintain production of
good British films in the future." Alex was deeply touched by
this truly spontaneous expression of his collaborators' affection
and support. He had more than once described his philosophy of

film-making—but perhaps summed it up most concisely when he visited the Berlin Film Festival in 1953: "Whenever I made 'safe' films, I failed. Whenever I made 'crazy ones', I made a lot of money—and so did my backers . . ."

In November, 1953, Sir Arthur Jarratt was still speaking of making twenty top budget pictures in 1954 for British Lion. But a fortnight later it was announced that the net loss had been £150,330 for 1952/53 and that the total debit was now £2,217,035—more than two-thirds of the original Government loan.

The chill winds that were blowing in the glades and valleys of the British film industry heralded another crisis—and this time it seemed more serious than ever. Rank was slowly and doggedly reducing his enormous overdraft; commercial television was about to enter the scene; there had been no real relief in the entertainment tax and the Government was getting restive about the losses of the N.F.F.C. for the third or fourth year running.

The blow that fell in June, 1954, was perhaps the harshest, if not the most unexpected, in Korda's life. The Government decided to call in the loan, to terminate the support which it had given to British Lion. Four years later Mr. Davenport summed up what had really happened:

> "It was on a morning in June, 1954, that Mr. Harold Drayton woke up to find that he was no longer chairman of the British Lion Film Corporation. The Treasury which had lent the Corporation £3 million from public funds and seen it virtually go down the studio drain, had applied to the court for the appointment of a receiver in voluntary liquidation . . . He (Mr. Drayton) had only accepted chairmanship of British Lion out of a sense of public duty, for he knew that the Corporation was on the financial rocks, having previously given it a loan from BET (British Electric Traction Co.) secured on two Korda film epics which had

flopped. I have always thought that the Treasury treated
Mr. Drayton with scant consideration, but when financial
revolutionaries draw the gun, like all others they shoot on
sight. In this case they not only shot down Mr. Drayton
but all the innocent subscribers to the original British Lion
issue of four million 1s. shares at 5s. made in 1946 by the
merchant banking house of Hambro and sponsored by
leading brokers in the City . . ."

Mr. Davenport thought that "faulty organization and inadequate financial control on the part of both borrower and lender
were certainly to blame—as well as bad films." Before he had
resigned from the board of the N.F.F.C., he had suggested that the
Treasury should take over Korda's controlling shares immediately
(with his consent)—but Sir Wilfred Eady would not agree at
that time. He called British Lion films "the baby which was born
of the unholy wedlock between public funds and private (Korda)
enterprise". The baby almost died in 1954 and it is still rather
sickly in 1959—but Korda no longer had anything to do with
its further career.

Some time before, a trade paper spoke of the "old lion seeking
a new lair". These were tense and terrible days for Korda. Yet
his courage never faltered. It wasn't he but Tom O'Brien, M.P.,
who revealed that Korda himself had lost £500,000 in the
British Lion débâcle. Characteristically, the newly-appointed
receiver came to Alex and asked him whether he could suggest
anybody to succeed him as chief of production. Korda smiled his
slow smile and said: "It isn't easy . . . you see, I don't grow on
trees . . ."

A few days later he announced that he was continuing his work
with London Films. Not without cause, he added: "I am proud of
my record. In five years we have produced sixteen films—let
those speak for themselves."

British Lion and the 'old lion' went their separate ways. Once
again Korda had to rebuild a shattered empire—once again,

though for the last time, he gathered his courage and skill to fight the overwhelming odds.

*   *   *   *

So many films and fights; so many attacks and honours; so many plans and frustrations, successes and failures. These seven years in Alexander Korda's life were perhaps the most active and the most heart-breaking.

He still had the gift which so few other film-magnates in Britain possessed—the gift of helping and inspiring directors. One of his men at Shepperton Studios said of him: "Korda's an old rascal . . . you'd do anything for him." And there was always a special, almost electric feeling when he was down at Shepperton; as if every man throughout the studios had become alert.

Brian Worth, who appeared in several Korda pictures, though he was never directed by him, firmly believes that this atmosphere, created by Alex, endured even after his death. "Shepperton, to me," he said, "represents a place that still carries Korda's aura. I would work there at any time with the people he trained—rather than at some other studio . . ."

Korda's magic worked in many ways. When Sir Laurence Olivier was making a picture for him, he took a dislike to the painted forest background. "We want real trees," he demanded.

"Only God and Alexander Korda can make a tree," replied the art director.

They called the Piccadilly headquarters. Olivier got his trees.

Michael Powell supported Brian Worth's view, though he put it differently: "He was a giant—but he used his giant's strength as a child . . . or as a very wise and tolerant father . . ."

As an illustration, Powell told me the story of the Lost Test Films and the Frightened Third Assistant Director. It sounds like one of those cautionary tales in medieval books with capitals to make the words all significant—but it is a most illuminating incident.

Korda had discovered an actress. He was very hopeful of her future and decided to direct her tests himself. Shepperton was in full operation and time could only be found on a Sunday. The whole apparatus of the studio was mobilized, Alex went down and spent about ten hours on the job. At last it was finished, to his and everybody else's satisfaction.

A day or two later he demanded to see the result on film. The laboratories denied having ever received the negative. The whole studio was searched—and not a trace of the precious celluloid could be found.

Korda grew very angry and ordered a thorough investigation. By the end of the week it was discovered that the negative had been given to a young third assistant, the 'gofer boy'. (Gofer is film-slang for the lowest grade on the directorial side, the errand boy who is always told to 'go for' this or that.) And he had forgotten to deliver it! Then, realizing the enormity of his crime, he threw the film into the lake in the studio grounds.

When Alex was told of this, he descended upon Shepperton in Olympian wrath. But it was the studio manager at whom his anger was directed. "How can you give a boy such a responsible job?" Korda thundered. "What sort of an organization is this where a third assistant is so frightened that he'd rather destroy a negative than confess he'd forgotten about it?"

There was no question of dismissing the unfortunate young man; he kept his job and the dispatch department of Shepperton was completely reorganized.

In these last years loneliness seemed to draw upon Korda like a chilling shadow. This famous man who was, directly or indirectly, responsible for the livelihood of a couple of thousand people, who had friends and associates in five continents, appeared to be almost pathetically grateful for companionship. Sir Carol Reed told me how Korda would ring through on the house-telephone in the Piccadilly mansion and ask him: "What are you doing, Carol? Come up for lunch."

Then he would talk, about films, about his life, about people.

Sometimes he became depressed and his mind wandered, pre-occupied with its private concerns; then he would ask a question, something that was obviously just a springboard. It helped him to snap out of his dark moods and a few moments later he was talking with great animation. He seemed to delight in returning to the memories of his youth; he told Sir Carol how once he had undertaken to write and direct thirty films in thirty weeks. The scripts all had to be fitted to the existing costumes of the theatrical company that supplied his casts. When he had finished, he could only put together twenty-eight, though he had definitely shot thirty pictures—somehow two had got 'lost in the wash'. It was the kind of story that wasn't to be taken seriously; but he liked to tell tales against himself.

Sidney Gilliat and Frank Launder also used to receive such summons at lunch-time. There were weeks when Alex was punishing himself for rich living (he was beginning to have dizzy spells after too lavish a meal) and lunched on tea and toast. Those he invited for a chat had to do the same. Gilliat and Launder sometimes grew a little rebellious over such enforced austerity.

He could still be a most charming and entertaining host. In his social life, as Anthony Kimmins remembered, Alex was a wonderful actor. Mrs. Kimmins (an Admiral's daughter) and the director-producer would be invited to dinner as 'respectable people' whenever Korda had to entertain a high-ranking civil servant or some other, rather dull personage. The Kimminses played their parts, following Alex's lead. Then, with the important guests gone, they would sit down, take off their coats—and have a 'really wonderful time'.

*   *   *   *

In 1949 Korda bought himself a yacht. Characteristically, he named it *Elsewhere*.

Owning a yacht—even a comparatively modest, reconditioned

one—had been a long-standing dream of Korda. Steven Pallos told me how once, while they were both in Hollywood, Nicholas Schenck, the film-tycoon, had lent his yacht to Alex for a week-end. They sailed to Catalina Island and Korda came back full of enthusiasm for a sailor's life. When he thanked Schenck for 'the most enjoyable weekend of my life' and sang the praises of the boat, Schenck said: "You like it? It's yours, Alex."

Korda thought this a joke—the gesture was a royal one, even for a film-mogul. But Schenck insisted. The more Korda protested, the more serious his friend became. And in the end Korda accepted the gift.

He had to return to England but asked Pallos to make arrangements for bringing the yacht from Los Angeles to London. Pallos discussed the matter with a firm specializing in such services. They said they would quote a special price for the great producer—a trifle of ten thousand dollars. This was a bit too steep for Alex—and he decided to return the gift to Schenck. Later Pallos used to ask him how much he was spending on the upkeep of *Elsewhere*? Korda quoted the legendary answer of one of the Vanderbilts to the same question: "If you want to know how much the upkeep of a yacht is, you can't afford to keep one . . ."

He loved his yacht but he didn't have much time to use it. In 1952 he attended the Cannes Festival and then took his boat from the Côte d'Azur to Italy and then on a cruise to Greece. On the first leg of the journey Moira Shearer and her husband Ludovic Kennedy were among the passengers. The weather was rather stormy but Alex proved a wonderful sailor. He enjoyed it as if he had been born to the sea and not in a landlocked country.

In Naples the Kennedys disembarked; Graham Greene and the Oliviers joined Alex. Lady Olivier told me about the magic days they spent cruising among the Greek islands—how Alex really managed to forget his troubles for a short while even though he hadn't got away from films. In Athens rumours were ripe that this cruise would 'put Greece on the map' of the film world; Graham Greene was reported to be writing the screen-play of the *Iliad* with Sir Laurence and Lady Olivier heading the cast. They visited Epidaurus, with its magnificent ancient theatre; they called in at the Piraeus and spent some halcyon days among the Cyclades. The plan—if there was a plan—never came to anything but those taking part in the cruise certainly had a happy and restful time.

In May 1953, London Films celebrated its 21st birthday— almost a Methuselah age for a film company. 'Gilbert & Sullivan' was chosen as the birthday picture; after the gala première there was a party with three hundred guests. Mr. Dowling had sent a huge cake, decorated with figures of Korda's most famous films, and Alex cut it with a sword. Vincent and Zoltan were at the party; so were most of the men and women who were Alex's friends and associates, with David Selznick, Jennifer Jones, Olivia de Havilland and many others from overseas. It must have been a warm and satisfactory experience which touched his cynic's heart. The newspapers and trade publications paid tribute to his work and his genius.

Honours came to Alex in these final years, too; honours he never sought but still appreciated. The President of France decorated him personally with the Legion of Honour; the investiture marked, according to the citation, 'many years of devotion to French culture and the art of cinematography'. This was, indeed, well deserved; apart from his deep sympathy for French culture, Alex had also been instrumental in introducing many of the French films to England at the Rialto Cinema, his West End 'showcase'. I remember that it was at his invitation I saw the uncut version of 'Les Enfants du Paradis', perhaps the finest picture made in France during the war. Alex financed the exchange of students at the Sorbonne with Oxford undergraduates just as he endowed with a gift of £5,000 ten scholarships at the Academy of Dramatic Art for ex-service men and women and gave Oxford a similar sum to send a drama study group to the United States.

He was the first winner of the Golden Laurel Award which had been founded by David Selznick for 'a contribution to international goodwill and understanding through films'. Their lawsuits and arguments were forgotten over this occasion. The award was made at the 1953 Edinburgh Festival by Winthrop Aldrich, the American Ambassador who hailed Korda as the European film-maker "whose work through the years has made the most important contribution to the purpose of the awards." Before he died, he was made a Commander of the Italian Order of Merit; in June 1955, he received the Freedom of the City of Berlin. The boy from the *puszta* had come very far indeed.

* * * *

In 1952 a young blonde Canadian girl arrived in London to study singing. Her name was Alexa Boycun. She was born and raised in Fort William, Ontario. She met Alex at a party and they became close friends.

In June, 1953, Alex was relaxing in the South of France after the strenuous 21st birthday celebrations and his trip to India, where he had gone in connection with the planned 'Taj Mahal' picture. Alexa and her mother were his guests on *Elsewhere*.

Rumours of their forthcoming marriage had been going around for some time; but Alexa was silent and Alex denied it. On June 3rd, however, they announced their engagement—though Korda a few days earlier had told some reporters that they wouldn't get married for two or three months. Then, on June 8th, the wedding took place at Saint Paul de Vence—not very far from the place where Alex had married Merle Oberon in 1939. There were only a very few people present: General Edouard-Flaminio Corniglion-Molinier, the ex-chief of the Free French Air Force and now deputy for Saint Paul de Vence, who had become Alex's friend during the war—and Korda's old friend and associate, Baroness Moura Budberg. Though this was Coronation Week and Alex had hoped to escape the notice of the press, there were dozens of reporters and photographers outside the Town Hall and more than a hundred local inhabitants cheered them as they came out. Korda, seeing the throng, grinned. "I'm certainly surprised to see you here in strength," he told the pressmen. "I never guessed you'd find us out."

They asked him about his bride and he said: "She's never been in films and never will be . . ."

After a brief honeymoon, the newly-married couple settled down in an apartment in Millionaire's Row, Kensington. When somebody asked Alex about the difference in their ages, he grinned and said: "Now I know why I must pay my young lovers so high!" But then he added, softly: "I have never been so happy with anyone as with Alexa; I never knew a real home life until I married her—and yet I think she would like to leave all this and move with me into two furnished rooms . . ."

*　　*　　*　　*

What was the achievement and what was the failure of Korda in these seven years? Someone very close to him told me: "All his life he had been fighting and struggling, his quicksilver mind working at the highest pitch. All his life he wanted to be a father to all the world. And when he reached sixty and achieved fame and wealth, he was tired. His mind slowed down, his memory faltered; and he found the vultures gathering . . ."

As I said before, no doubt Korda made serious mistakes of judgment in these years. He allowed films to be made that never should have been made; he was also governed, to a certain extent, by a fierce and not always conscious, personal rivalry. The directors, producers, actors, writers who left the Rank Organization and came to him did this partly because London Films gave them more freedom and artistic independence; but also because Korda paid them a good deal more money. Sometimes far more than they were worth. The Anglo-American film war, the recurrent crisis—all this wasn't Korda's doing or fault. He could make pictures cheaply and well though he wasn't overmuch interested in them. British Lion lost almost three million pounds of public money. Not all of this, by any means, was lost on Korda pictures, but he was blamed equally for the mistakes of others; and under Korda's executive leadership a score or so fine films were made. Who could strike a balance here? Those films, given the right chance, might still earn back their production cost though with the spread of television and the falling-off of cinema attendances this is less likely today than it was with the films Korda bought back from Prudential. I have no intention of denying or glossing over Korda's mistakes. But I believe that without him British film production would have died in those critical years.

CHAPTER XI

NOT AS A FAILURE

SHORTLY after the collapse of British Lion, John Woolf, the young producer, met Korda in the South of France. C. M. Woolf, John's father, had been connected with Korda's early days in England, as we know—and when the young man followed in his father's footsteps, Alex took a paternal interest in his progress. To John Woolf he was something of a hero, a shining example.

"Why don't you retire, Alex?" the younger man asked Korda as they basked in the Riviera sunshine. "You have everything you could possibly want—a charming home here in the South of France, a beautiful young wife, your lovely pictures, enough money . . ."

"No," said Alex. "I couldn't retire. Not now. *I don't want to die a failure* . . ."

He wasn't afraid of death; he was rather bored by the thought of it. Once his doctor, complaining about his own problems, had said to him: "Life is difficult, Alex." And Korda had replied: "No, my friend. Life isn't difficult. It is exciting and wonderful. Dying is difficult—it's long and tedious . . ."

Many people thought they knew Korda. But they all knew only a part of him—and he was, like every genius, not one man but many. His doctor made a study of him for many years because he thought him such an extraordinary creature. His whole constitution, his physiology was that of a placid, almost lethargic human being. He used that part of the nervous system which others employ for rest and relaxation for the opposite—for stimulation and excitement. Every morning, lying in bed, with the telephones snakily criss-crossing their cords over the coverlet, he would seek for something to make him angry. Deliberately and systematically. Then would come a beautiful, almost theatrical outburst of temper, an Olympian discharge of lightning wrath. It began as sheer acting to turn into something real. He needed it. It was his way of recharging the batteries, soaking up new energy.

He was no hypochondriac; but illness made him impatient and difficult to handle. He hated exercise and never took it. Once he was in bed with shingles and his doctor tried to keep him quiet —an almost impossible task. The phone rang—it was Sir Winston Churchill, enquiring after the patient. Alex told him he wasn't at all well. Sir Winston began to scold him:

"The trouble with you, Alex," he said, "is that you never take any exercise—never use your hands. Look at me—I used to lay bricks, I still paint, I'm active . . . What do you do with your hands?"

"I talk with them," replied Alex—and that was the end of the conversation.

He took an almost impish delight in treating death playfully; as if the disrespect he showed for the end of all men would take the proverbial sting out of dying. Once, at a dinner, he sat next to a medical statistician and picked his brains through a long evening. The next time he met his doctor, he told him gleefully that he had worked out the actuarial percentages for three people —Sir Winston, the doctor and himself. According to the available data and the figures, the doctor had the worst life-expectation. Alex came next—and Sir Winston would live longest.

For once, mathematics lied; at least as far as Alex and the physician were concerned.

When Korda told John Woolf: "I don't want to die a failure," he knew that he was going to die. He knew that he might die any minute.

Apart from his skin-trouble, which was clearly of psycho-somatic origin (for his burdens had begun to weigh too heavily),

Korda was a remarkably healthy man. About 1952, however, there were signs that his circulatory system was beginning to deteriorate. Nothing alarming, nothing serious. But in the late summer of 1954 he had a heart-attack. It was coronary thrombosis. For the last eighteen months of his life he lived familiarly with death. He had lived as a Bohemian, as a spendthrift and as a cynic; he was to die as a *grand seigneur*, as a truly Roman Stoic. Many things he did puzzled and dismayed people during these months. They did not know, they could not guess that Alex was looking at the world, at life, from the almost Olympian height of a man who has been sentenced to death but does not know the date of his execution. Yet this was only part of his attitude. He did not want to distress or burden his family, his friends, his associates with his dying; and so to those who did not know of his doom, he said nothing; to those few who knew, he pretended that *he* himself was unaware of it. To live even a week in this condition needs inhuman strength, or perhaps what is more, the 'courtesy of the heart', the Italian *cortesia del cuore*, one of the rarest human qualities; to live under the shadow for eighteen months needs a high and noble stoicism—especially for a man who did not have the consolation of religious faith.

"Not as a failure"—that was the guiding thought in his mind, and success to him wasn't the game of capital gains and preferential dividends, of tax losses and paper assets. He was playing a far subtler and far more fundamental game—that of life and death. He had dreamed of a 'ripe old age', of peace 'from 60 to 95', as he wrote to Lajos Biro twenty-five years earlier—that dream was gone. What remained was to do his duty to himself, his friends and associates.

*   *   *   *

If he felt bitter after the British Lion débâcle, he recovered his spirits with amazing speed. He had to live with the very special pain which coronary thrombosis means, a pain unlike any other;

but it wasn't constant and he could often pretend that it wasn't there.

Less than five weeks after the appointment of the Official Receiver for British Lion, Mr. Robert Dowling flew to London and it was announced that a $15m. deal had been completed between him and Korda. "Sir Alexander and I are partners now," Mr. Dowling told the Press. "Korda has the talent for the films I'm interested in. I don't want the ordinary routine pictures at the rate of ten or twenty a year."

During his London visit, Korda's new partner expressed his wish to see a typical English home—as he had never been inside one.

Alex rang up Ann Todd and asked her to invite the American tycoon.

"What'll I serve him?" Miss Todd asked.

"Oh, anything," replied Korda.

A little mischievously, Ann served tea and crumpets, pretending that there was no alcohol in the house. Dowling admired the decor and his hostess in equal measure; but he was puzzled by the refreshments. When Alex asked him how he had enjoyed his first visit to an English home, he replied: "Beautiful, beautiful—but a little dry!"

Soon after the Dowling-Korda partnership, John Woolf became Korda's associate. Their business connection began when Deutsche London Films took over the German distribution of 'Moulin Rouge'. They both made a very satisfactory profit on it. A little later, when Woolf was preparing 'I am a Camera', he needed about £50,000 worth of German marks for location work. He went to Alex, knowing that he had money available in Germany. They began to talk—and at the end of the long session Woolf found himself committed to £500,000 and a partnership in four films. The £50,000 was quite forgotten . . .

It was typical of Korda to turn disaster if not into triumph, at least into a new beginning—even if he knew that he could never see its full flowering. John Woolf certainly had no reason to regret that visit to 146 Piccadilly. In September 1954, Alex announced that he would make a film in Cinemascope in association with 20th Century–Fox—a London Films Production, based on Terence Rattigan's hit play 'The Deep Blue Sea'. Anatole Litvak, the veteran Hollywood director, was coming over to direct it. Other ambitious plans were in the offing, resulting in the successful films of 1955.

* * * *

Of the last seven pictures of Korda all but one were conspicuous financial and artistic triumphs. 'The Constant Husband' had been shot still under the British Lion–London Films tie-up; it was another polished, satirical comedy from Frank Launder's and Sidney Gilliat's fertile brain. It starred Rex Harrison with Margaret Leighton and Kay Kendall; it had a well-deserved success both in Britain and America.

So had Carol Reed's last Korda film, 'A Kid For Two Farthings', the legend which Wolf Mankowitz wove from the teeming and vivid material of London's East End.

"At first Alex couldn't see it as a film at all," Sir Carol told me. "But he read the book again, slept over it and rang me to say that he had changed his mind."

Scripted by Mankowitz, one of the most robust and original writers of our post-war generation, the film had a brilliant cast. Carol Reed's magic touch brought extraordinary performances from such new and old stars as Celia Johnson, Diana Dors, David Kossoff, Brenda de Banzie, Jonathan Ardmore (the small boy who finds a fairy-tale unicorn in Petticoat Lane), Sydney Tafler, Primo Carnera, Sidney James and others. London herself acquired a new beauty and dimension; Korda's co-operation with John Woolf and his American backers started most auspiciously.

Undoubtedly the most important film in this final phase of Korda's career was Laurence Olivier's third Shakespeare picture —the triumphant screen-version of 'Richard III'. Sir Laurence's own performance of the crookback king was worthy to set beside his great 'Henry V' and 'Hamlet'. John Gielgud and Ralph Richardson, Sir Cedric Hardwicke and Claire Bloom, Alec Clunes and Helen Hayes, Pamela Browne and Stanley Baker—to mention only some of the large cast—all kindled to the superb challenge of Shakespeare. There was great visual beauty in the film, and though Lancastrian and Yorkist history still puzzled some of the viewers, the film repeated the triumph of 'Henry V'. It was the first major motion picture that had its American première on television—an astute move that didn't endear Korda to the exhibitors yet proved that such an 'exposure' to millions of viewers in a single night did *not* hurt the subsequent box-office receipts in the cinemas. It was a bold experiment which came off.

'The Deep Blue Sea' when it came to be made had a less happy career. Though Rattigan wrote a sensitive screenplay and Anatole Litvak brought all his experience and understanding to directing it, the film did not do well. The cast was impeccable —headed by Vivien Leigh, who came back to Korda for the first time since 'Anna Karenina', starring with Kenneth More, Eric Portman, Emlyn Williams and Moira Lister. It was expensively mounted and beautifully photographed—but the tale of the tormented lovers somehow failed to ring the bell.

Extremely successful was the remake of Zoltan Korda's 'Four Feathers' (now called in some countries, 'Storm Over the Nile') and remade by Zoltan himself. Various attempts were made to bring the story 'up to date' but in the end it was decided to keep to the original. According to some wits, Zoltan Korda insisted that even the same rocks should be photographed as in the first, well-tried and popular version.

Alex was also concerned with the David Lean picture, 'Summer Madness', which Ilya Lopert produced and which was shot against the never-cloying beauty of Venice. It introduced to the Anglo-Saxon public Rosano Brazzi, the handsome Italian star, who was co-starred with Katherine Hepburn. Though it did not make a large profit, the picture had most enthusiastic reviews (especially in the States) and comfortably recovered its production cost.

* * * *

Those last eighteen months of Korda's life, between June 1954 and January 1956, were full of planning and activity—even though he knew that most of those plans could not come to fruition. They were also full of somewhat nostalgic journeys. In June 1955 he went to the Berlin Film Festival with his brother Zoltan. He was not very well and Zoltan insisted that he should be back in their hotel every night by ten—which meant that Alex did turn up not later than eleven. His caustic humour never deserted him. When he visited the Hamburg offices of Deutsche London Films, he ordered champagne and asked the pretty secretaries to join him in a glass. One of the girls said, enthusiastically: "You ought to come to Germany every week, Sir Alexander!" Korda turned to Karl Klär and said: "You see, I'm getting an old man. A few years ago she would have said: 'Come every day!'"

He made a brilliant speech in his 'Mikosch-Deutsch' (that is the German expression for 'Hungarian' or 'pigeon'-German) at the Festival. Later that evening some women journalists wanted to interview him. Korda asked whether they were pretty. Klär assured him that they were. But Alex looked at his watch and said, with a little sigh: "It's only half-past ten. For men of my age that is much too early!"

His post-war visits to Germany always seemed to have put Korda in a reminiscent mood. During one of them he said in an interview:

"It would be fine if I could say that as soon as I saw the first talkie, I forecast enthusiastically: this is the future of the cinema! But unfortunately this would be untrue. I was interested in sound as a 'craftsman'—but neither more nor less than in any other technical equipment or invention in the cutting rooms. You can therefore imagine how I felt when they told me in Hollywood: 'Your next film will be a talkie!' I had already seen in Germany, in 1923 or 1924, an experimental talking film. There was a barnyard in it with all kinds of poultry and it sounded most natural. But I had no special interest in it . . . As a young man, all my ambitions were literary. At eighteen I wanted to write a great novel—at least as great as *War and Peace*. Or a thin volume of poetry with a dozen immortal sonnets. Though these youthful dreams never matured, something remained of them and I approached films more from the literary than from the pictorial angle. This might be also a 'fault' of my later films; it depends on the point of view of the critic. I still remember how unhappy I was when I made 'The Private Life of Helen of Troy' and had to use sub-titles to make certain ideas tangible. With the talkies this annoying crutch could be thrown away for ever . . ."

There were other journeys and plans. Korda had joined the original board of A.B.D.C., the first British commercial TV company. In October 1955 he resigned; he had little faith in sponsored television even in the modified form Britain had adopted. He formed two new subsidiaries and acquired the television rights of Somerset Maugham's short stories. He announced that in 1956 he would start a television film series based on famous trials. He had already sold several of his films to American television at a price reported to be £20,000 each.

He had many interesting plans for feature films, too—among them 'Arms and the Man' with Alec Guinness; the long-deferred 'King's General', the screen-version of Daphne du Maurier's novel for which he was supposed to have paid £60,000; 'The Admirable Crichton', in which he planned to star Robert Morley and Kenneth More. He was also planning a fourth Shakespeare film with Sir Laurence Olivier—the first choice was 'Macbeth'.

It is another proof of the great gap left by Alex that up to now no one has had the courage and vision to finance this picture.

The last film which bore Korda's name was finished a few days before Christmas 1955. It was 'Smiley', based on Moore Raymond's delightful book of an Australian boy's life in the 'outback'. The film had been planned for a long time but various difficulties postponed it again and again. Korda loved the book, in which he felt the freshness of Mark Twain, and he made arrangements with Spyros Skouras, head of 20th Century–Fox for a co-production. Unfortunately he also mentioned a provisional budget figure—£125,000—which would have been enough for a normal, black-and-white version but proved to be very tight for the Cinemascope and Technicolor format which was finally chosen.

They were stuck with the original budget. Anthony Kimmins, who produced and directed the film, tried very hard to pare it down, even deferring his own fees; but there was still the sum of eight or nine thousand pounds which they couldn't cut. Kimmins had made all the arrangements to go to Australia and still there was no decision. Then one day Alex sent for him. He had the budget on his desk. With a stroke of his pen he deleted the sum of £8,000—the cost of the completion guarantee from the N.F.F.C. on which, of course, all distributors and executive producers must insist.

"Tony, I've never done this for anybody before," he told Kimmins, "but it's the only way. Now you must really finish that bloody picture—on time and within the budget!"

Kimmins did. In Australia he found Sir Ralph Richardson on a theatrical tour. For him he enlarged the part of a bush parson and Sir Ralph gave a delightful performance—as did the small, tow-headed and freckled boy whom Kimmins discovered after a country-wide search. A few days before Christmas the last scene was shot in the wilds of the Australian bush. Kimmins drove to the nearest tiny post-office to send a cable. The old postmistress had never sent an international one before and it took quite some time to look up all the regulations. '*Smiley finished*,' the telegram ran, '*well under schedule and well under budget. Love, Tony*.' Back came a warmly congratulatory message from Alex. Kimmins returned to England via Hollywood. It was on the way that he received the news of Alexander Korda's death.

*   *   *   *

In November 1955 Alex had to go to America. He was to sign contracts, finalize various production plans. A few days before he had a medical check-up. His personal physician and an eminent heart specialist were present. Korda stood behind the screen in the darkened part of the room while they faced the X-ray screen. The two doctors did not have to exchange a single word or even a look—the X-ray picture told the story clearly. The heart-muscle was practically gone. The end might come at any moment—in a day, in a month, in a year.

Korda went to get dressed and then returned. He told them that he had to go to New York, where a week of concentrated effort awaited him. Was it all right for him to go? The doctors said yes, of course. They knew that nothing could make the slightest difference.

"I'm planning to start this picture on February 16th," Alex went on. "I'll have to go to the studio every day—spend six or eight hours there. Will that be all right?"

"Yes, Sir Alex," replied the heart specialist.

Korda asked a few more questions, seeking reassurance—or so it sounded. The doctors gave him all he wanted. He thanked them warmly, then drove back to Piccadilly. He turned out everybody from his office; he sat down and wrote his will, his final letters—preparing everything, putting all in order. *For he knew*. He knew that the picture in February would have to be made, if it were made, without him; he knew that the end was near. But he played the game, the elaborate, beautiful game with his doctors, with the whole world. He might have thought that dying was a long and tedious business; but he was going to tackle it in the manner of a *grandseigneur*, of a modern Stoic.

The end came suddenly but not unexpectedly.

The day before he died, David Lewin, the *Daily Express* columnist, lunched with Alex and his wife.

> "There were just the three of us—and Korda's bulldog, Buttons. We chatted through the afternoon, Alex in his white silk monogrammed pyjamas and dressing gown, because he was not feeling well and had stayed in bed until one o'clock when his doctor had left him . . . He joined me in a brandy—although he was not supposed to drink—and said: 'You know, David, I came into the show business forty years ago knowing nothing. Then I learned everything. Now I know nothing again. That is films. Sometimes I think of retiring but then I go to my desk again and I know I cannot. When you have been on the treadmill as long as I have it goes faster and faster and it is not possible to step off . . .'"

That morning his wife had chided him gently because he had taken to going out alone, dismissing his car and the faithful Bailey, his driver. His doctor was with him when Lady Korda made these solicitous remarks. Alex looked at them and smiled his slow, wise, cynical smile. The doctor always wore a bow-tie; he also happened to wear a suit which Korda had given him.

"Don't worry, my dear," Alex said. "Should anything happen to me, they'll phone you from the morgue . . , I've got a label with my name inside my suit . . ." Then he paused and grinned. "Even then you may have a pleasant surprise. . . ."

"A pleasant surprise?" asked his wife. "Really, Alex . . ."

"Yes. You should ask whether the body's wearing a bow-tie or not . . . If he does, even though my label's in his suit, it isn't me. . . ."

The final heart-attack came in the evening of January 22, 1956. The doctors arrived within a few minutes; Korda fought death for over eight hours though it was obvious that nothing could save him. He had almost no pulse, he was in great pain and unconscious part of the time. Yet he rallied again and again and his brain was still as clear and nimble as it had always been. When one of the three doctors left, he thanked him courteously and apologized for keeping him up so late.

Near the end his wife bent over him. "Go to bed," he whispered. "You must rest . . ."

"God bless you, Alex . . ." she faltered.

A tiny smile flickered across the dying man's face.

"Don't bother the Old Man up there," he said. "He's done enough already for me. . . ."

He turned to his doctor:

"If I say good night to you now, my friend . . . will you promise that I won't wake again?"

The doctor nodded as he gave him another injection. As dawn broke over Kensington Gardens, Alexander Korda died.

*   *   *   *

Ann Todd was having lunch that day with Madame Pandit Nehru at the Indian Embassy opposite Korda's house. A sudden storm lashed the trees in Millionaire's Row, lightning flashed, then the clouds burst and the heavens seemed to be rent by the violence of the hurricane. Ann felt frightened and oppressed by a sense of disaster. Then, as she left the Embassy, she saw the headlines of the evening papers: ALEXANDER KORDA DIES.

The obituaries paid tribute to his genius, his charm, his vision; so did the leading figures in the film industry. But to those of us who gathered in St. Martin-in-the-Fields, the finest tribute, the most perfect summary of Alex was given by his friend and star, Sir Laurence Olivier:

"This is a memorial service," Sir Laurence said, "and a memorial should be a fusion of prayer and thanksgiving.

First then, let us offer thanks for his godlike yet unobtrusive generosity; for his perceptive and informative intellectuality; for the intelligence he used every bit as much for his friends as for himself.

He was wise, he was kind, he was clever—clever with the gift of a shepherd, and there were times when he could be a very angry shepherd indeed. He was not soft. He was gentle and he was strong. He managed the difficult and rare mixture of artist and businessman with an extraordinary virtuosity. He had a joyous humour and an enchanting imagination. He was a wonderful mixer and great company with his shrewd wit and fascinating conversation. Though he never really mastered the English language, he improved it; and if our country may feel some pride in his anglophilia, the rest of the world can apprehend and praise the internationality of his instinct and purpose.

Artistically he was always remarkable for his individual and original angle of approach. In working association we loved him as actors and craftsmen because he loved us, and loved our problems, too. The warm radius of his friendship ranged from the humblest studio technician to the highest personages in the land.

With a backward eye, perhaps, to those beginnings from which he became such an international figure, he relished what life had to offer and lived it in a beautiful and enviable style; and with an inward eye to humanity he was capable and experienced in deep suffering and compassionate understanding. When his back was against the wall, he was quite magnificent. In the last year of his life he made five successful pictures and last week, when he must have felt the cold sergeant's hand upon him, he was busily planning four feature films.

In deep gratitude and pride will he be kept for ever by the devotion he inspired in his loved ones, his friends and his personal servants.

So much then, and most inadequately expressed for you, I'm afraid, so much for the thanksgiving part of our Memorial.

For our prayer, let it be that we may bear our bereavement and face what cold newness and strange changes his passing is to bring about with the like courage and resourcefulness that he would have shown, for—take him for all in all—we shall not look upon his like again . . ."

* * * *

"When Korda died, I died too," Montague Marks told me. After the war, which he had spent in hush-hush work in Spain, Marks had returned to Korda as an executive. But when Alex died, he retired and refused to have anything more to do with films.

When Korda died, London Films, his empire, died with him. Perhaps he had done it deliberately, perhaps unconsciously—but he made a will whose terms made it impossible for anybody to carry on after him. When his will was admitted to probate, it was found that his estate amounted to £385,684 (£158,160 net). He left £10,000 to his son, Peter, to be paid at once; £2,000 to his first wife, Maria; £500 to his faithful chauffeur, Ernest Bailey. To his wife Alexa he left all his personal belongings—including the valuable collection of paintings which he had gathered through many years as a most discerning connoisseur—and one-quarter of the residue of his estate. As executors he named his brothers Vincent and Zoltan (the latter resigned immediately for health reasons) together with Sir David Cunynghame and Harold Boxall. The will stipulated that if any of the beneficiaries disputed its terms, he or she was to forfeit his or her share.

In spite of this, a whole series of court actions followed, some of which are still pending. Both Maria Korda and Peter sued the executors; these actions, up to the date of writing, have all been unsuccessful. Nor has the estate been wound up yet, more than three years after Korda's death. He owned a good many valuable story and script properties; his old films are still playing in the cinemas of the world. In Britain twenty-five of his films have been sold to commercial television at a reported price of £50,000. London Film International has earned more than a million pounds since 1956. Alex also had a number of artists under contract and these had to be disposed of. Altogether, his executors have a complex and difficult task to carry out; but the production side of his companies ended its work when he died.

Few men can foresee what will happen to their estate, their work, their reputation after their deaths. But Korda left both a great legacy and a great vacuum. More than a score of directors and producers learned the craft of film-making under his wings. The best of them—and the most successful—carry on in their individual ways the Korda tradition even though the British film industry has again reached one of its periodical crises which even the drastic reduction of the Entertainment Tax hasn't been able to solve. Almost everybody to whom I spoke about Korda, agreed with Sir Laurence's summing up: "Take him for all in all, we shall not look upon his like again . . ." There is literally no one to fill his place. His enemies and detractors, of whom he had his share, cannot deny his leadership and unique vision. "There were four or five people who played an important part in my life," Sir Carol Reed told me. "Of these Alex was the most important. I would have done anything for him—anything—and one of the greatest sorrows of my life is that he is no longer here that I could do his bidding."

*   *   *   *

His house in Kensington Palace Gardens has been sold to the European Coal and Steel Community. After a year, his wife remarried. The mansion in Piccadilly is now divided up into various offices, though it still serves the making of films, for it houses, among others, Joseph Somlo, Douglas Fairbanks jr.,

Anthony Kimmins, Sir Carol Reed and several others. But the finest and most enduring memorials to Alexander Korda are his films. Hardly a week passes that they are not being shown somewhere in England; his name crops up again and again at film society meetings, festivals and lectures, in the pubs around Wardour Street, in the studios. The man dies, his work lives—even in the most ephemeral form of the creative arts.

There was a question I asked every star, director, producer, technician or friend about Korda: "Was he a happy man?" If I wanted to take a poll, the result would have been overwhelmingly in the negative. One of his secretaries, who loved him dearly, cried almost indignantly: "How could a great man expect to be happy?" At the most, they said, he had moments of happiness— but many of them saw him in moments of dejection and thought him, fundamentally, a very unhappy man indeed.

What was the source of this unhappiness? He had the good things of life, luxury, comfort, fame. He had to fight for these— but without a good, hard fight he wouldn't have felt alive. His personal relationships weren't happy but sometimes he found companionship and peace. Though he had the healthy appetites of a Central European, he wasn't what one would call 'a ladies' man' and he had a deep reserve in his most intimate life which few had been able to penetrate.

John Grierson, who never worked with him but was his friend for many years, told me: "Of course he was unhappy. He was like a tigron—the half-lion, half-tiger I once saw in a zoo. Pacing restlessly, up and down, circling the cage—it looked to me the most miserable animal I had ever seen. It reminded me of Alex in all his strength and power. He was half-artist and half-businessman; and he wanted to be an artist, pure and simple. He couldn't resist manipulating large sums of money—and I suppose, with the kind of pictures he made, he had to. But this always created a feeling of guilt as if he had betrayed the funda-mental Korda . . . He knew it and he couldn't help it; and even so there was enough of the artist left to wipe the floor with any other film-producer I had ever met . . ."

So many of his friends and associates felt the same; though they all agreed that he wasn't interested in money for money's sake. Indeed, he despised it. The story, used so often to sum up his character, was more than a facile joke: when he handed one of his young nephews a five-pound note, he told him: "Don't spend it —waste it. That's what money is for." But he was fascinated by high finance as he was by politics; knowing the great, being on intimate terms with them, wasn't a feeding of snobbery; it was part of his way of life.

Yet, as Grierson pointed out, could he have functioned as an artist without being a financier? I met a writer who told me how wonderfully humble and understanding Korda was.

"He sat and listened to me for two hours," the screenwriter said, "while I told him what was wrong with all his pictures. I'm sure, he would've listened even longer, only his secretary came in to tell him that his Rolls was waiting. He was to be driven to the airport to fly to Antibes and board his yacht."

"And you?" I asked, a little maliciously.

"Oh, me?" he replied ruefully. "I caught the bus back home to Brixton . . ."

*　　*　　*　　*

He wasn't a happy man; but I believe he was a great man. Somebody quoted a saying of Winston Churchill about Korda to me. "Alex would make a wonderful Prime Minister of Hungary," Sir Winston had said, "if he had Rockefeller for his Chancellor of Exchequer." I don't think that Korda ever had any political ambitions; and he had to be his own Chancellor of Exchequer. His greatness was not in his charm, in his talent or skill; it was in his imagination and artistic sensitivity, in his courage and tenacity. That is why he has a place of honour in the history of film-making which few can equal.

KORDA'S FILMS

This list is as complete as I could make it and has been checked by Korda's various associates. The dates are approximate as sometimes there was considerable delay between completing a picture and its release. Korda has been connected with these films in various capacities and I have used a simple code to mark these: D = Director; P = Producer; S = Screenplay; EP = Executive Producer. The titles are given in the original language with an English translation where necessary.

(1)	Egy tiszti kardbojt (An Officer's Swordknot)	1916	D - S
(2)	Fehér éjszakák (White Nights)	1916	D - S
(3)	Vergödö szivek (Struggling Hearts)	1916	D - S
(4)	Nagymama (Grandmama)	1916	D - S
(5)	Mesék az irógépröl (Tales of the Typewriter)	1916	D - S
(6)	Egymillió fontos bankó (The Million Pound Banknote)	1916	D - S
(7)	Mágnás Miska (Mike the Magnate)	1917	D
(8)	A kétszivü férfi (Man with Two Hearts)	1917	D
(9)	Szent Péter esernyöje (St. Peter's Umbrella)	1917	D
(10)	A gólyakalifa (The Stork Caliph)	1917	D
(11)	Mágia (Magic)	1917	D
(12)	Faun	1917	D
(13)	Az aranyember (Man of Gold)	1918	D
(14)	Harrison & Barrison	1917	D
(15)	Mary-Ann	1918	D
(16)	Ave Caesar	1919	D
(17)	A kétlelkü asszony (Woman with Two Souls)	1917	D
(18)	Se ki se be (Neither in Nor Out)	1918	D
(19)	Fehér rózsa (White Rose)	1919	D
(20)	A 111 - es (The No. 111)	1919	D
(21)	Yamata	1919	D
(22)	Seine Majestät das Bettelkind (The Prince and the Pauper)	1920	D

(23)	Herren der Meere (Masters of the Sea)	1922	D
(24)	Eine versunkene Welt (Lost World)	1922	D
(25)	Samson und Delila (Samson and Delilah)	1922	D
(26)	Jedermanns Frau (Everybody's Woman)	1924	D
(27)	Das unbekannte Morgen (Unknown Tomorrow)	1923	D – S
(28)	Tragödie im Hause Habsburg (Tragedy in the House of Hapsburg)	1924	D
(29)	Der Tänzer meiner Frau (Dance Mad)	1925	D – S
(30)	Eine Dubarry von Heute (A Modern Dubarry)	1926	D
(31)	Madame wünscht keine Kinder (Madame Doesn't Want Children)	1926	D
(32)	The Stolen Bride	1927	D
(33)	The Private Life of Helen of Troy	1927	D
(34)	The Yellow Lily	1928	D
(35)	Night Watch	1928	D
(36)	Love and the Devil	1929	D
(37)	The Squall	1929	D
(38)	Her Private Life	1929	D
(39)	Women Everywhere	1930	D
(40)	The Princess and the Plumber	1930	D
(41)	Rive Gauche	1931	D
(42)	Marius	1931	D
(43)	Service for Ladies	1931	D
(44)	Women Who Play	1932	D
(45)	Wedding Rehearsal	1932	D – P
(46)	Men of Tomorrow	1933	P
(47)	That Night in London	1933	P
(48)	Strange Evidence	1933	P
(49)	Counsel's Opinion	1933	P
(50)	Cash	1933	P
(51)	The Girl from Maxims	1933	D
(52)	The Private Life of Henry VIII	1933	D – P
(53)	Catherine the Great	1934	P
(54)	The Private Life of Don Juan	1934	D – P
(55)	The Scarlet Pimpernel	1935	P
(56)	Sanders of the River	1935	P
(57)	The Ghost Goes West	1935	P
(58)	Moscow Nights	1935	P
(59)	The Private Life of the Gannet	1935	P
(60)	The Fox Hunt	1935	P

(61)	Forget-me-not	1936	P
(62)	Rembrandt	1936	D – P
(63)	Men Are Not Gods	1936	P
(64)	Things to Come	1936	P
(65)	The Man Who Could Work Miracles	1936	P
(66)	Knight Without Armour	1936	P
(67)	The Squeaker	1936	P
(68)	Paradise for Two	1937	P
(69)	Fire Over England	1937	EP
(70)	Farewell Again	1937	P
(71)	Elephant Boy	1936–37	P
(72)	Dark Journey	1937	EP
(73)	Storm in a Teacup	1937	EP
(74)	Action for Slander	1937	EP
(75)	The Drum	1938	P
(76)	The Challenge	1938	EP
(77)	The Divorce of Lady X	1938	P
(78)	Prison Without Bars	1938	EP
(79)	The Return of the Scarlet Pimpernel	1938	P
(80)	South Riding	1938	EP
(81)	Twenty-one Days (The First and The Last)	1939	EP
(82)	Over the Moon	1939	P
(83)	Rebel Son	1939	EP
(84)	The Four Feathers	1939	P
(85)	The Lion Has Wings	1939	P
(86)	The Spy in Black	1939	EP
(87)	Q Planes	1939	EP
(88)	Old Bill and Son	1940	EP
(89)	The Thief of Baghdad	1939–40	P
(90)	Lady Hamilton	1941	D – P
(91)	Lydia	1941	P
(92)	Jungle Book	1941	P
(93)	Perfect Strangers	1944	D – P
(94)	Night Beat	1947	EP
(95)	Man About the House	1947	EP
(96)	An Ideal Husband	1947	D – P
(97)	Mine Own Executioner	1947	P
(98)	Anna Karenina	1948	P
(99)	Bonnie Prince Charlie	1948	EP
(100)	The Fallen Idol	1948	P
(101)	The Winslow Boy	1948	EP

(102)	The Small Back Room	1949	EP
(103)	The Last Days of Dolwyn	1949	EP
(104)	Saints and Sinners	1949	EP
(105)	That Dangerous Age	1949	EP
(106)	The Third Man	1949	EP
(107)	The Cure for Love	1949	EP
(108)	My Daughter Joy	1950	EP
(109)	State Secret	1950	EP
(110)	The Elusive Pimpernel	1950	EP
(111)	The Angel With the Trumpet	1950	EP
(112)	Gone to Earth	1950	EP
(113)	Seven Days to Noon	1950	EP
(114)	The Happiest Days of Your Life	1950	EP
(115)	The Wooden Horse	1950	EP
(116)	The Bridge of Time	1950	EP
(117)	The Wonder Kid	1951	EP
(118)	Cry The Beloved Country	1951	EP
(119)	The Tales of Hoffmann	1951	EP
(120)	An Outcast of the Islands	1951	EP
(121)	The Sound Barrier	1952	EP
(122)	Home at Seven	1952	EP
(123)	The Holly and the Ivy	1952	EP
(124)	Who Goes There?	1952	EP
(125)	The Ringer	1952	EP
(126)	The Road to Canterbury	1952	EP
(127)	Edinburgh	1952	EP
(128)	The Story of Gilbert and Sullivan	1953	EP
(129)	The Heart of the Matter	1953	EP
(130)	The Captain's Paradise	1953	EP
(131)	Hobson's Choice	1953	EP
(132)	The Man Between	1953	EP
(133)	Three Cases of Murder	1954	EP
(134)	The Man Who Loved Redheads	1954	EP
(135)	The Teckman Mystery	1954	EP
(136)	The Constant Husband	1955	EP
(137)	A Kid For Two Farthings	1955	EP
(138)	The Deep Blue Sea	1955	EP
(139)	Storm Over the Nile (Four Feathers)	1955	EP
(140)	Richard III	1955	EP
(141)	Smiley	1956	EP

AUTHOR'S NOTE

WRITING this biography was like assembling a tremendous jigsaw puzzle without a pattern. For almost two years I journeyed through the colourful and bewildering continent of show-business where appearances are real and realities often dissolve under closer inspection. I sat in dressing rooms and Mayfair apartments, in executive offices and maisonettes, in hotel-halls and on the stages of film-studios. Some of my quarries I had to pursue for several months before running them to earth in the wings of a theatre, an espresso bar or the lounge of an airport. Some I never caught. There were very few people in the European and American theatre, cinema and literature who did not cross Alexander Korda's path at one time or other. Most of them were helpful; though a handful refused to talk for reasons best known to themselves.

I have always hated footnotes and so I am giving here, chapter by chapter, the names of all those who so generously and kindly helped me. Some of them I cannot name as their aid was given on this stipulation. But every word and every fact was checked by two men who have been as close to Alex as any living human being.

Here, then, is my list of acknowledgments:

Chapter II: The details of Korda's childhood and school-days were supplied by his cousins Ferenc Pajor and Sandor Klein, together with his class-mates Julius Mandy, Simon Darvas (who took him to his first film-show) and Andor Zsoldos. Alexander Incze gave me valuable data about his collaboration with his former film-editor.

Chapter III: The story of Korda's first film was given to me by its star, Gabor Rajnay. Alexander Incze and Mrs. Lilly Janovics-Poor provided details about his meeting with Mr. Janovics and his work in Transylvania. His cousin, Alexander Klein, added information about the building of Corvin Studios and Korda's alarming habits in the cutting-room. Ila Loth recalled for me her work with Korda in 'Yamata'. Andor Zsoldos and others filled in the details about Korda's work during the final years in Hungary.

Chapter IV: Memories of Korda's start in Vienna and his subsequent pictures in Austria and Germany were generously recalled for me by Karl Hartl, his assistant and friend. Alfred Deesy, temporarily in Vienna at the same time, added some details. Ines Blanco helped me with data about Capozzi and the Italian plans of Alex. Mrs. Lajos Biro and her daughter Mrs. Vera Holländer, gave me the facts about his co-operation with the late playwright and screenwriter. Karl Klär, Julius Aussenberg's assistant, Mrs. Kitty Bee (Koloman Zatony's daughter), Miss Maie Hanbury, Joseph Somlo, John Loder were equally helpful. Alexander Incze also clarified some points.

Chapter V: Korda's early days in Hollywood were described for me by Clive Brook, Charles Vidor and Harold Young. His letters to the late Lajos Biro were very kindly put at my disposal by Mrs. Biro; Mrs. Vera Holländer, Biro's daughter, added some important dates and facts. Some anecdotes about his First National and Fox pictures I found in a series of articles written by H. W. Seaman. Andor Zsoldos, Alexander Incze and Victor Katona also supplied me with helpful information. Margaret Chute was present at the Malibu Beach house when Korda spoke of his frustrating final months in California.

Chapter VI: Details of the short Berlin stop-over were given to me by Andor Zsoldos and Steven Pallos. About Paris and the early beginnings of London Films my informants were Mrs. Vera Holländer, Steven Pallos, Mrs. Lily Veidt and Nicholas Bela. The early days and months in London were described by John Loder, Victor Savile, Sir Michael Balcon and Dorothy Holloway. Miss Holloway also lent me Merle Oberon's file card and told the incident about 'Women Who Play'. John Sutro kindly gave details about his father's association with Korda; George Grossmith jr., Emlyn Williams and Steven Pallos about the first seven London Films pictures. I found in Alan Wood's *Mr. Rank* a valuable and clear summary of the first Quota Act and its effects. On the film 'Henry VIII' I used the personal reminiscences of Charles Laughton, Gibb McLaughlin, Wally Patch, Miss Binnie Barnes (Mrs. Mike Francovich) and Dorothy Holloway. John Myers told his own story.

Chapter VII: The most important material for this chapter was supplied by Mr. Montague Marks, the architect of the Korda-Prudential co-operation. The story of the Hungarian cook was told by Steven Pallos. Melchior Lengyel, Douglas Fairbanks jr., Flora Robson gave me details about 'Catherine the Great'. The United Artists story is based on contemporary records and on Mr. Fairbanks's recollections. The building of Denham was related by Mr. Marks and Jack Okey. James Mason wrote a long letter from Hollywood telling how Korda started him in pictures. Dorothy Holloway contributed amusing details about 'The Scarlet Pimpernel', Sir Carol Reed told me himself about his first memorable meeting with Alex and so did Jeffrey Dell about his bewildering but enjoyable years with the Kordas. Mrs. Holländer lent me the memorandum which her father, Lajos Biro, wrote about H. G. Wells's 'Things to Come'; Margaretta Scott, Sophie Stewart, Sir Ralph Richardson, John Clements all recalled for me their parts in the picture. Ann Todd gave me many fascinating glimpses of Korda. Charles Laughton, Raymond Huntley and Allan Jeayes invoked the memories of 'Rembrandt'. Steven Pallos gave me the story about the first night of 'The Ghost Goes West'. Lothar Mendes, Wally Patch, Anthony Asquith, Christopher Brunel (Adrian's son) all added important information or colour to this chapter.

Chapter VIII: Some of the background material in this chapter I found in Alan Wood's admirable *Mr. Rank* (Hodder & Stoughton). Lothar Mendes contributed the story of the three City gentlemen and Korda's "snake-charming act". Mr. Montague Marks supplied the details about the final Prudential phase. Charles Laughton, Dorothy Holloway, Donald Taylor, Anthony Asquith, Flora Robson, Vivien Leigh, John Clements, Nicholas Rozsa, Victor Savile, Rex Harrison, Kay Kendall, Allan Jeayes, Valerie Hobson, Basil Dean, Brock Williams, Brian Desmond Hurst contributed their personal experiences either in writing or during the meetings I had with them.

Chapter IX: John Justin told me the story of his first starring rôle and the difficulties he had with his name, his service in the R.A.F. and his return to England. Nicholas Rozsa sent a long letter, every word of which showed his affection and admiration for Korda. Karl Klär contributed the tale about Ludwig Berger's post-war visit to Alex. Andor Zsoldos, Miles Malleson, Michael Powell, Brian Worth and others gave me information about 'The Lion Has Wings' and Steven Pallos himself told me about his adventure in Rome. Sir Michael

Balcon recalled the bitter arguments about British film-makers in Hollywood; Steven Pallos described the Congressional hearing in connection with 'Lady Hamilton'. Vivien Leigh, R. C. Sherriff, Melchior Lengyel, C. S. Forester, Donald Taylor, Basil Dean, Sir Carol Reed, Catherine de la Roche, Ann Todd were others who kindly supplied bits of the vast jigsaw puzzle. Steven Pallos gave the authentic details about the Prudential-Korda deal on the re-issues of former Korda films.

Chapter X: The first part of this chapter is based on official records, *Hansard*, the film trade papers and other public material. Joseph Somlo supplied some details; Anthony Asquith and Donald Taylor told me about Korda's trade union relationships and his attitude to smaller producers. I have given credit to Mr. Alan Wood in the text where I quoted his Rank biography. Sir Carol Reed, Mr. Nicholas Davenport, Karl Klär, Leslie Arliss, Guy Morgan, Commander Anthony Kimmins, Ronald Adam, James Mason, Michael Powell, Moira Shearer, Emlyn Williams, John and Roy Boulting, Leo Genn, Denholm Elliott, and Steven Pallos were among those who also supplied details and anecdotes, most generously.

Chapter XI: John Woolf supplied many interesting details about his association with Korda. Dr. Tibor Csato, his physician, gave me invaluable material about Alex's health, illness and death. Ann Todd, Sir Carol Reed, Karl Klär, Anthony Kimmins, and John Grierson also provided details and anecdotes. I am gratefully acknowledging my thanks to Sir Laurence Olivier for permission to quote his moving memorial speech.

There are a few others who gave me general help: Mr. Joachim Kreck who did research work in the German official film archives at Wiesbaden; Mrs. Ines Blanco who did the same work in Rome while Messrs. Paul Hollander and Robert Gati saved me immense trouble by ploughing through dozens of volumes of *Hansard*, cinema trade papers and other publications.

Writing this book has been a great privilege and pleasure. I have known Korda only for the last thirteen years of his life and I had to discover the man and artist step-by-step. I have suppressed nothing and invented nothing. The record of a great man and a great artist speaks for itself.

INDEX

Titles of films, books and plays are in *italic* type

Health Improvement Library
Law House
Airdrie Road
Carluke
ML8 5ER
ML8 5EP

Caring for Older People in Nursing

Transforming Nursing Practice series

Transforming Nursing Practice is the first series of books designed to help students meet the requirements of the NMC Standards and Essential Skills Clusters for degree programmes. Each book addresses a core topic, and together they cover the generic knowledge required for all fields of practice.

Core knowledge titles:

Series editor: Professor Shirley Bach, Head of the School of Nursing and Midwifery at the University of Brighton

Acute and Critical Care in Adult Nursing	ISBN 978 0 85725 842 7
Becoming a Registered Nurse: Making the Transition to Practice	ISBN 978 0 85725 931 8
Communication and Interpersonal Skills in Nursing (2nd edn)	ISBN 978 0 85725 449 8
Contexts of Contemporary Nursing (2nd edn)	ISBN 978 1 84445 374 0
Dementia Care in Nursing	ISBN 978 0 85725 873 1
Getting into Nursing	ISBN 978 0 85725 895 3
Health Promotion and Public Health for Nursing Students	ISBN 978 0 85725 437 5
Introduction to Medicines Management in Nursing	ISBN 978 1 84445 845 5
Law and Professional Issues in Nursing (2nd edn)	ISBN 978 1 84445 372 6
Leadership, Management and Team Working in Nursing	ISBN 978 0 85725 453 5
Learning Skills for Nursing Students	ISBN 978 1 84445 376 4
Medicines Management in Adult Nursing	ISBN 978 1 84445 842 4
Medicines Management in Children's Nursing	ISBN 978 1 84445 470 9
Medicines Management in Mental Health Nursing	ISBN 978 0 85725 049 0
Nursing Adults with Long Term Conditions	ISBN 978 0 85725 441 2
Nursing and Collaborative Practice (2nd edn)	ISBN 978 1 84445 373 3
Nursing and Mental Health Care	ISBN 978 1 84445 467 9
Passing Calculations Tests for Nursing Students (2nd edn)	ISBN 978 1 44625 642 8
Patient and Carer Participation in Nursing	ISBN 978 0 85725 307 1
Patient Assessment and Care Planning in Nursing	ISBN 978 0 85725 858 8
Patient Safety and Managing Risk in Nursing	ISBN 978 1 44626 688 5
Psychology and Sociology in Nursing	ISBN 978 0 85725 836 6
Safeguarding Adults in Nursing Practice	ISBN 978 1 44625 638 1
Successful Practice Learning for Nursing Students (2nd edn)	ISBN 978 0 85725 315 6
Using Health Policy in Nursing	ISBN 978 1 44625 646 6
What is Nursing? Exploring Theory and Practice (3rd edn)	ISBN 978 0 85725 975 2

Personal and professional learning skills titles:

Series editors: Dr Mooi Standing, Independent Academic Consultant (UK and International) & Accredited NMC Reviewer and Professor Shirley Bach, Head of the School of Nursing and Midwifery at the University of Brighton

Clinical Judgement and Decision Making in Nursing	ISBN 978 1 84445 468 6
Critical Thinking and Writing for Nursing Students (2nd edn)	ISBN 978 1 44625 644 2
Evidence-based Practice in Nursing (2nd edn)	ISBN 978 1 44627 090 5
Information Skills for Nursing Students	ISBN 978 1 84445 381 8
Reflective Practice in Nursing (2nd edn)	ISBN 978 1 44627 085 1
Succeeding in Essays, Exams & OSCEs for Nursing Students	ISBN 978 0 85725 827 4
Succeeding in Research Project Plans and Literature Reviews for Nursing Students	ISBN 978 0 85725 264 7
Successful Professional Portfolios for Nursing Students	ISBN 978 0 85725 457 3
Understanding Research for Nursing Students (2nd edn)	ISBN 978 1 44626 761 5

Mental health nursing titles:

Series editors: Sandra Walker, Senior Teaching Fellow in Mental Health in the Faculty of Health Sciences, University of Southampton and Professor Shirley Bach, Head of the School of Nursing and Midwifery at the University of Brighton

Assessment and Decision Making in Mental Health Nursing	ISBN 978 1 44626 820 9
Mental Health Law in Nursing	ISBN 978 0 85725 761 1

You can find more information on each of these titles and our other learning resources at www.sagepub.co.uk. Many of these titles are also available in various e-book formats, please visit our website for more information.